G·I·V·I·N·G
OFFENSE

G·I·V·I·N·G OFFENSE

ESSAYS ON CENSORSHIP

J. M. COETZEE

THE UNIVERSITY OF CHICAGO PRESS

CHICAGO AND LONDON

The University of Chicago Press, Chicago 60637
The University of Chicago Press, Ltd., London
© 1996 by The University of Chicago
All rights reserved. Published 1996
Printed in the United States of America

05 04 03 02 01 00 99 98 97   5 4 3 2

ISBN: 0-226-11174-1 (cloth)
ISBN: 0-226-11176-8 (paperback)

Library of Congress Cataloging-in-Publication Data

Coetzee, J. M., 1940–
    Giving offense / essays on censorship / J. M. Coetzee.
        p.   cm.
    Includes bibliographical references (p.   ) and index.
    ISBN 0-226-11174-1 (cloth)
    1. Censorship.   I. Title.
    Z657.C658   1996
    363.3'1—dc20   95-37389
                                                    CIP

Contents

Preface and Acknowledgments

The essays here collected constitute an attempt to understand a passion with which I have no intuitive sympathy, the passion that plays itself out in acts of silencing and censoring. They also constitute an attempt to understand, historically and sociologically, why it is that I have no sympathy with that passion. They do not, therefore, amount to any kind of history of censorship (which is not to say that I treat censorship as an institution without a history). Nor do they embody any strong theory of censorship. As a phenomenon, censorship belongs to public life; the study of censorship sprawls across several disciplines, including law, aesthetics, moral philosophy, human psychology, and politics—politics in the philosophical sense but more often in the narrower, more pragmatic sense.

As there is a world of difference between subversive ideas and morally repugnant representations (to say nothing of blasphemous utterances), so, in theory, there ought to be a world of difference between the censorship brought into being to supervise the media and the censorship that polices the arts. In practice, however, the same censors patrol the boundaries of both politics and aesthetics. In drawing no sharp line between censorship on political and on moral grounds, I thus follow the censor as he tracks "the undesirable," the category under which he uneasily and even haphazardly assimilates the subversive (the politically undesirable) and the repugnant (the morally undesirable).

Undesirable is a curious word. In the meaning "not to be desired" (OED) it is out of line with most English adjectives beginning un-/in- and ending -able/-ible. Inexplicable means "not able to be explained" but undesirable does certainly not mean "not able to be desired." On the contrary, an eager appetite for the books or pictures or ideas under interrogation is precisely what the censor seeks to curb. In his lexicon, undesirable means "that ought not to be desired" or even "that may not be desired."

The point can be pressed further. What is undesirable is the desire of the desiring subject: the desire of the subject is undesired. If we take the morphological liberty of reading undesired not as un(desired) but as (undesire)d, then we can think of undesire as a verb whose meaning is something like "to curb the desire of X for Y."

An undesirable object—object Y—is an undesired object, an object desire for which is to be forbidden. It is also, in the extended sense I suggest above, an object desire for which, on the part of the subject X, itself becomes the object of an active anti-desire whose essence is cold (chilling) rather than hot (ardent).

The undesired objects treated in this book are, for the most part, the productions of writers; my concern is less with why they are undesired in each case than with the ways in which their authors have responded to the attentions of the censor. In extreme cases (Osip Mandelstam commanded to compose an ode in praise of Stalin, Breyten Breytenbach writing poems under and for the eyes of his prison guards) the censor looms over the writer and cannot be ignored. But in most cases the contest with the censor is more private, a matter of keeping an unwelcome, censorious reader from invading the writer's inner, creative life.

Censorship is not an occupation that attracts intelligent, subtle minds. Censors can and often have been outwitted. But the game of slipping Aesopian messages past the censor is ultimately a sterile one, diverting writers from their proper task.

The only case I take up of an artist wholeheartedly engaged in a trial of wits with the organs of the state is that of Aleksandr Solzhenitsyn, in the years before his expulsion from the Soviet Union in 1974. The Solzhenitsyn of those years was a skillful and redoubtable polemicist; by any criterion save that employed by the Soviet state itself—the criterion of who disposed over most force—

he won. I have no reason to think that Solzhenitsyn looks back on his efforts with any self-doubt.

The punitive gesture of censoring finds its origin in the reaction of being offended. The strength of being-offended, as a state of mind, lies in not doubting itself; its weakness lies in not being able to afford to doubt itself. To the self-certainty of the state of being-offended I apply an Erasmian critique whose strength and whose weakness lies in that it is an uncertain critique—not wavering, but not certain of itself either. To the extent that my own critique of the censor is an uncertain one (I am not sure, for instance, what to think about artists who break taboos and yet claim the protection of the law), this book is dominated by the spirit of Erasmus.

The single instance I take up from wholly within the sphere of politics is that of Geoffrey Cronjé, one of the early theorists of apartheid. Cronjé was both an unwilling censor of his own work (a reluctant practitioner of Aesopian writing for an audience so ill-attuned to the mode that, having first veiled his meanings, he then had to signal them vigorously) and, later in his life, when apartheid had begun to hanker after respectability, the object of the machinations of colleagues eager to consign him to the darker recesses of the archive. But the real reason why I take up Cronjé is that I am struck by the blankness of contemporary political science about the deeper motives behind apartheid, a blankness to which the prudence of old believers on the one side, too wary to stick out their necks, and moral disapprobation amounting to horror on the other, both contribute. It is only by returning to the founding fathers, it would seem, that we can catch sight of the passions underlying apartheid in their full, original force.

Wholly aware that the line between journalism and "writing" is hard to draw, particularly in the late twentieth century, I nevertheless do not address the situation of journalists practicing their profession under regimes exercising press censorship or otherwise restricting the flow of information. Nor do I take up the question of bans operated, openly or covertly, by private bodies such as publishing houses, film studios, and television networks. I do so on the basis of the argument that in such cases artists have alternative avenues by which to disseminate their work. I recognize, however, that this is not a strong argument: the bans effected by monopolies or near-monopolies can in practice be no less complete than those implemented by bodies of censors with the force of the law behind them.

Nor, finally, do I have much to say about "undesirable" pictures and films, despite the fact that, as visual pornography has become cheaper and more widely available, the attentions of the censors have shifted almost entirely from print to the various visual media. Legal and critical debate about visual pornography faces a special problem: no matter how plausibly one may plead that what the viewer sees is a constellation of signifiers calling up other, intertexted constellations of signifiers whose total meaning is anything but obvious, this position is always in danger of being overwhelmed by the viewer's conviction—a conviction which it is in a sense the business of the film industry, by every means at its disposal, to bolster—that what he or she sees is the thing itself. This is the critical impasse I face in my chapter on Catharine MacKinnon.

Ten of the chapters in this book have already appeared in print, as listed below; most have been extensively revised. I am grateful to the editors and proprietors in each case for permission to republish.

Chapter 2 in *Salmagundi* 100 (1993).

Chapter 3 in *Mosaic: A Journal for the Interdisciplinary Study of Literature*, 21/1 (Winter 1988), and in *Doubling the Point* (Cambridge, Mass.: Harvard University Press, 1992).

Chapter 5 in *Neophilologus* 76 (1992).

Chapter 6 in *Representations* 35 (1991). Copyright © 1991 by the Regents of the University of California; reprinted by permission.

Chapter 7 in *Pretexts* 2/2 (1990).

Chapter 8 in *Salmagundi* 88–89 (1990–91).

Chapter 9 in *Social Dynamics* 17/1 (1991).

Chapter 10 in *English in Africa* 17/1 (1990), and in *Doubling the Point*.

Chapter 11 in *Research in African Literatures* 21/3 (1990); reprinted by permission of Indiana University Press.

Chapter 12 in *Raritan* 10/4 (Spring 1991); reprinted by permission of *Raritan: A Quarterly Review,* copyright © 1991 by *Raritan,* 31 Mine St., New Brunswick, N.J. 08903.

I am grateful to Breyten Breytenbach for permission to publish translations of various of his poems, as I am indebted to the Human Sciences Research Council (South Africa) and the University of Cape Town for supporting the research on which this book is based.

CHAPTER ONE

Taking Offense

OFFENSE

In the early 1990s, an instructive shift took place in public discourse in South Africa. Whites, who for centuries had been genially impervious to what blacks thought about them or called them, began to react touchily and even with outrage to the appellation *settler*. One of the war-chants of the Pan-Africanist Congress struck a particularly sensitive nerve: "ONE SETTLER ONE BULLET." Whites pointed to the threat to their lives contained in the word "bullet"; but it was "settler," I believe, that evoked a deeper perturbation. Settlers, in the idiom of white South Africa, are those Britishers who took up land grants in Kenya and the Rhodesias, people who refused to put down roots in Africa, who sent their children abroad to be educated, and spoke of England as "Home." When the Mau Mau got going, the settlers fled. To South Africans, white as well as black, a settler is a transient, no matter what the dictionary says.

When Europeans first arrived in southern Africa, they called themselves *Christians* and the indigenous people *wild* or *heathen*. The dyad *Christian/heathen* later mutated, taking a succession of forms, among them *civilized/primitive, European/native, white/ nonwhite*. But in each case, no matter what the nominally opposed terms, there was a constant feature: it was always the Christian (or white or European or civilized person) in whose power it lay to apply the names—the name for himself, the name for the other.

The heathens, the nonwhites, the natives, the primitives of

1

course had their own names for the Christian/European/white/civilized others. But to the extent that those who did this counternaming did not do so from a position of power, a position of authority, their naming did not count.[1]

From the mid-1980s onwards, however, as their political authority ebbed away, the power of those who called themselves whites to name and make the name stick, but more tellingly to resist or ignore naming, dwindled. There is nothing inherently insulting in the name *settler*. It is a word from one of the whites' own languages. But in the discourse of contemporary South Africa it is a word appropriated; it comes from another's mouth, with a hostile intentionality behind it, and with historical baggage that whites do not like. For the first time in their history (a history which, in important senses, was no longer theirs to make or to write) the whites who heard "ONE SETTLER ONE BULLET" found themselves in the position of the ones named. Part of their outrage was at tasting an impotence of which being-named is the sign. Part was also a firsthand discovery that naming includes control over deictic distance: it can put the one named at a measured arm's length quite as readily as it can draw the one named affectionately nearer.

It is not obvious why neutral-seeming terms like *native* (or *Negro* in the United States), instead of becoming more and more empty as they become embedded in usage—the fate of most names—on the contrary build up power to offend and anger, to the point where only the obdurate or thick-skinned continue to use them. It is only when we see their use as a verbal act, a gesture of distance-marking, that we understand their resistance to semantic entropy. The content (the blackness of *negro*, the autochthonousness of *native*) may dwindle until the word is a mere shell, but brought out into the open in an act of speech, wielded as a name, the word regains all its symbolic power, the power of its user to nominate. *Settler* seems to be as neutral in its denotation as *native*. But in the ritualized chant "ONE SETTLER ONE BULLET" it becomes outrageous and outraging; it is part of an enactment by the chanters of distance-assertion as well as of historical superordination over their object.[2] For whites hearing it, powerless to ignore it, powerless to put a stop to it, there was nothing left to do but take offense.

Taking offense is not confined to those in positions of subordination or weakness. Nevertheless, the experience or premonition of being robbed of power seems to me intrinsic to all instances of taking offense. (It is tempting to suggest that the logic of provocative name-calling, when used as a tactic of the weak against the strong, is that if the strong can be made to take offense, they thereby put themselves at least momentarily on the same footing as the weak.)

The Intellectual

Rational, secular intellectuals are not notably quick to take offense. Like Karl Popper, they tend to believe that

> I must teach myself to distrust that dangerous intuitive feeling or conviction that it is I who am right. I must distrust this feeling however strong it may be. Indeed, the stronger it is, the more I should mistrust it, because the stronger it is, the greater is the danger that I may deceive myself; and, with it, the danger that I may become an intolerant fanatic.[3]

Convictions that are not backed by reason (they reason) are not strong but weak; it is the mark of a weak position, not a strong position, that its holder, when challenged, takes offense. All viewpoints deserve a hearing *(audi alteram partem)*; debate, according to the rules of reason, will decide which deserves to triumph.

Such intellectuals also tend to have well-developed explanations ("theories") of the emotions—of which my own explanation of taking offense and Popper's analysis of "fanaticism" are instances—and to apply these explanations in a self-conscious way, as far as they can, to their own emotions. When they do take offense, they try to do so programmatically, setting (or believing themselves to set) their own thresholds of response, and allowing themselves (or believing themselves to allow themselves) to respond to triggers only when such thresholds are exceeded. The belief in fair play (that is, the belief that under the rules of fair play they win more often than they lose) that constitutes one of their more deeply entrenched values also encourages sympathy for the underdog, the subordinate, and discourages jeering at losers.

The combination of a close, rational watch over the emotions with sympathy for the underdog tends to produce a twofold response to displays of outrage on the part of other people. On the

one hand, the kind of intellectual I describe sees outrage as preratio-
nal or irrational and suspects it of being no more than a self-
deceiving disguise for a weak debating position. On the other hand,
to the extent that he or she recognizes outrage as a response of the
powerless, the intellectual may well take the side of the outraged,
at least ethically. That is to say, without empathetic participation in
the feeling of outrage, and perhaps even privately deeming outrage
in itself to be backward, a too-easy slide into self-serving emotionalism, yet out of a belief in the right of the other to take offense,
and particularly out of conviction that underdogs should not have
their subordination redoubled by having it prescribed to them in
what form they should object to being subordinated, the intellectual is prepared to respect and perhaps even defend other people's
taking offense, in much the same way that he or she might respect
someone's refusal to eat pork, while privately feeling the taboo is
benighted and superstitious.

This tolerance—which, depending on how you look at it, is either deeply civilized or complacent, hypocritical, and patronizing—
is a consequence of the security intellectuals feel about the rational
secularism within whose horizons they live, their confidence that
it can provide explanations for most things, and therefore—in its
own terms, which attach ultimate importance to being able to explain things—that it cannot itself be the object of some other
method of explanation more all-inclusive than itself. As the un-
framed framer, reason is a form of power with no in-built sense of
what the experience of powerlessness might be like.

Complacent and yet not complacent, intellectuals of the kind I
describe, pointing to the Apollonian "Know yourself," criticize and
encourage criticism of the foundations of their own belief systems.
Such is their confidence that they may even welcome attacks on
themselves, smiling when they are caricatured and insulted, responding with the keenest appreciation to the most probing, most
perceptive thrusts. They particularly welcome accounts of their enterprise that attempt to relativize it, read it within a cultural and
historical framework. They welcome such accounts and at once set
about framing them in turn within the project of rationality, that
is, set about recuperating them. They are in many ways like the

chess grandmaster who, confident in his powers, looks forward to opponents worthy of him.

I myself am (and am also, I would hope, to a degree not) an intellectual of this kind, and my responses to moral outrage or outrage at offended dignity are framed from within (though again, I would hope, not wholly from within) the procedures of thinking and the system of values I have outlined. That is to say, my responses are those of someone whose first reaction to the stirrings of being-offended within himself is to subject these incipient feelings to the scrutiny of skeptical rationality; of someone who, though not incapable of being offended (for instance, at being called a settler), does not particularly respect his own being-offended, does not take it seriously, particularly as a basis for action.

In *Notes from Underground* Dostoevsky's underground man, another rational intellectual, though perhaps more irascible of temperament than most, identifies the ability to feel sincere outrage and take sincere offense (along with the ability to feel unreserved love and experience uncomplicated happiness) as a feature of the kind of integrated, unselfconscious personality he would prefer to have. At the same time, he despises uncomplicated happiness and the unexamined life in general, and has no trouble detecting the worm of complacency at the heart of sincerity; his mordant analysis identifies taking offense as the blustering move of the soldier-bully and the last resort of the threadbare clerk. However, his very ability thus to frame taking offense historically and sociologically saps him of any sense of conviction when he tries to take offense himself. Conversely, the incisiveness of his diagnosis of rationality as an endless chess-game with the self betrays him as a bred-in-the-bone rationalist. These are two heads of a hydra-headed paradox in whose grip he struggles in vain.

For someone who does not respect his own being-offended, it is hard to respect in the deepest sense other people's being-offended. One respects it only in the sense that one respects the adherence of other people to creeds one regards as superstitious, that is to say, respecting their right to the creed of their choice while retaining every reserve about the creed itself, and maintaining this split attitude on the basis of the pragmatic, Lockean principle that if we do not interfere in the private lives of others, then they will be less likely to interfere in ours. It is a compromise between private conviction and public expression undertaken in the interests of civil order and neighborliness, a much less than ethical stance requiring no more of us than that we take note of the feelings of fellow-citizens and behave scrupulously, at all points, as though we respect them. It does not require us to go further and actually, in our hearts, respect those feelings—respect, in particular, when these arise, feelings of outrage.[4]

The Offense of the Powerful

In my analysis of being-offended I have pointed to the powerlessness of the affected party as a cardinal element in the genesis of outrage. The powerlessness of a subordinated religious sect or ethnic minority is easy to see. But when at the other extreme a national government or dominant church or powerful class is offended by some or other teaching or representation to the extent that it sets about suppressing it, how can I claim that it reacts out of powerlessness?

State censorship offers a clue. State censorship presents itself as a bulwark between society and forces of subversion or moral corruption. To dismiss this account of its own motives by the state as insincere would be a mistake: it is a feature of the paranoid logic of the censoring mentality that virtue, *qua* virtue, must be innocent, and therefore, unless protected, vulnerable to the wiles of vice. Powerlessness is thus not necessarily objective powerlessness: the fears of the powerful dare not speak their name precisely because, as fears of the powerful, they must seem groundless.

Furthermore, the power of the powerful to defend themselves against representations of them is surprisingly limited; and the more accurate the representation, the more limited this power. Ortega suggests that *mimesis* is guided by the spirit not of fidelity but of mockery.[5] As a generalization this may not hold water; nevertheless, from the viewpoint of the one imitated the motive may certainly seem so. For, the closer the imitation, the more immediately and irresistibly it evokes laughter in the onlooker. Simply by virtue of their prominence, the powerful become objects of imitations which mock or seem to mock them, and which nothing but force

can suppress. Yet the moment they act against these representations as the misrepresentations they intrinsically are, they betray
(or seem to betray) a vulnerability to mockery.

The logic I have traced illuminates not only the helplessness of
power—helplessness in the sense that power is taken to its wits'
end—but the essential heartlessness of the enterprise of representation (and I have in mind here not only satirical or caricatural
representation). People who engage themselves daily in the manufacture of representations see nothing magical in them, and therefore nothing worthy of respect in people who credit them with
magical powers. The more seriously the artist sees his work being
taken by the represented and offended party, and the more his work
is denounced, the less he is likely to take that party seriously. (Of
course this does not mean he will disregard the power of the offended party to exact revenge.)

Censorship Today

In the seven years that have passed since I wrote the earliest of the
essays collected in this book, the context in which I write has been
affected by two historical and perhaps even historic shifts in the
political landscape. On the one hand, in the course of the handover
of power in my home country that began in 1990, the apparatus of
state censorship has fallen into virtual disuse; while at the same
time the corresponding systems in the USSR and the old East European bloc were crumbling. On the other hand, the liberal consensus
on freedom of expression that might once have been said to reign
among Western intellectuals, and that indeed did much to define
them as a community, has ceased to obtain. In the United States,
for instance, institutions of learning have approved bans on certain
categories of speech, while agitation against pornography is not
limited to the Right. Even in South Africa, where one might have
expected resistance among an intelligentsia with firsthand experience of censorship, the tide has begun to turn. For instance, academics and publishers, groups formerly firm in their opposition to
censorship, have as a contribution to a general *Säuberungsaktion*
collaborated with education authorities to expunge racially offensive words from new editions of Afrikaans classics.[6]

In the mid-1980s I could assume that the intelligentsia broadly shared my sentiment that the fewer legal restraints there were on speech, the better: if it turned out that some of the forms assumed by free speech were unfortunate, that was part of the price of freedom. Institutional censorship was a sign of weakness in the state, not of strength; the record of censorship world-wide was ugly enough to have discredited it forever. In 1995 this assumption can no longer be made. There are reputable intellectuals who advocate legal and institutional sanctions against publications and films of the kind that in the old South Africa used to be called undesirable and are now generally called offensive; while the thesis that, in conflicts between the writer and the law, right has always to be on the side of the writer is itself in the process of being historically framed and set aside as ahistorical, as a feature of "the heady liberalism of thirty years ago."[7]

AGAINST CENSORSHIP

The essays collected here do not constitute an attack on censorship (the polemics of writers against censors seldom do the profession credit). It is not my concern to take up instances of extreme offensiveness, moral or political, that is, limit cases of the kind that form the bread and butter of philosophers and academic lawyers. I barely address the two liveliest issues in censorship debates today, (racist) race and (misogynist or homophobic) sex.

Nor do these essays confront the issue of blasphemy. It is a measure of the degree to which Western society has become secularized that Muslim outrage against *The Satanic Verses* and its author, Salman Rushdie, should have met with widespread bewilderment. The United Kingdom, of which Rushdie is a citizen, still has laws against blasphemy; but these laws, and indeed the very notion of entrusting the name of the Almighty to the protection of the law courts, have taken on an increasingly anachronistic air.[8] For believing Muslims, the burning question has been whether *The Satanic Verses* is blasphemous, and, if it is, what the fate of its author should be. For most Britons, on the other hand, the question has been one of jurisdiction: do foreigners—and foreign clergy at that—have the right to pass sentence of death on a fellow citizen? Sympathy for the underdog Rushdie has been strengthened by a suspicion that years of accumulated anti-Western resentment are being vented on him—that, though the publication of the *Verses* lit the spark, Rushdie has been made to stand for an entire intellectual establishment that by celebrating the book compounded its outrage.[9]

The censor acts, or believes he acts, in the interest of a community. In practice he often acts out the outrage of that community, or imagines its outrage and acts it out; sometimes he imagines both the community and its outrage. Though I try to treat censorship as a complex matter with psychological as well as political and moral dimensions, the essays here published are in no way sympathetic to the institution of censorship. I cannot find it in myself to align myself with the censor, not only because of a skeptical attitude, in part temperamental, in part professional, toward the passions that issue in taking offense, but because of the historical reality I have lived through and the experience of what censorship becomes once it is instituted and institutionalized. Nothing in either my experience or my reading persuades me that state censorship is not an inherently bad thing, the ills it embodies and the ills it fosters outweighing, in the long run and even in the medium run, whatever benefits may be claimed to flow from it.

This judgment is not a disinterested one. There are good historical reasons why, ever since the invention of printing—with the enormous increase in disseminative power that printing allowed— at least until the decline of print from its dominant position as a medium of communication, writers have had an uneasy relationship with governmental authority. Hostility between the two sides, which soon became settled and institutional, was exacerbated by the tendency of artists from the late eighteenth century onward to assume it as their social role, and sometimes indeed as their vocation and destiny, to test the limits (that is to say, the weak points) of thought and feeling, of representation, of the law, and of opposition itself, in ways that those in power were bound to find uncomfortable and even offensive. Into the tail end of this historical movement I, as a writer and intellectual, was so to speak born.

But aside from this historical explanation of my position, I have more pragmatic grounds for mistrusting censorship. The chief of these is that, in my experience, the cure is worse than the disease.

The institution of censorship puts power into the hands of persons with a judgmental, bureaucratic cast of mind that is bad for the cultural and even the spiritual life of the community. The point was made long ago by John Milton. If we are to have proper, professional censors, says Milton, they need to be persons "above the common measure, both studious, learned, and judicious." But for such studious, learned and judicious persons,

> there cannot be a more tedious and unpleasing journey-work . . . than to be made the perpetual reader[s] of unchosen books. . . . Seeing therefore those who now possess the employment . . . wish themselves well rid of it, and that no man of worth . . . is ever likely to succeed them . . . we may easily foresee what kind of licensers [i.e., censors] we are to expect hereafter, either ignorant, imperious, and remiss, or basely pecuniary.[10]

That is to say, the people we get as censors are the people we least need.

At an individual level, the contest with the censor is all too likely to assume an importance in the inner life of the writer that at the very least diverts him from his proper occupation and at its worst fascinates and even perverts the imagination. In the personal records of writers who have operated under censorship we find eloquent and despairing descriptions of how the censor-figure is involuntarily incorporated into the interior, psychic life, bringing with it humiliation, self-disgust, and shame. In unwilling fantasies of this kind, the censor is typically experienced as a parasite, a pathogenic invader of the body-self, repudiated with visceral intensity but never wholly expelled.[11]

The most law-abiding countries are not those with the highest prison populations but those with the lowest offender rates. The law, including the law of censorship, has a dream. In this dream, the daily round of identifying and punishing malefactors will wither away; the law and its constraints will be so deeply engraved on the citizenry that individuals will police themselves. Censorship looks forward to the day when writers will censor themselves and the censor himself can retire. It is for this reason that the physical expulsion of the censor, vomited forth as a demon is, has a certain symbolic value for the writer of Romantic genealogy: it stands for a rejection of the dream of reason, the dream of a society of laws founded on reason and obeyed because reasonable.

Writing does not flourish under censorship. This does not mean that the censor's edict, or the internalized figure of the censor, is the sole or even the principal pressure on the writer: there are forms of repression, inherited, acquired, or self-imposed, that can be more grievously felt. There may even be cases where external censorship challenges the writer in interesting ways or spurs creativity.[12] But the Aesopian ruses that censorship provokes are usually no more than ingenious; while the obstacles that writers are capable of visiting upon themselves are surely sufficient in number and variety for them not to invite more.

Nevertheless, for the common good, for the good of the state, apparatuses of regulation and control are from time to time set up, which grow and entrench themselves, as is the wont of bureaucracies. It is hard for any writer to contemplate the scale of such apparatuses without a disbelieving smile. If representations, mere shadows, are indeed so dangerous, one reflects, then surely the appropriate countermeasures are other representations, counter-representations. If mockery corrodes respect for the state, if blasphemy insults God, if pornography demeans the passions, surely it will suffice if stronger and more convincing countervoices are raised defending the authority of the state, praising God, exalting chaste love.

This response is wholly in accord with the teleology of liberalism, which believes in throwing open the marketplace to contending forces because in the long run the market tends to the good, that is to say, to progress, which liberalism understands in a historical and even metaphysical light. It is wholly at odds with the outlook of the more austere branches of Islam, Judaism, and Protestant Christianity, which, detecting a seductive and devilish force at the root of the power of representation, and thus having no reason to expect that, in a war of representations, a war without rules, good representations will triumph, prefer to ban graven images.

We have here reached the entry-point into a debate about the rights of the individual as against the rights of the collectivity which is familiar enough not to need extended rehearsal and to which I have nothing to contribute except perhaps a caution against the kind of moral vigilance that defines vulnerable classes of people and sets about protecting them from harms whose nature they must be kept blind to because (the argument goes) merely to know the harm is to suffer it. I refer here primarily to children, though the same argument has been made in respect of so-called simple believers. We are concerned to protect children, in good part to protect them from the consequences of their limitless curiosity about sexual matters. But we should not forget that children experience control of their explorations—control which by its own premises cannot spell out exactly what it is that is forbidden—not as protection but as frustration. From the measures adults take to deny the satisfaction of children's curiosity, may children not legitimately infer that their curiosity is censurable; and from the explanations with which they are provided for being constrained—explanations riddled with holes—may they not infer that they are not respected as moral agents? May the ethical wrong done to the child in the process not be more durable than any harm it may suffer from following wherever curiosity leads?[13]

This is neither an argument for keeping sexually explicit materials away from children nor an argument against it. It is a reflection on how harms weigh up against each other, on balancing imponderables, choosing between evils. In making such choices we might include in our reckoning the consideration that to a small child the things that adults do with or to each other's bodies are not only intriguing and disturbing but ugly and funny too, even silly; the consideration, too, that whether or not the child succeeds in blocking the thought that what the people do in the picture its parents may do too, it is hard for the parent not to project this thought upon the child, and, reexperiencing it through the child, to be embarrassed, ashamed, and even angry. Nor should we forget who is most embarrassed when to the candid gaze of a child spectacles of gross adult nakedness are exposed. The moment is a complex one; but included in our desire to keep such sights from the child may there not be a wish not to descend, by association, in the child's esteem, not to become the object of the child's disgust or amusement? Max Scheler distinguishes between the nakedness of an Aphrodite sculpted with such awe that she seems to have a veil of modesty about her, and the "deanimation," or loss of soul, that occurs when primitive or childish wonder is lost, and the naked body is seen with knowing eyes. He links deanimation to what he calls the "apperceptive breaking out" of the sexual organs from the body: no longer seen as integral with the body, nor yet as "fields of expression of inner and passionate movements," the sexual organs—particularly, one might note, the male apparatus, with its appearance of extruded viscera—threaten to become objects of disgust.[14] It is not strange that we should wish to preserve the childhood of children by protecting them from such sights; but whose sensibilities are we in the first place guarding, theirs or our own?

The sexual organs, observes Saint Augustine, move independently of the will. Sometimes they respond to what we do not want them to respond to; sometimes they remain "frozen" when we want to employ them.[15] From this disobedience of the flesh, mark of a fallen state, none are exempt, not even the guardians of our morals. A censor pronouncing a ban, whether on an obscene spectacle or a derisive imitation, is like a man trying to stop his penis from standing up. The spectacle is ridiculous, so ridiculous that he is soon a victim not only of his unruly member but of pointing fingers, laughing voices. That is why the institution of censorship has to surround itself with secondary bans on the infringement of its dignity. From being sour to being laughed at for being sour to banning laughter at what is sour is an all-too-familiar progression in tyranny, one that should give us further cause for caution.

In the above similitude, I need hardly point out that the one who pronounces the ban does not have to be male. The one who pronounces the ban by that act lays claim to the phallus, but the phallus in its mundane form as penis. Taking up the position of censor, this one becomes, in effect, the blind one, the one at the center of the ring in the game of blind man's buff. For a time, until the blindfold that at the same time marks him, elevates him, and disables him can be passed on, it is his fate to be the fool who stumbles about, laughed at and evaded. If the spirit of the game, the spirit of the child, is to reign, the censor must accept the clownship that goes with blind kingship. The censor who refuses to be a clown, who tears off the blindfold and accuses and punishes the laughers, is not playing the game. He thereby becomes, in Erasmus's paradox, the true fool, or rather, the false fool. He is a fool because he does not know himself a fool, because he thinks that, being in the center of the ring, he is king.

Children are not, *qua* children, innocent. We have all been children and know—unless we prefer to forget—how little innocent we were, what determined efforts of indoctrination it took to make us into innocents, how often we tried to escape from the staging-camp of childhood and how implacably we were herded back. Nor do we inherently possess dignity. We are certainly born without dignity, and we spend enough time by ourselves, hidden from the eyes of others, doing the things that we do when we are by ourselves, to know how little of it we can honestly lay claim to. We also see enough of animals concerned for their dignity (cats, for instance) to know how comical pretensions to dignity can be.

Innocence is a state in which we try to maintain our children; dignity is a state we claim for ourselves. Affronts to the innocence of our children or to the dignity of our persons are attacks not upon our essential being but upon constructs—constructs by which we live, but constructs nevertheless. This is not to say that affronts to innocence or dignity are not real affronts, or that the outrage with which we respond to them is not real, in the sense of not being sincerely felt. The infringements are real; what is infringed, however, is not our essence but a foundational fiction to which we more or less wholeheartedly subscribe, a fiction that may well be indispensable for a just society, namely, that human beings have a dignity that sets them apart from animals and consequently protects them from being treated like animals. (It is even possible that we may look forward to a day when animals will have their own dignity ascribed to them, and the ban will be reformulated as a ban on treating a living creature like a thing.)

The fiction of dignity helps to define humanity and the status of humanity helps to define human rights. There is thus a real sense in which an affront to our dignity strikes at our rights. Yet when, outraged at such affront, we stand on our rights and demand redress, we would do well to remember how insubstantial the dignity is on which those rights are based. Forgetting where our dignity comes from, we may fall into a posture as comical as that of the irate censor.

Life, says Erasmus's Folly, is theater: we each have lines to say and a part to play. One kind of actor, recognizing that he is in a play, will go on playing nevertheless; another kind of actor, shocked to find he is participating in an illusion, will try to step off the stage and out of the play. The second actor is mistaken. For there is nothing outside the theater, no alternative life one can join instead. The show is, so to speak, the only show in town. All one can do is to go on playing one's part, though perhaps with a new awareness, a comic awareness.

We thus arrive at a pair of Erasmian paradoxes. A dignity worthy of respect is a dignity without dignity (which is quite different from unconscious or unaffected dignity); an innocence worthy of respect is an innocence without innocence. As for respect itself, it is tempting to suggest that this is a superfluous concept, though for the workings of the theater of life it may turn out to be indispensable. True respect is a variety of love and may be subsumed under love; to respect someone means, inter alia, to forgive that person an innocence that, outside the theater, would be false, a dignity that would be risible.

PORNOGRAPHY

Conservatives and Their Critics

On issues of pornography and in general of legal sanctions in the moral realm, there is a range of positions that can broadly be called conservative. The most extreme of these is that, morality being valuable in itself, whatever steps need to be taken against immorality in any of its manifestations are justified. A more moderate position would maintain that, because a shared morality—whether or not it is an inherently admirable morality—is what holds society together, breaches of morality constitute an offense against society as a whole, against which society is entitled to defend itself. In particular, when breaches of morality arouse the public to a pitch of intolerance, indignation, and disgust, the law has a positive duty to respond. This moderate thesis is not itself considered to be part of the shared morality, but is put forward as an autonomous, rationally defensible principle.[16]

When applied to the arts, the assertion of the sovereignty of moral principle or, more moderately, of moral consensus lays the onus on the artist and on the publishers or distributors of the artist's work to avoid giving offense. To H. L. A. Hart, as a liberal critic of conservatism, this onus is unfair: by accepting the role of *custos morum*, he argues, courts sacrifice the essential principle of legality that requires criminal offenses to be as precisely defined as possible, "so that it can be known with reasonable certainty beforehand what acts are criminal and what are not."[17] In taking this stance, Hart reiterates the opposition of the Mills, father and son, to the tyranny of popular morality: James Mill had distinguished between truly injurious actions, public disapproval of which is justified, and actions that evoke simply "groundless antipathies."[18]

In the moderate conservative position—a position he chooses to associate with the British jurist Patrick Devlin—Ronald Dworkin distinguishes two arguments. The first is that, when public feeling rises to intolerance, indignation, and disgust, society has a right to protect itself by imposing its standards. Since, according to this argument, nothing more than "passionate public disapproval" (James Mill's "groundless antipathy") is needed before the law is invoked, it does not in Dworkin's eyes have the status of a moral argument at all.[19] The second strand is that every society has a right to protect its central social institutions, that is, that as a matter of democratic principle legislators have to follow whatever "consensus of moral position" obtains in the community at large. Here, Dworkin contends, conservatives like Devlin use morality and the notion of a moral position in a merely "anthropological" sense: the consensus appealed to need not have a properly moral basis, but may be a compound of "prejudice. . . , rationalization. . . , and personal aversion (representing no conviction but merely blind hate. . .)."[20]

This is not to argue—Dworkin stresses—that the legislator should ignore community sentiment. But unless the consensus he heeds is one of "moral conviction" rather than of "moral position," the legislator who adheres to it will be behaving merely strategically rather than on the basis of moral principle. Furthermore, moral conviction must be demonstrated, not only asserted—for instance, in the form of "moral reasons or arguments which the average member of society might sincerely and consistently advance."[21]

Here one might dubiously ask, if we cannot be sure what we ourselves *sincerely* believe, as distinct from what we merely *believe*, how can we know what other people sincerely believe? By historicizing or deconstructing the notion of sincerity, we can with a little ingenuity show anyone's sincerity, including our own, to be a mask for self-interest. The conclusion seems inescapable: if only to avoid the anarchy of wholesale skepticism, we must, when people say they believe something, accept that they believe it, or at least respond on such a basis, no matter what private reservations we may entertain.

Liberal Standards

To John Stuart Mill, it is not society that requires protection against the deviant individual but the individual whose rights need to be protected, not only against "the tyranny of the magistrate" but against "the tyranny of the prevailing opinion and feeling," that is to say, the tendency of society to impose its own ideas and practices as rules of conduct for all. The recurring theme of *On Liberty* is "that the sole end for which mankind are warranted, individually or collectively, in interfering with the liberty of action of any of their number is self-protection." Intervention in the name of safeguarding the moral welfare of the individual can never be justified.[22] The state should be neutral in the arena of morals, neither promoting the morally admirable nor sanctioning the morally deplorable, as long as no one is harmed.

Can we define sanctionable harms, and thus specify under what circumstances society may be justified in restricting the freedom of the individual? Here Mill follows Jeremy Bentham: no act should be treated as sanctionable "which is not liable, in some way or another, to be detrimental to the community." Detriment is to be tested by the calculus of utility. "An action . . . may be said to be conformable to the principle of utility . . . when the tendency it has to augment the happiness of the community is greater than any it has to diminish it." As for the principle of utility itself, this "neither requires nor admits any other regulator than itself"; it is outside the system.[23]

People sometimes feel, or claim to feel, distress at what they take to be the immorality or depravity of the actions of others, even when such actions do not directly and unambiguously touch them. Do actions causing pure moral distress of this kind (rising to moral outrage, Devlin's "intolerance, indignation, and disgust") diminish the sum of happiness and therefore count as sanctionable harms in Mill's book?[24] Should any distinction be drawn between actions of this kind and such actions as cause or may be claimed to cause "long-lasting or permanent disorientations or impairments" and are thus more demonstrably harmful?[25]

Mill does not confront this question directly. As Jeremy Waldron points out, Mill tends to identify obedience to prevailing public standards with stagnation, and action based on private conviction with progress: this is the point at which Mill's romantic ethic of self-development and his historical evolutionism come together. "The contest between the morality which appeals to an external standard, and that which grounds itself on internal conviction," says Mill, "is the contest of progressive morality against stationary—of reason and argument against the deification of mere opinion and habit."[26] Thus in the larger picture, Waldron suggests, moral distress is to Mill "actually a *positive* feature of deviant actions and lifestyles; the outrage and disturbance that deviance evokes is something to be welcomed, nurtured and encouraged in [a] free society." One of the tests of a free and progressive society is its readiness to accept what Waldron calls "ethical confrontation." He paraphrases Mill as follows: "If . . . widespread moral distress *is* detectable in the community, then far from being a legitimate ground for interference, it is a positive and healthy sign that the processes of ethical confrontation . . . are actually taking place."[27] This reading suggests that Mill's understanding of harm would be extremely narrow, and would certainly not include actions causing distress or outrage, no matter how personally disorienting.

To Mill, freedom of speech includes immunity from censorship, specifically from prepublication censorship, but also freedom from societal pressures, "the tyranny of the prevailing opinion and feeling." Mill conflates censorship with social pressures (sometimes called *censure*) in ways I am reluctant to follow. Censure, as Frederick Schauer points out, is not strictly speaking a free-speech issue. Social intolerance is different in kind from official sanctions backed by the force of law: people have a choice not to follow orthodoxy.[28]

Mill's faith in the long-term value of free speech is very much the basis of the report of the committee headed by Bernard Williams in 1979, charged with proposing reforms to British legislation on obscenity and film censorship:

> The more basic idea, to which Mill attached the market-place model, remains a correct and profound idea: that we do not know in advance what social, moral or intellectual developments will turn out to be possible, necessary or desirable for human beings and for their future, and free expression, intellectual and artistic—something which may need to be fostered and protected as well as permitted— is essential to human development, as a process which does not merely happen (in some form or another, it will happen anyway) but so far as possible is rationally understood.[29]

Ronald Dworkin defines the approach enunciated here as "goal-based" rather than "rights-based." The stance taken by the Williams Report is that, in the long run, exercising censorship is worse for society than permitting pornography a free run. It is *not* that it would be wrong to censor pornography—irrespective of whether it is bad for society or not—because that would violate the rights of some individuals (including, presumably, its producers and its consumers). It backs up its position with the so-called "slippery slope" argument: that anyhow it would be difficult if not impossible to devise a form of words that would reliably separate trash from work of redeeming value.[30]

Just as Mill is vague about why we should endorse progress, the Williams Report does not define the goal in whose name it opposes censorship more narrowly than to call it "human development." Yet this quintessentially liberal faith that free speech must be in the long-term interest of communities has been widely questioned. Whatever its liberatory value in Mill's own day, Herbert Marcuse suggests, such faith is no longer justified in the twentieth century, when states have developed techniques of using tolerance for subtly repressive ends.[31] Dworkin calls the liberal argument for the overriding value of free speech "highly problematical, speculative, and in any case marginal" (in the case of pornography he finds it "not only speculative and marginal, but implausible as well").[32]

Terms

"Pornography" is of course not a neutral appellation but a term of opprobrium. People who make sexually explicit books and films routinely deny that their products are pornographic. For my purposes here I will ignore such denials and accept as pornographic what most educated secular Westerners, men and women, regard as pornographic. John Ellis points to the omnivorousness of the category of the pornographic, an omnivorousness it is futile to decry:

> "Pornography" as a label always threatens to engulf any sexual representation that achieves a certain level of explicitness. There is no way that any representation—especially if it involves photography—can insure itself against such labelling.[33]

We cannot hope for a consensus on what *the pornographic* means. In the general field defined by the pornography industry and its attempts at self-legitimization; by courts enforcing obscenity laws as well as by institutions enforcing their own standards; and by what Ellis (p. 148) calls "the general mobilization of moral and philosophical positions" at any particular social moment, there will always be rival definitions striving for command.

Nevertheless, there are some terminological distinctions worth observing. One is that the obscene and the pornographic are not coreferential.[34] Scenes of evisceration, for instance, may be obscene but not pornographic; while as long as the obscene, as one of the varieties of the offensive, involves what Joel Feinberg calls "disliked mental states," a subject cannot react with unmixed pleasure to pornography yet at the same time call it obscene.[35]

Obscenity has a particular kind of impact on the offended subject: it produces repugnance, shock, or disgust (though, as Feinberg points out, the offending materials can paradoxically be alluring at the same time).[36] Because the offended typically feels resentment against the offender, we infer that an intentionality is perceived behind the obscene act. An intention may indeed be present: Max Scheler points to a component impulse behind the obscene act that seeks out other people's sense of shame or modesty in order to violate it for its own ends.[37] On the other hand, it is precisely at the point at which an intention to offend is detected behind every action giving offense that the gates of paranoia are opened.

Furthermore, while an obscenity is an offense, it is not necessarily a harm. In particular, an offense is not a minor harm: the two are different in nature. To a jurist in the tradition of Mill, an offended party, even an "extremely" or "deeply" offended party, is not necessarily thereby harmed.[38]

Liberal Standards: The Feminist Critique

Under a liberal regime, the legal position of pornographers and consumers of pornography is quite strong. It is predicated upon three overlapping principles. (1) All persons without exception are entitled to freedom of expression. (2) This freedom may not be curtailed unless it can be demonstrated that its exercise entails harm to the interests of others (where harm is to be construed quite narrowly). (3) Pornography is anyway a private transaction between purveyors and consumers.

In recent years, all of these principles have been questioned by critics—and particularly feminist critics—of liberalism. Regarding the right of pornographers to freedom of expression, it has been argued that in the wake of speech-act theory any simple distinction between expression and action is untenable: in their perlocutionary force, pornographic representations, like public insults, are more actlike than speechlike and therefore not *per se* entitled to protection.[39]

Principles (2) and (3), which state that pornography is a private matter, usually between men and men, causing no demonstrable harm to anyone, have been rejected on a number of grounds. First, the validity of the entire private/public distinction has been denied, and with it the defense that pornography need not intrude itself into one's private space unless one allows it in.[40] Second, some feminists have claimed that there is an empirically verifiable link of causation between the consumption of pornography and violent acts against women.[41] The argument that pornography indeed causes harm also comes in an extended form, namely that it harms not only women as a class but the mores of the whole of society (one is reminded of the conservative argument that the right of a society to protect its structuring principles transcends the rights of individuals).[42]

Principles (2) and (3) have also been rejected on the basis of a false-consciousness argument: that a woman who maintains that pornography does her no harm, for instance, may very well hold this view because she has internalized a version of female sexuality constructed by men. Thus, in denying the harm of pornography she may in fact be displaying a symptom of a more all-embracing harm that has been done to her.[43]

Pornography objectifies: this thesis is common ground among its feminist critics. In pornography women are regarded as sexual objects; men who consume pornography learn to regard real-life women likewise. The question is, what kind of wrong is objectification? In the tradition inherited from Kant, it is the wrong of treating persons as less than persons, as means to ends rather than as ends in themselves. For Jacqueline Davies, pornography (which is so pervasive nowadays that for most people, she contends, it constitutes the effectual form of sex-education) treats women as means rather than as ends in that it predetermines how their behavior is to be interpreted, thereby in effect robbing their behavior of its freedom and constituting them as an unfree class.[44]

The liberal position on pornography and its right to free-speech protection is thus challenged at its roots by feminist critics. Indeed, when liberals can be drawn back from their preoccupation with such aridities as whether one can claim to be offended to the point of being wronged by materials that are not thrust upon one but on the contrary are easily avoided,[45] and confronted with the sweepingly political attacks on pornography by antagonists like Catharine MacKinnon, the juxtaposition bears out to a remarkable degree the pessimistic analysis of contemporary moral discourse given by Alasdair MacIntyre in *After Virtue:*

> From our rival conclusions we can argue back to our rival premises; but when we do arrive at our premises argument ceases and the invocation of one premise against another becomes a matter of pure assertion and counter-assertion.[46]

It is characteristic of modern debates on morality, MacIntyre continues, that as the philosophical rivals lose common ground, each begins to accuse the other of adopting his/her position unreasonably. "Corresponding to the interminability of public argument there is at least the appearance of a disquieting private arbitrariness." Hence the common tendency nowadays to fall back on emotivism, the doctrine that "all moral judgments are *nothing but* expressions of preference, expressions of attitude or feeling" (p. 11).

Within a framework of emotivism, judgments on pornography are expressions of attitude and therefore incontestable. Thus for instance Susan Mendus presents Andrea Dworkin's relation to pornography as a prephilosophical matter, an *attitude:* "Such material is corrupt whether she encounters it or not. She wants it not to exist."[47] This is not a moral judgment, says Mendus: moral judgments are based on reason, whereas Dworkin's judgment is based on feelings. By their nature, nonmoral judgments remove us from the realm of moral philosophy and thus from debate under the rules of reason. She quotes Mary Warnock: "The intolerable is the unbearable. And we may simply feel, believe, conclude without reason that something is unbearable and must be stopped."[48]

Another name for MacIntyre's emotivism, the doctrine that moral judgments have no basis save in emotional attitudes, that is, save in the emotional orientation of the subject toward the world, is *perspectivism*. As a particular form of relativism, perspectivism may be more characteristic of moral discourse today than the pure emotivism Warnock alludes to. Perspectivism is writ large all over the work of Catharine MacKinnon—indeed, it is an ingrained mannerism of her polemical style:

> Sexual liberation in the liberal sense frees male sexual aggression in the feminist sense. What looks like love and romance in the liberal view looks a lot like hatred and torture in the feminist view.[49]

But it is also a common feature of post-liberal moral philosophy, with its deep suspicion of foundational principles and in particular of the axioms of liberalism:

> What liberalism represents as the neutral requirement of preventing harm to others will be perceived by those with different conceptions of what is harmful as the enforcement of a morality they do not share. Liberalism itself embodies substantial moral precepts and ideals and its conception of what is harmful has no self-evidently greater claim to primacy than that of other moral viewpoints.[50]

> Viewed from the perspective of the would-be consumer of pornography, the principle of moral independence dictates a policy of tolera-

tion. Viewed from the feminist perspective it dictates a policy of re-
striction.[51]

The abandonment of a quest for common principles in favor of
the perspectivism of "viewpoints" is as marked in the debate on
pornography as elsewhere in moral philosophy. As for pornographic discourse itself, from that quarter we can expect no aid in
the form of philosophical self-defense: the pornographic is an entirely unreflective mode, perhaps because, unlike the erotic, where
self-awareness may generate further frissons of pleasure, pornography stands to gain nothing thereby.

Recourse to the Law

It is possible to dislike pornography, to find it offensive (which is
not quite the same as being offended by it), to believe that spending
a lot of time watching pornographic films is not good for people,
particularly for young people, and yet not to take the next step,
namely, to conclude that the manufacturers or distributors or ex-
hibitors of pornographic materials should therefore be liable to be
prosecuted or sued. Instead, one might settle for wishing unhappily
that pornography had less of a hold over people, as one might wish
that alcohol had less of a hold. That is, insofar as one might grant
there is a pornography problem, one might identify the source of
the problem as a weakness (not necessarily a moral weakness) in
humankind, rather than the ready availability of certain enticing
visual materials.

This is something like the conclusion Susan Sontag reaches in
her well-known essay "The Pornographic Imagination." While admitting that she has an aversion to pornography and is uncomfortable about its increasing availability, Sontag questions whether pornography should be distinguished from other freely obtainable
materials for which people may not have the "psychic preparation."
"Pornography is only one item among the many dangerous com-
modities being circulated in this society, and, unattractive as it may
be, one of the less lethal, the less costly to the community in terms
of human suffering."[52]

What has happened between 1967, when Sontag wrote the essay,
and the present is that (a) a boom has taken place in the pornography industry, (b) the incidence of violence against women, criminal

and domestic, has either increased or been uncovered in its enormity (or both), and (c) feminists have drawn connections between (a) and (b). In the process, Sontag's attitude has come to seem out of date or based on ignorance of the facts.

In nations founded on laws, there is a tendency to imagine that social problems must have legal solutions, and thus that the courts can be used to right historic wrongs and correct social imbalances.[53] "The idea that law has the power to right wrongs is pervasive," writes Carol Smart. "Just as medicine is seen as curative rather than *iatrogenic,* so law is seen as extending rights rather than creating wrong." In a warning vein, she continues: "We need to consider that in exercising law we may produce effects that make conditions worse, and that in worsening conditions we make the mistake of assuming that we need to apply more doses of legislation."[54]

Smart's caution reflects some difference of approach between feminist lawyers from Britain, like herself, and their North American counterparts. The difference is particularly noticeable in approaches to pornography. This may in part be because the Puritan project of legislating moral standards has not died out in America; but there are jurisprudential grounds as well. In a country where freedom of speech is constitutionally guarded (via the First Amendment), pornography has in the recent past enjoyed an unusual degree of protection, based, some of its opponents would say, on sophistical arguments; while the very narrow definition given to the concept of harm in British jurisprudence makes it difficult for feminists there to argue that pornography causes harm.[55] But even so skeptical a commentator on legal activism as Carole Pateman, who sees it as the proper goal of feminism not to destroy the pornography industry but to "undermine" the representation of women given by pornography, concludes that, taking into account the scale of the pornography industry, "perhaps the law is a necessary recourse for women."[56]

It is as well to spell out what Smart means by "iatrogenic" medicine and "juridogenic" law. Just as medicine not only cures disease but creates a medical profession and a pharmaceutical industry, so law not only judges cases but creates a legal profession and a law industry. In particular, censorship laws create a bureaucracy of censors and a parallel legal industry (legal departments in publishing houses and film studios, lawyers specializing in free-speech cases). In states that take their censoring role seriously, censors outnumber writers (the old Soviet Union) and more money is spent on policing the arts than on fostering them (the old South Africa, massively).

While in theory the problem may be formulated as whether or not pornographers have a right to free expression, the practical question, as anyone with experience of censorship knows, is how to distinguish the censorable from the permissible in an equitable fashion. Neither in countries where the ideological brief of the censor has been overt (as in the Soviet Union and South Africa) nor in countries where relations between political power and juridical orthodoxy have been more complexly mediated (as in the United States) does either the history of censorship legislation or the application of that legislation give cause for confidence.[57]

Recourse to the Law: Irigaray

In a larger conspectus, should women be looking for redress to the law, a system whose origins are deeply imbricated with patriarchy? Is recourse to the law and to the categories of the law compatible with feminism as a philosophical enterprise?

One obvious response is that women are entitled to further their interests by whatever means they find best, including the courts. In the process of confronting women's issues it can be expected that the courts and even the law will give up a certain degree of their bias.

A more cautious response is expressed by Carol Smart: the price of using the law to enforce "feminist standards," which entails adapting feminist theory to fit the legal grid, will inevitably be the loss of much of the complexity of that theory. Furthermore, the move may be strategically unwise: on issues of censorship feminists too often find themselves in alliance with the moral Right. Of Catharine MacKinnon—whose political orientation is left-wing and indeed Marxist—Smart writes: "Ultimately [hers] becomes a position virtually indistinguishable from the moral right in terms of its antithesis to sexuality and its reliance on blunt modes of legal censorship." Smart recalls the paradox of censorship enunciated by Annette Kuhn (a paradox of which MacKinnon herself is well aware), that in a sense pornography needs censorship to increase its allure, to make it into the forbidden and desired object, and thus to give it the status of a repressed truth, whereas "it is the very idea that pornography is the truth of sex . . . that needs to be challenged."[58]

But the most general articulation of the problem of the relation of women to the law has been set out by Luce Irigaray. In Irigaray's view, women start in an impossible position. "Women are in a position of exclusion. . . . Man's discourse, inasmuch as it sets forth the law . . . [knows] what there is to know about that exclusion." The exclusion of women is "*internal* to an order from which nothing escapes: the order of (man's) discourse." It is futile to imagine that, from a pocket within man's discourse—for instance, from within the legal system—women can substitute feminine power for masculine power: while seeming to be a reversal, this "phallic 'seizure of power'" would leave women still "caught up in the economy of the same." "There is no simple manageable way to leap to the outside of phallogocentrism, *nor any possible way to situate oneself there* [on the outside], *that would result from the simple fact of being a woman.*" Man's discourse can be taken over only via the path of "mimicry." Unless the woman's utterances are to remain "unintelligible according to the code in force," they must be "borrowed from a model that leaves [her] sex aside."[59]

All of which does not mean, however, that the law, as part of the discourse of the masculine imaginary, has to remain a closed and forbidden book. On the contrary, once a woman has reconnoitered it and demarcated its "outside," she can situate herself with respect to it as woman, "implicated in it and at the same time exceeding its limits." But her implication in it cannot be unambivalent, and therefore cannot be taken with unequivocal seriousness. To inhabit the male imaginary seriously is to commit herself to a simple reversal of power, to fall back into "the economy of the same."

To Irigaray, feminism and jurisprudence are thus not incompatible. But a feminist jurisprudence that is not ludic, that in return for access to the law concedes the claim of the law to its dignity and respects that dignity, by that concession gives up its independence. "Isn't laughter the first form of liberation from a secular oppression? *Isn't the phallic tantamount to the seriousness of meaning?*"

"To escape from a pure and simple reversal of the masculine position means . . . not to forget to laugh."[60]

Outrage

The language of the law, in its dealings with the emotions, is markedly clumsy. How do we feel when we feel offended, asks Joel
Feinberg? His answer (the collective answer of the law, gathered
from centuries of introspection on the part of lawyers): we feel any
or all of a miscellany of states of unpleasure, including but not limited to disgust, shame, hurt, and anxiety; also a measure of resentment against the one on whom this unpleasure is blamed.[61]

The unpleasure of being-offended is not necessarily a form of
pain. Pornography may cause sexual arousal; this arousal may be
indulged and, to an extent, enjoyed; yet the experience may even-
tuate in disgust and an urge to repudiate whatever precipitated it.
This ambivalence—and, from a moral point of view, this hypoc-
risy—no doubt reflects disturbance at deeper psychic levels. Nevertheless, it is a common progression and a common response.[62]

The nuances of emotional states are personal and perhaps private; they interact and combine quasi-chemically. Shame is shame,
hurt is hurt, but shame plus hurt make up a new compound for
which we have no name except the sum of the names of its con-
stituents. Shame plus hurt plus resentment yield an even
more complex compound whose synthetic name might include at
the very least shame-at-feeling-resentment and resentment-at-
feeling-shame, two highly reactive compounds in themselves.

But the very project of defining the component elements of the
feeling of being offended—the project of getting to the bottom of
offense—can be put in question. In his account of the moral emotions, based on Adam Smith's theory of the moral sentiments, Edward Westermarck makes moral indignation (offense, outrage) a
sister-emotion to the complex anger-revenge, and locates the origin
of both in the primitive retributive emotion of resentment. He
writes:

> It is the instinctive desire to inflict counter-pain that gives to moral
> indignation its most important characteristic. . . . The reason why
> moral judgments are passed on volitional beings, or their acts, is not
> merely that they are volitional but that they are sensitive as well;

and however much we try to concentrate our indignation on the [offending] act, it [the moral judgment] derives its peculiar flavor from being directed against a sensitive agent.

No moral judgment can therefore, logically speaking, be passed on retributive urges, since retribution is the basis of moral judgment itself.[63]

Like the taxonomy of the emotions embodied in Western law, the account of the emotions given by Smith and Westermarck is free of the machinery of psychoanalytic psychology; to this extent the two systems cohere. If, as Westermarck claims, group emotions—"public indignation and public approval"—are the prototypes of the moral emotions,[64] then the feelings of people coming together in groups to denounce or applaud are the primes of moral judgments, and it would be misguided to try to separate out even more primitive flavors (disgust, shame, hurt, anxiety, or whatever) in the denunciatory spirit. It may make practical sense to treat anger (indignation, outrage, being-offended) as the primitive emotion out of which condemnatory action springs, and to give up trying to elaborate a morally tasteful basis for that anger. In other words, within the field of legal psychology it may make sense to be as little self-reflective as feminists of the Andrea Dworkin–Catharine MacKinnon school, who have hitherto been criticized for their unthinkingness: to them, complains Carol Smart, "anger *is* the analysis"; if they find an image "problematic and distasteful, . . . this sufficiently identifies the problem [for them] and provides a basis for censorship."[65]

To doubt the value, in a *legal* context, of trying to distinguish shades of emotion behind the censoring reflex is not to concede *ethical* justification to anger and unthinking action flowing from anger. Anger is an emotion that stifles questioning and self-questioning: in the very blindness of blind anger we identify its ethical fragility. There is something paradoxical about anger: at the same time that it concentrates the forces of the body and overrides all inner checks, turning the body into a tower of strength, it stiffens thought, forfeits mobility, becomes vulnerable to the sly dart (the arrow of Paris shot into Achilles' heel), to mockery, laughter. Once one has viewed anger coolly from the outside, it is hard to inhabit states of anger or indignation from the inside in any spirit of authenticity. Anger is thereafter not necessarily a lost resource; but one can be angry only in a spirit of what Irigaray calls mimicry: half inside the state, half outside. This perhaps why the first goal of anger is to make its antagonist angry too—to blind him (or her).

The Pornographic Project

In the shoddiness of their execution, their lack of creative but even more of erotic imagination, their blank incomprehension of the human issues they poke their fingers into, the everyday products of the pornography industry seem unworthy of the attention accorded them by scholars and lawyers. Yet the very qualification implied in the word "everyday" raises the question: what is there in the range of pornography that is not everyday?

There does, of course, exist something called erotic art (erotic verse, erotic fiction, erotic pictures, erotic films) that is meant to put commercial pornography in its place by demonstrating that sex can be handled with imagination, intelligence, and even taste. Yet in the very act of falling back on the protection of the law (claiming a redeeming aesthetic value) and thus measuring its distance from the pornographic, the erotic seems to dodge the test, to settle for being daring but ultimately only chic, for being outrageous without evoking real outrage; whereas the pornographic, though oafish, at least retains a certain raw, wild quality.[66]

The truth is that it is not in the erotic mode but in the pornographic mode that real assaults have taken place, not only on moral norms and indeed on norms of human conduct, but on the limits of representation itself, or at least on the idea that representation must have limits. There is nothing admirable about such assaults: in fact, because of the extramoral position from which they are launched, the admirable is an accolade they must reject. Nevertheless, and despite the excesses of her language, Susan Sontag is right to point to the importance of the pornographer-writers Sade, Lautreamont, and Bataille, and the hostility or derision with which they confront the rational ideal of integrating sex into a pleasant, happy, ordered, and productive life—of taming sex and setting it to work for personal enjoyment. In their work, says Sontag, the obscene becomes "a primal notion of human consciousness" and sexuality asserts itself as "something beyond good and evil, beyond

love, beyond sanity . . . one of the demonic forces in human consciousness," driving people to "taboo and dangerous desires" extending from "the impulse to commit sudden arbitrary violence"
to a voluptuous yearning for death itself.[67]

Sontag thus sees the great pornographers as restoring the demonic truth of desire that civility tends to cover over. But she
makes a slip—a slip all the stranger for occurring in an essay called
"The Pornographic Imagination"—in conflating the ambitions of
pornography with the ambitions of sexual desire itself. It is one
thing to acknowledge the demonic, another to act it out. There is a
deep sense in which Jane Austen finds sex as demonic as Sade does.
She finds it demonic and therefore locks it out. What she emphatically does not share with Sade is any faith in the capacity of the
rituals of writing, in acting out the motions of demonic desire, to
break down the bounds of the self. This entirely metaphysical ambition, linked to but to be distinguished from the ambition of transcending the self by the route of sexual excess, is what animates
the frenziedly repetitive pornography of Sade, of whom Bataille
writes: "He had the misfortune to live [that] dream, whose obses-
sion is the soul of philosophy, [namely] the unity of subject and
object. The identity is the transcendence of the limitations of beings, of the object of desire and the subject which desires."[68]

Pornography is a form of warfare: it is absurd to imagine Sade
appealing to the law for protection against taboos on exhibiting ob-
scenities. By the standards of a project as Luciferian (or satanic) as
Sade's, it is also absurd to think of the taboo as a trick mechanism
used by pornography to make itself desirable, or, in MacKinnon's
word, "sexy."[69] In both senses of the locution, Sade is *behind* the
taboo. An alignment of forces is thus conceivable which would lo-
cate a Sadean philosophy of the bedroom, including a Sadean feminism, on one side—the outlaw side—of the bar on pornography,
and ancestral patriarchy and normative feminism on the other, the
side of the law. Such an alignment would reflect—paradoxically—
the position of feminists who warn against a ban on pornography.
"Feminists and moral majoritists," writes Linda Williams, should
look beyond the violence against women in pornography to the diversity of sexual practices represented in pornography, a diversity
which "contributes to the defeat of the phallic economy's original

desire to fix the sexual identity of the woman as the mirror of its own desire"—that is, to define woman as the object of male desire. "In the multiplication of . . . diverse [sexual] practices, [pornography] undermines its original goal of fixing and representing the linear and visible narrative truth of female sexual pleasure."[70]

What is here endorsed is a Sadean and therefore *perverse* pornography running counter to the "phallic economy." While she accepts a simplistic conception of male desire as a desire that knows its object (she does not reflect, for instance, on the more Hegelian conception of desire that desires the other's desire), Williams at least cautions against a form of censorship that takes it as its task to isolate, judge, and grade the scenes of the pornographic work, setting aside as irrelevant their diversity and their formal juxtapositions—in other words, ignoring the work as a whole.

Pornography and Advertising

In the popular songs, fiction, and films of the past thirty or forty years, sex has become steadily more explicit; in advertising, the sexualization of imagery has steadily grown more blatant. These cultural phenomena and the growth of the pornography industry are undoubtedly related. The question is, how should the relation be expressed? Are both the sexualization of the environment and the spread of pornography to be understood as manifestations of a single, broad historical current, or is pornography the pioneer art, and are the other arts infected with the pornographic virus?

To this question—in essence a question about the social significance of pornography—feminists respond variously. Carol Smart, for instance, finds advertising, soap operas, and romantic fiction more influential than pornography as vehicles for fixing and conveying representations of women.[71] On the other hand, Rosalind Coward sees pornography as a pervasive force: "It seems to me that the look now [in 1984] dominating women's magazines in general has come direct from pornography"; "The more routinely available images of women . . . all draw on the conventions by which women are represented in pornography." To Coward, it is pornography above all that has created the regime and the codes within which images of women, and hence women's bodies, are read. This way of looking at women had its origin in the appropriating and dominating gaze of the man, particularly the urban *flâneur*, but today it is the camera that teaches men, as well as other women, how to see her.[72]

The latter analysis, which in a broader form makes of pornography a kind of testing ground for techniques of sexualization and objectification that are then exploited in the popular media, particularly in advertising, and thence gradually infuse both social and private life, leads naturally to the conclusion that, for feminists, pornography should be the first target to attack.

A more cautious alternative analysis, one that attributes less of a leading role to pornography, would see both visual pornography and visual advertising as expressions of commercial forces that are as much concerned to define, whip up, commodify, package, and sell desire itself as to propagate new, or reinforce old, models of how to desire (through the eyes, for instance) or to sell images. In the desire business, where the fashion photographer and the pornographer move in the same circles and may indeed be the same person, advertising may even hold a lead over pornography, not only because it involves bigger money but because it has a more coherent theoretical program. Advertising undertakes no more than to promise, while at some level pornography takes it upon itself to do what no representation can in fact do: to deliver. The advertisement remains wholly within the constitution of the sign: it is something standing for something else; whereas, in offering to be the thing itself, pornography violates its own constitution. Hence its characteristic frenzy and hence perhaps its increasing violence, to be understood as the violence of frustration. In its use of taboo, too, advertising is more canny than pornography. Knowing that it cannot deliver, it points to the taboo: But for that, it says, I could show you what you want; for the present you will have to be satisfied with less, with only a glimpse. Pornography, on the other hand, first violates the taboo and then, for its own survival, has to resurrect it elsewhere.

As Roland Barthes observes, the glimpse is more erotically charged than the thing bared.[73] The nature of desire is promise, not delivery. Advertising *employs* desire in a way that pornography does not (pornography wastes desire). To this extent advertising is central to the business of desire, pornography peripheral.

CHAPTER TWO

Emerging from Censorship

From the early 1960s until about 1980, the Republic of South Africa operated one of the most comprehensive censorship systems in the world. Called in official parlance not censorship but "publications control" (*censorship* was a word it preferred to censor from public discourse about itself),[1] it sought to control the dissemination of signs in whatever form. Not only books, magazines, films, and plays, but T-shirts, key-rings, dolls, toys, and shop-signs—anything, in fact, bearing a message that might be "undesirable"—had to pass the scrutiny of the censorship bureaucracy before it could be made public. In the Soviet Union, there were some 70,000 bureaucrats supervising the activities of some 7,000 writers. The ratio of censors to writers in South Africa was, if anything, higher than ten to one.

Paranoids behave as though the air is filled with coded messages deriding them or plotting their destruction. For decades the South African state lived in a state of paranoia. Paranoia is the pathology of insecure regimes and of dictatorships in particular. One of the features distinguishing modern from earlier dictatorships has been how widely and rapidly paranoia can spread from above to infect the whole of the populace. This diffusion of paranoia is not inadvertent: it is used as a technique of control. Stalin's Soviet Union is the prime example: every citizen was encouraged to suspect every other citizen of being a spy or saboteur; the bonds of human sympathy and trust between people were broken down; and society fragmented into tens of millions of individuals living on individual islets of mutual suspicion.

The Soviet Union was not unique. The Cuban novelist Reinaldo Arenas wrote of an atmosphere of "unceasing official menace" in his country that made a citizen "not only a repressed person, but also a self-repressed one, not only a censored person, but a self-censored one, not only one watched over, but one who watches over himself."[2] "Unceasing official menace" punctuated with spectacles of exemplary punishment inculcates caution, watchfulness. When certain kinds of writing and speech, even certain thoughts, become surreptitious activities, then the paranoia of the state is on its way to being reproduced in the psyche of the subject, and the state can look forward to a future in which the bureaucracies of supervision can be allowed to wither away, their function having been, in effect, privatized.

For it is a revealing feature of censorship that it is not proud of itself, never parades itself. The archaic model for the censor's ban is the ban on blasphemy, and both bans suffer an embarrassing structural paradox, namely, that if a crime is to be satisfactorily attested in court, the testimony will have to repeat the crime. Thus it used to be that in the public sessions of the rabbinical courts witnesses to blasphemy were supplied with codified euphemisms to utter in place of the banned name of the Holy; if the actual blasphemy had to be repeated to make conviction conclusive, the court moved into closed session, and testimony was followed by rituals of purgation on the part of the judges. Embarrassment went even further: the very notion that the name of the Holy as a blasphemous word could curse the Holy was so scandalous that for "curse" the word "bless" had to be substituted.[3] Just as a chain of euphemisms came into being to protect the name of the Holy, so in an age when the state was worshipped the office that protected its name had to be euphemized. That office waits for the day when, its functions having been universally internalized, its name need no longer be spoken.

The tyrant and his watchdog are not the only ones touched by paranoia. There is a pathological edge to the watchfulness of the writer in the paranoid state. For evidence one need only go to the testimony of writers themselves. Time and again they record the feeling of being touched and contaminated by the sickness of the state. In a move typical of "authentic" paranoids, they claim that their minds have been invaded; it is against this invasion that they express their outrage.

The Greek writer George Mangakis, for instance, records the experience of writing in prison under the eyes of his guards. Every few days the guards searched his cell, taking away his writings and returning those which the prison authorities—his censors—considered "permissible." Mangakis recalls suddenly "loathing" his papers as he accepted them from the hands of his guards. "The system is a diabolical device for annihilating your own soul. They want to make you see your thoughts through their eyes and control them yourself, from their point of view."[4] By forcing the writer to see what he has written through the censor's eyes, the censor forces him to internalize a contaminating reading. Mangakis's sudden, revulsive moment is the moment of contamination.

Another passionate account of the operations of introverted censorship is given by Danilo Kis:

> The battle against self-censorship is anonymous, lonely and unwitnessed, and it makes its subject feel humiliated and ashamed of collaborating. [It] means reading your own text with the eyes of another person, a situation where you become your own judge, stricter and more suspicious than anyone else. . . .
>
> The self-appointed censor is the *alter ego* of the writer, an *alter ego* who leans over his shoulder and sticks his nose into the text . . . It is impossible to win against this censor, for he is like God—he knows and sees all, he came out of your own mind, your own fears, your own nightmares. . . .
>
> This *alter ego* . . . succeeds in undermining and tainting even the most moral individuals whom outside censorship has not managed to break. By not admitting that it exists, self-censorship aligns itself with lies and spiritual corruption.[5]

The final proof that something has, so to speak, gone wrong with writers like Arenas or Mangakis or Kis is the excessiveness of the language in which they express their experience. Paranoia is not just a figurative way of talking about what has afflicted them. The paranoia is there, on the inside, in their language, in their thinking; the rage one hears in Mangakis' words, the bafflement in Kis's, are rage and bafflement at the most intimate of invasions, an invasion of the very style of the self, by a pathology for which there may be no cure.

Nor am I, as I write here, exempt. In the excessive insistency of its phrasing, its vehemence, its demand for sensitivity to minutiae of style, its overreading and overwriting, I detect in my own language the very pathology I discuss. Having lived through the heyday of South African censorship, seen its consequences not only on the careers of fellow-writers but on the totality of public discourse, and felt within myself some of its more secret and shameful effects, I have every reason to suspect that whatever infected Arenas or Mangakis or Kis, whether real or delusional, has infected me too. That is to say, this very writing may be a specimen of the kind of paranoid discourse it seeks to describe.

For the paranoia I address is not the imprint of censorship on those writers alone who are singled out for official persecution. All writing that in the normal course of events falls under the censor's eye may become tainted in the manner I have described, whether or not the censor passes it. All writers under censorship are at least potentially touched by paranoia, not just those who have their work suppressed.

Why should censorship have such contagious power? I can offer only a speculative answer, an answer based in part on introspection, in part on a scrutiny (perhaps a paranoid scrutiny) of the accounts that other writers (perhaps themselves infected with paranoia) have given of operating under regimes of censorship.

The self, as we understand the self today, is not the unity it was assumed to be by classical rationalism. On the contrary, it is multiple and multiply divided against itself. It is, to speak in figures, a zoo in which a multitude of beasts have residence, over which the anxious, overworked zookeeper of rationality exercises a rather limited control. At night the zookeeper sleeps and the beasts roam about, doing their dream-work.

In this figural zoo, some of the beasts have names, like figure-of-the-father and figure-of-the-mother; others are memories or fragments of memories in transmuted form, with strong elements of feeling attached to them; a whole subcolony are semitamed but still treacherous earlier versions of the self, each with an inner zoo of its own over which it has less than complete control.

Artists, in Freud's account, are people who can make a tour of the inner menagerie with a degree of confidence and emerge, when they so wish, more or less unscathed. From Freud's account of creative work I take one element: that creativity of a certain kind involves inhabiting and managing and exploiting quite primitive parts of the self. While this is not a particularly dangerous activity, it is a delicate one. It may take years of preparation before the artist finally gets the codes and the keys and the balances right, and can move in and out more or less freely. It is also a very private activity, so private that it almost constitutes the definition of privacy: how I am with myself.

Managing the inner selves, making them work for one (making them productive) is a complex matter of pleasing and satisfying and challenging and extorting and wooing and feeding, and sometimes even of putting to death. For writing not only comes out of the zoo but (to be hypermetaphorical) goes back in again. That is to say, insofar as writing is transactional, the figures *for whom* and *to whom* it is done are also figures in the zoo: for instance, the figure-of-the-beloved.

Imagine, then, a project in writing that is, at heart, a transaction with some such figure of the beloved, that tries to please her (but that also tries continually though surreptitiously to revise and recreate her as the-one-who-will-be-pleased); and imagine what will happen if into this transaction is introduced in a massive and undeniable way another figure-of-the-reader, the dark-suited, bald-headed censor, with his pursed lips and his red pen and his irritability and his censoriousness—the censor, in fact, as parodic version of the figure-of-the-father. Then the entire balance of the carefully constructed inner drama will be destroyed, and destroyed in a way that is hard to repair, since the more one tries to ignore (repress) the censor, the larger he swells.

Working under censorship is like being intimate with someone who does not love you, with whom you want no intimacy, but who presses himself in upon you. The censor is an intrusive reader, a reader who forces his way into the intimacy of the writing transaction, forces out the figure of the loved or courted reader, reads your words in a disapproving and *censorious* fashion.

One of Stalin's principal victims among writers was Osip Mandelstam. From the case of Mandelstam—which I take up in greater detail in Chapter 6—I extract certain important and appalling lessons about the paranoid state.

In 1933, Mandelstam, then 42 years old, composed a short but powerful poem about a tyrant who orders executions left, right, and center, and relishes the deaths of his victims like a Georgian munching raspberries. Though the tyrant is not named, the reference is clearly to Stalin.

Mandelstam did not write the poem down, but recited it several times to friends. In 1934, his home was raided by security police looking for the poem. Though they did not find it—it existed solely inside the heads of the poet and his friends—they arrested him. While he was under arrest, the poet Boris Pasternak had a telephone call from Stalin. Who is Mandelstam, Stalin wanted to know? In particular, is he a *master*? (The word is the same in Russian as in English.)

Pasternak correctly inferred the second half of the question: Is Mandelstam a master or is he disposable? Pasternak replied, in effect, that Mandelstam was a master, that he was not disposable. So Mandelstam was sentenced to internal exile in the city of Voronezh. While he was living there, pressure was brought to bear on him to pay tribute to Stalin by composing a poem in his honor. Mandelstam gave in and composed an adulatory ode. What he felt about this ode we will never know, not only because he left no record, but because—as his wife persuasively argues—he was mad when he wrote it, mad with fear, perhaps, but mad too with the madness of a person not only suffering the embrace of a body he detests, but having to take the initiative, day after day, line after line, to caress that body.

From this story I isolate two moments: the moment when Stalin asks whether Mandelstam is a master, and the moment when Mandelstam is ordered to celebrate his persecutor.

"Is he a master?" We can be sure Stalin was not asking because he regarded great artists as above the state. What he meant was something like, Is he dangerous? Is he going to live, even if he dies? Is his sentence on me going to live longer than my sentence on him? Do I have to be careful?

Hence the command later on that Mandelstam write an ode.

Making the great artists of his day kowtow to him was Stalin's way of breaking them, of making it impossible for them to hold their heads up—in effect, of showing them who was master, and of making them acknowledge him as master in a medium where no lie, no private reservation, was possible: their own art.

Side by side with the case of Mandelstam let me set a case from South Africa (dealt with more fully in Chapter 12), comparable in dynamic if not in scale.

In 1972 the poet Breyten Breytenbach published a poem in Afrikaans entitled "Letter to Butcher from Foreign Parts." As the poem made clear, the butcher to whom the letter was addressed was Balthazar John Vorster, then prime minister of the Republic of South Africa, the man who had done most to create a security-police empire with huge powers over life and death, untouchable by the law, above the courts.

At the end of the poem, Breytenbach lists the names of men who had died, probably under torture at the hands of the security police, and for whose deaths the courts had found no one culpable. The poem baldly lists the names, as if asserting, "It is I that will live in memory and in history, not the court records." The heart of the poem, however, is a passage addressed to the butcher himself in which Breytenbach asks Vorster in the most intimate of ways what it is like for him to use fingers red with blood to fondle his wife's private parts. It is a shocking and obscene question, all the more obscene when uttered in a highly puritanical society. The poem was, of course, banned in South Africa.

Two years later the tables were turned. Breytenbach found himself under arrest and in the dock. Though the substantial charge was that he had tried to recruit saboteurs, his writings, particularly the poem against Vorster, soon emerged as a subtext to the proceedings. The goal of the prosecution, as it emerged, was to break him in much the same way that Mandelstam had been broken. This goal was attained: Breytenbach was brought to apologize to Vorster in open court, repudiating his own poem as "crass and insulting."

Confronting the vast machinery of the state, including its well-developed machinery of censorship, both Mandelstam and Breytenbach were clearly powerless. Yet their respective heads of state—

both, as it happened, philistines—responded to their writings as if deeply offended, and deemed the cases important enough to merit personal attention. Why could the two poems in question, however insulting, not have been ignored like the pinpricks they were? Why need the antics of writers concern the state at all?

To answer this question, to understand the troubled relations between writers and the state in all their long history, we need to reflect not on single cases but on authorship as an institution, with a history going back to the beginnings of the modern age, and on the ambitions opened up to individuals by a career in authorship.

The notion that, by dint of writing, a person could aspire to and attain fame, was neither invented nor fostered by scribal culture, the culture of the West before the invention of printing. Such ambitions belong to print culture. We begin to see evidence soon after the invention of printing, as printers make it their practice to attach authors' names to the books they put out. Certainly this signing of the book had its commercial and legal side: the originator of the book laid claim to a share of the profits from its sale while accepting a share of the legal responsibility for its publication.[6] Since copyright law would not arrive until the eighteenth century, what forced the writer to accept definition as a legal entity—to become an *author* with all the legal responsibilities thereby entailed—was the institution and the power of censorship.[7]

But signing a book also has a symbolic meaning. A book can be seen as a vehicle used by an author to project his signature—and indeed sometimes his portrait—into the world, in a multiplied form. It is this potentially endless multiplication of traces of himself that gives to the author in the early modern age intimations of a power to cross all spatial and temporal boundaries. In visions of fame and immortality authorship and the mystique of the author as we know it today is born.[8]

The word of the author echoes in the ear of the reading public. Without his public, the author is nothing. This reading public is a creation less of authors themselves than of the early printer-publishers. It is also a model of the people as imagined in the philosophy of the early modern state: literate, integrated (as a body is integrated), receptive to direction. Thus it is no accident that, as habits of reading spread, state censorship takes on a more systematic, pervasive, and rigorous character, as though in printers and their authors the state had identified not so much an enemy (though in fact that is what they were often labeled) as a rival for power. From the sixteenth century onward we begin to detect in the language of the state, when it turns to authors and their powers, a note of distinctly modern paranoia, a paranoia that, as Tony Tanner reminds us, is predictable in and, indeed, necessary to a regime of censorship.[9] Here, for instance, is Sir Nicholas Bacon, England's Lord Keeper in 1567:

> These books . . . [make] men's minds to be at variance one with another, and diversity of minds maketh seditions, seditions bring in tumults, tumults make insurrections and rebellions, insurrections make depopulations and bring in utter ruin and destruction of men's bodies, goods and lands.[10]

Repressive censorship is usually thought of as part of the apparatus of absolutist or totalitarian states: the Russia of Nicholas I, Stalin's Soviet Union. But the rulers of early modern Europe, civil and clerical, viewed the book as a vehicle for sedition and heresy at least as seriously, and operated systems of censorship that were sweeping, draconian, and surprisingly sophisticated in their mechanisms.[11] As early as the sixteenth century, authors and printer-publishers were viewed from above as not only an interest group with a strong (and self-justifying) sense of historical mission but an elite with an ability to create a following among the influential literate sector of society in a way that was unsettlingly similar to the ambitions of the state itself.

The history of censorship and the history of authorship—even of literature itself, as a set of practices[12]—are thus intimately bound together. With the advent of printing and the rapid multiplication of copies, the fortunes of the author rose; he grew in power, but also became the object of suspicion and even envy on the part of the state. It is only in the late twentieth century, with the rise to dominance of new, electronic media and the decline of the book, that the state has lost interest in the author and his waning powers.

II

There is nothing that raises the hackles of writers like the threat of censorship, no topic that calls forth a more pugnacious instinctive response. I have suggested why the threat of censorship is felt so intimately; I turn to the rhetoric in which that response is typically framed.

"Is he a master?" asked Stalin. Whether Mandelstam was a master writer or not, what had Stalin to fear from him? I raise this question again in the framework of a contest between state and author to spread their respective words of authority by their respective powers.

In this framework, the object of the state's envy is not so much the rival content of the author's word, or even specifically the power he gets from the press to spread that word, as a certain disseminative power of which the power to publish and have read is only the most marked manifestation. While the power of authors in general is slight without the multiplier effect of the press, the word of the master author has a disseminative power that goes beyond purely mechanical means of dissemination. The master's word, particularly in cultures where an oral base survives, can spread by word of mouth, or from hand to hand in carbon copies (*samizdat'*, literally, "self-publication"); even when the word itself is not spread, it can be replaced by rumors of itself, rumors that spread like copies (in the case of Mandelstam, the rumor that someone had written a poem about which the Leader was furious).

Furthermore, a logic seems to spring into operation that works to the state's disadvantage. "A tyrant cannot take notice of a Fable without putting on the cap that fits," remarked a nineteenth-century editor of Aesop.[13] The more draconically the state comes down on writing, the more seriously it is seen to be taking writing; the more seriously it is seen to be taking writing, the more attention is paid to writing; the more attention is paid to writing, the more the disseminative potential of writing grows. The book that is suppressed gets more attention as a ghost than it would have had alive; the writer who is gagged today is famous tomorrow for having been gagged. Even silence, in an environment of censorship, can be eloquent, as Montesquieu observes.[14]

No matter what the state does, writers always seem to get the last word. The craft-solidarity of men and women of letters—the intellectual community, the academic community, even the journalistic community—can be surprisingly strong. And those who write the books, in an important sense, make history.

Underlying the confidence among intellectuals in the inevitability of a reversal of power in their favor lies the Judaeo-Christian teaching of the vindication of the truth in the fullness of time. There are many instances of this confidence in our own age. In the old South Africa, writers, no matter how much marginalized and repressed, knew that in the long run the censors would lose—not only because the regime of which censorship was an arm was doomed to collapse, not only because puritanical moral standards were on the wane in a worldwide economy of consumption, but because, as a community, writers would outlast their foes and even write their epitaph.

It is the very vitality of this myth of the inevitability of the emergence of the truth—a myth that intellectuals as a class have annexed and made their own—that leads me to ask whether writers under censorship are wholly disinterested in presenting themselves as embattled and outnumbered, confronting a gigantic foe. Since South Africa, where durable ties had long existed between writers—at least those to whom writing in English was an option—and foreign (principally British) publishers, may have been a special case, let me seek from farther abroad instances of how the conflict between writer and censor has been represented as a battle between David and Goliath.

In 1988, Seamus Heaney published an essay on the poets of Eastern Europe, particularly the Russian poets who suffered under Stalin, and on the effect upon the West of their exemplary lives. Tsvetaeva, Akhmatova, the Mandelstams, Pasternak, Gumilev, Esenin, Mayakovsky, says Heaney, have become "heroic names [in] . . . a modern martyrology, a record of courage and sacrifice which elicits . . . unstinted admiration." Even though they were silenced, the quality of their silence held an exemplary force. Their refusal to compromise their art "expose[d] to the majority [of Soviet citizens] the abjectness of their [own] collapse, as they [fled] for security into whatever self-deceptions the party line require[d] of them."[15]

To Heaney, these great persecuted writers were heroes and martyrs despite themselves. Neither seeking glory nor aspiring to bring about the downfall of the state, they merely remained true to their calling. In the process, however, they drew upon themselves the guilty resentment of those many who had given in to the menaces of the state, and so were left in vulnerable and ultimately tragic isolation.

There can be no question about the power of these life-stories to evoke our pity and terror. What I draw attention to, however, is the language of Heaney's account: to metaphors of battle, to the radical opposing of victory and defeat, suffering and triumph, courage and cowardice. Is the staging of the opposition between Russian writers and the Soviet state in terms of a metaphorics of battle not in itself a declaration of war that strangely betrays what Heaney admires in these writers: their unshakeable (but not wholly unshakeable—they were human, after all) fidelity to their art?

The idea that the poet at his desk could be a hero seems to have been invented by Thomas Carlyle. Carlyle singles out poetry as the path that religious energies must follow in the modern age, and the poet as the world-historical figure who, taking over the roles played earlier in human history by the god-man and the prophet, must define the patterns by which ordinary mortals will live. Though Carlyle evokes Dante and "Shakspeare" as precursors of the poet-hero, his conception remains essentially Shelleyan.[16]

To modern ears, the notion of poet as superman sounds quaint—quaint enough to have had to go underground.[17] Lionel Trilling certainly took up the challenge of keeping Carlyle's flame alive, but did so only at the cost of redefining and internalizing the heroic as a "moral energy" (which he glosses as a "mature masculinity") of a kind exhibited most clearly in Keats.[18] In his conception of the poet-hero as a figure of stubborn, principled resistance rather than as a prophet-pioneer, Heaney is closer to Trilling than to Carlyle. Yet his tribute to the poets who suffered under Stalin calls upon a particularly intransigent metaphorics of black and white without shades of gray. It describes a historical dynamic in which there are finally only two positions left open: for or against, good or bad, the self-censored cowardice of the herd or the uncensored heroism of the few. As a reading of life under Stalin, it seems, in its firm grasp on the handle of rhetorical power, to issue a challenge to all gray, toned-down readings of those times, perhaps even to nuanced readings. It constructs the relationship between writer and tyrant (or writer and censor) as that of a power-rivalry that can only grow more and more naked. It dooms the state to the same no-win dilemma that Ben Jonson triumphantly identified:

> Nor do they aught, that use this cruelty
> Of interdiction, and this rage of burning;
> But purchase to themselves rebuke, and shame,
> And to the writers an eternal name.[19]

If the state in extremis suffers from paranoia, then does the writer as hero of resistance, implacably attending to the voice of his daimon, not run an analogous psychic risk? Consider the following boast by Mario Vargas Llosa:

> The congenital unsubmissiveness of literature is much broader than is believed by those who consider it a mere instrument for opposing governments and dominant social structures: it strikes equally at everything [that] stands for dogma and logical exclusivism in the interpretation of life, that is, both ideological orthodoxies and heterodoxies. *In other words, it is a living, systematic, inevitable contradiction of all that exists.*[20]

I take the liberty of reading this claim, nominally on behalf of literature, as in fact on behalf of writers as a professional and even vocational group, against both the bureaucrat-censor in the hire of the tyrant, and the tyrant's foe, the revolutionary scheming to enroll the writer in the grand army of the revolution. In their attitude to the writer, says Vargas Llosa, tyrant and revolutionary are more alike than they are different. Their opposition is, from the point of view of the writer, spurious or illusory or both. The writer's opposition, true opposition, means "systematic . . . contradiction" of them and their totalizing claims.

The maneuver executed by Vargas Llosa here—namely, shifting his own opposition to a logical level one floor higher than the ground-level political battle—implies that the writer occupies a position that simultaneously stands outside politics, rivals politics, and dominates politics. In its pride, this claim is quite Marlovian; however unwittingly, it suggests that the risk run by the writer-as-hero is the risk of megalomania.

CHAPTER THREE

Lady Chatterley's Lover: The Taint of the Pornographic

THE TRIAL OF *LADY CHATTERLEY*

In 1960 Penguin Books decided to publish the full text of *Lady Chatterley's Lover*, the text of the private (Florence) edition of 1928, replacing the expurgated (British) edition. In response, the Crown announced that it would prosecute. The affair was conducted in a thoroughly gentlemanly way as a test case for the newly ratified British Act on Obscene Publications (1959).

Though this act preserves the key feature of nineteenth-century British legislation on obscenity—the test of whether the publication "tends to deprave and corrupt persons likely to read it"—it introduces side by side with it certain not entirely compatible criteria drawn from literary criticism, namely, that the work has to be judged as a whole, and that literary merit, to which expert witnesses may testify, has to be taken into consideration; it directs that there should be no conviction if publication can be "justified as being for the public good on the grounds that it is in the interests of science, literature, art or learning, or any other objects of general concern."[1]

The defense of *Lady Chatterley's Lover* was conducted by a legal team with the resources of Penguin Books behind it, able to call in a stream of eminent witnesses to the merits of the book. The prosecution, by contrast, either could find no prominent witnesses to support its case or deemed it impolitic to call such witnesses.

Expert witnesses for the defense included an Anglican bishop who asserted that in *Lady Chatterley's Lover* Lawrence was trying

48

to portray the sexual relationship between man and woman as "something essentially sacred," and a director of religious education who suggested that reading the book would help young people to grow up "mature and responsible."[2]

> [The gamekeeper] stroked her tail with his hand. . . .
>   "Tha's got a nice tail on thee," he said, in the throaty, caressive dialect. "Tha's got the nicest arse of anybody. It's the nicest, nicest woman's arse as is! . . ." His fingertips touched the two secret openings to her body, time after time, with a soft little brush of fire.
>   "An' if tha shits an' if tha pisses, I'm glad. I don't want a woman as couldna shit nor piss."[3]

In his own commentary on the book, Lawrence writes:

> The words that shock so much at first don't shock at all after a while. . . . We are today . . . evolved and cultured far beyond the taboos which are inherent in our culture. . . . The evocative power of the so-called obscene words must have been very dangerous to the dim-minded, obscure, violent natures of the Middle Ages, and perhaps are still too strong for slow-minded, half-evoked lower natures today. . . . [But] culture and civilization have taught us . . . [that] the act does not necessarily follow on the thought.[4]

In this uncharacteristically enlightened, progressive dismissal of taboo, Lawrence is invoking the backing of the anthropology of his day, the anthropology of J. G. Frazer. In particular, Lawrence is using the notion of *survivals*, which Frazer takes over from Henry Burnett Tylor. Survivals are "customs . . . which have been carried by force of habit into the new society . . . and . . . thus remain as proofs and examples of an older condition of culture out of which the newer has evolved."[5] Taboos on words with sexual or excretory reference are thus survivals from a less highly evolved stage of European culture.

What harm is there in such survivals? Why should we be iconoclasts of the old taboos? The answer given by both Lawrence and his expert defenders is that to maintain taboos on words is to maintain an aura of shame around their reference, to the ultimate detriment of society. "Fifty yards from this court," testified the critic Richard Hoggart,

> I heard a man say "fuck" three times as he passed me. He was speaking to himself and he said "fuck it, fuck it, fuck it." . . . He [was

using] the word as a word of contempt, and one of the things Law-rence found most worrying was that the word for this important relationship had become a word of vile abuse. . . . [Lawrence] wanted to re-establish the meaning of [the word], the proper use of it.[6]

Whatever one's prior sympathies, it is hard to read the trial re-cord without sympathy for the prosecution. For, as the trial prog-resses, it becomes more and more clear that the prosecution is fighting with its hands tied. Witnesses are rarely prepared to stand up and testify that they have been depraved and corrupted by a book when such testimony evokes more ridicule than sympathy.[7] Only in the stuffiest, most venerable fora do we find the language of forthright moral condemnation—and, behind it, the tones of pa-ternalism and class hostility—still in use. In the wake of the acquit-tal of *Lady Chatterley's Lover,* the House of Lords debated a motion that the writings of D. H. Lawrence be banned in perpetuity. "I hold a very strong view," said Lord Teviot, who proposed the motion, "on giving unbridled licence to everybody in the country, and I am very anxious lest our world become depraved and indecent, to put it mildly." As for *Lady Chatterley's Lover,* it was a "disgusting, filthy affront to ordinary decencies."[8]

In the end, Lord Teviot was placated by his colleagues and with-drew his motion. But the House agreed that *Lady Chatterley's Lover* was an unfortunate business from beginning to end. Lord Gage summed up: it would certainly not be "very becoming" to find a book in such "very bad taste" on sale in public. As for the clerics who had lent themselves to the defense, their testimony evoked in him only "a considerable sense of the ridiculous" (p. 265).

Lord Gage's judgment was a representative conservative one, namely, that *Lady Chatterley's Lover* offends against decorum on a fairly gross scale. The problem for the Lords, however, was that rules of decorum depend on social consensus. In the England of Victoria to which they harked back, the terms of that consensus had been prescribed by the class to which they belonged. By 1960 their class had lost that prescriptive power, and lacked furthermore any way of appealing against the dismissal of its standards. For there is no logic, no body of evidence by which decorum can plead for and justify itself. It is of the essence of decorum to be tacit. Decorum marks off a domain about which there shall be silence, and preserves silence about how the boundaries of that domain are determined. Decorum can therefore be gestured towards but not codified. Once questioned, it turns to smoke.

Hence the dismay in the House as the Lords began to realize the implications of the 1959 act. By creating an overriding criterion of the public good, to be attested to by expert witnesses—in most cases, academics from outside the old consensus—the act demanded that decorum plead for itself. If the Lords shook their heads over the role the Church had played in the acquittal of *Lady Chatterley's Lover*, it was because the Church ought surely to understand that there are matters one does not debate: commandments, taboos. For taboo, too, has no defense against being questioned.

LAWRENCE'S DEFENSE OF *LADY CHATTERLEY*

The story Lawrence tells is of the wife of a member of the English aristocracy who has an affair with one of the servants of the estate, falls pregnant, and decides to run off with her lover. The intercourse of Connie Chatterley with the gamekeeper transgresses at least three rules: it is adulterous; it crosses caste boundaries; and it is sometimes "unnatural," i.e., anal. The second and third of these transgressions deserve comment.

Though we commonly speak of Sir Clifford Chatterley and his wife as belonging to an upper class, they more properly belong to an upper caste, part of a pan-European upper caste in the twilight of its days, characterized inter alia by endogamy and asymmetrical rules of sexual relations: men might freely cross caste boundaries in their sexual contacts, but for women this was interdicted, or, in the language of the caste, "not done." The rationale for this interdiction involved the notion of pollution: women carry the blood of the caste, and the blood-stock is polluted when it is invaded by the blood (or semen, which, in the language of pollution, is the same thing) of a man of lower caste. This interdiction is explicitly pointed to by the crippled Chatterley when he tells his wife he will give his name to any child she bears as long as she exercises her "natural instinct of decency and selection" and does not allow "the wrong sort of fellow [to] touch [her]" (*LCL*, p. 49).

The third transgression is carried out by the gamekeeper, Mellors, when he not only has intercourse with the lady of the manor but sodomizes her. Furthermore, Mellors' ex-wife spreads the news that he is a sodomist. Connie Chatterley is thus known all over the district to have had what used to be called a "crime against nature" committed upon her body—a crime whose transgressive nature was marked, in the British penal code of the 1920s, by draconian punishments, even for man and wife.

But besides these three transgressions, there is a fourth. Mellors, in the language of the day, *pollutes Connie's mind* by schooling her in the use of taboo words. In the Victorian mythology of pollution, "bad language" is the speech of a polluted mind. The only class of women in whose mouths bad language is expected to occur are so-called fallen women, women in a state of unredeemed defilement. Mellors' transgression is to teach a woman bad language. Bad language is harmless among men—when Mellors and Connie's father meet, the latter jovially applies taboo words to his daughter (*LCL*, p. 321)—but blasts the innocence of women and children.[9] (A language of men forbidden to women, and a language of women forbidden to men, are phenomena well attested in the literature of taboo, to say nothing of a language of adults forbidden to children.)

Lady Chatterley's Lover was followed by a series of prose pieces in which Lawrence defended himself against charges of being a pornographer: the introduction to the private edition of *Pansies* (1929), the essay "Pornography and Obscenity" (1929), the introduction to the 1929 book of paintings, and the pamphlet *A Propos of Lady Chatterley's Lover* (1930).[10] In these pieces he explores the origins of the pornographic imagination, origins that in his view lie in an excremental experience of sex. What does this mean?

Lawrence explains as follows. In "healthy" human beings, two kinds of flow take place: an excremental downward flow, in which form is dissolved and living matter becomes dirt; and a sexual upward flow which is both procreative and form-creating (cf. *LCL*, p. 316). In "degraded" human beings, however, the instinct to hold the polarities apart has collapsed, and the flow of the body is solely downward and decreative, issuing in dirt. Sexual play becomes a play with dirt; the body of the woman becomes the dirt the man plays with; sex, for the man, becomes an act of soiling. "Common individuals of this sort have a disgusting attitude towards sex, a disgusting contempt of it, a disgusting desire to insult it. If such fellows have intercourse with a woman, they triumphantly feel they have done her dirt" (*SLC*, pp. 38–39).

This is Lawrence's picture of the degraded or fallen state. When and how did the fall take place? With considerable tentativeness Lawrence situates it in the time of Elizabeth I. The shock of epidemic syphilis on England, particularly on the aristocracy, he suggests, resulted in a "rupture in human consciousness." "The pox entered the blood of the nation . . . After it had entered the blood, it entered the consciousness." But why should syphilis and no other disease have left this legacy? Because nothing can equal the horror of the realization that the issue of the sexual act may be a taint on the unborn (*SLC*, pp. 54, 55, 57).

In Lawrence's speculative fantasy, then, after a certain historical moment there is a fear that male seed may be tainted. The seed may be bad, the seed may be dirt: ejaculation becomes part of the excremental flux. From here it is a short step to Lawrence's next figure of sex in a fallen state. Sexual desire is no longer itself desired. Instead it is experienced as a suppurating wound in the body. The wound itches, is scratched, does not heal, oozes dirt, and adds its quota to the downward, excremental flow. Scratching is another name for masturbation, "perhaps the deepest and most dangerous cancer of our civilization." Introverted, self-enclosed desire expresses itself in an art of pure subjectivity (here Lawrence seems to have Proust and Joyce in mind, though he does not name them) (*SLC*, pp. 40–42).

What is the remedy? "The way to treat the disease is to come out into the open." We must have "a natural fresh openness about sex" (*SLC*, p. 40). Specifically, we must restore the fallen Word, the Word that has become "unclean." "To-day, if you suggest that the word arse was in the beginning, and was God and was with God, you will . . . be put in prison. . . . The word arse is as much god as the word face." The villain is the mind. The mind, hating the body, has turned the old body-words into scapegoats and driven them from consciousness. Now they haunt the margins of consciousness like jackals or hyenas, undying. They must be readmitted. The taboo must be lifted. If not, we will remain at the level of savages. "The kangaroo is a harmless animal, the word shit is a harmless word. Make either into a taboo and it becomes dangerous. The result of taboo is insanity." As an instance Lawrence cites Jonathan Swift, whose mind was "poisoned" as if by "some terrible constipation" by the thought that "Celia shits" (*SLC*, pp. 28–30).

Let us look further into the case of Lawrence's Swift, with his poisoned mind.

There are two poems of Swift's in which the phrase "Celia shits" occurs. They are about young men who play the idealizing game of pastoral love, but find that the pastoral will not contain the full reality of the beloved, body functions and all. The two poems belong to a group of four, all written about 1732, a decade before Swift was declared of unsound mind and placed under guardianship, which have attained a mild notoriety as the "excremental" or "scatological" poems.[11]

In the first of the "Celia shits" poems, the swain steals into Celia's dressing room and discovers with dismay the soiled underwear and makeup that lie behind her ethereal public front. Pressing on with his exploration of her private world, he gropes in the commode and fouls his hand in the pan. This experience unhinges him: in his tainted imagination the sight of a woman henceforth always calls up the smell of excrement.

In the second poem—a slighter piece—the swain (a student himself living in considerable squalor) finds that there is no place for "the blackest of all female deeds" in his Arcady, and similarly falls to raving.

In a straightforward reading, the two poems warn against idealizing the body, against closing the eyes and nose to the downward flow that is proof of its animal nature. What is repressed from consciousness inevitably returns to haunt us; the dirt whose existence is denied returns as dirty thoughts, dirty language. The poems present themselves as the work of a critic and moralizer who sets himself at an explicit distance from the idealizer with his fragile defenses against reality.[12]

In his dealings with Swift, Lawrence misremembers and misquotes these poems so badly, ignoring the moralizing distance, that one wonders whether he knew them at first hand or had simply heard of them from his friend Aldous Huxley.[13] But let me give Lawrence the benefit of the doubt and take up the most interesting possibility, namely, that Lawrence has given Swift a reading of genius, recognizing the moralizing as simply a screen—a screen erected by Swift to enable himself to represent a personal excremental crisis without the nakedness of overt confession.

In this reading, the true story is told by the bald narrative. A hand is plunged into a dark hole and comes out smelling of excrement; from hand via nose, the excremental taint invades and poisons the mind, as vengeance for penetration of the woman's sanctum.

> But Vengeance, goddess never sleeping,
> Soon punished Strephon for his peeping.
> His foul imagination links
> Each dame he sees with all her stinks. (Lines 119–22)

Lawrence comes back to these poems of Swift's several times in the late 1920s, always in order to hold Swift up as a terrifying example of what can happen if a taboo is taken to heart.[14] The word *shit* is harmless in itself, he says; but make it into a taboo and the result is insanity. Lawrence's Swift makes contact with his mistress's excrement, is flooded with contagion, and goes mad. Therefore—what? Therefore, says Lawrence, we must destroy the excremental taboo, not naively, as Laputans would do, by bringing the substance itself into the open, but symbolically, at one remove, by uttering the word *shit*, thereby purging the mind of the signified of the word, namely, the idea of shit-as-contagion.

Whether one treats Lawrence's understanding of Swift as gross or as inspired, his reading of the Celia poems can come only from a mind touched (or tainted) by something in the poem. What touches Lawrence, what takes control of his reading of Swift, is the idea of excremental taint. In the post-Chatterley essays he starts by denouncing Swift and anathematizing the excremental taboo, and ends by denouncing and anathematizing the idea of taint itself. The moral he claims for his tale of a commode—that *shit* ought to be just a word like any word—is a non sequitur. The moral he is really after is that only a mind already tainted can be touched by taint. Its converse is that it ought to be possible for an untainted mind to undertake any exploration whatsoever of the body, however tabooed, without suffering self-punishment. The question Lawrence does not face is, therefore: Is the very reading he gives Swift not made possible by a sharp nose for taint, a nose belonging to one acquainted with taint? Indeed, is any reading at all possible to a person without a nose? Where would such a reader begin reading? How would such a reader know, for example, that the point of entry into Swift's poem must be the word "taint" in line 112? Is there not a direct connection between reading, curiosity, and a nose for dirt? In a society without interdictions, without the Law—if such a society is imaginable—who would want to read or write?

(We may remember that in evolutionary biology the region of the cortex given over in lower mammals to olfactory discrimination assumes in *homo sapiens* the function of abstract discrimination. The activity in animals called smelling is in human beings called analytic thinking.)

At some point during the reign of Elizabeth I, says Lawrence, the horror of syphilis—of sexual taint—migrated from the blood to the deeper consciousness of the English people. After this rupture in consciousness "the real natural innocence of Chaucer" was no longer possible. Whereas Shakespeare is "morbid with fear," "nothing could be more lovely and fearless than Chaucer" (*SLC*, pp. 54, 57, 53).

The story of the rich, impotent nobleman with the lusty young wife who escapes from the manor house for bouts of energetic intercourse with the gamekeeper would seem to be material ready made for Geoffrey Chaucer. In Chaucer's hands, one might imagine, the story would receive comic treatment, with (after appropriately ironic apologies) splashes of *cherlish speche:* the lady's *queynte*, the gamekeeper's *sely thinge*, the pleasure of their *swyving* named without circumlocution. (Whether in Chaucer's treatment the lady's heart would "melt out of her with a kind of awe" at the "slow, momentous, surging rise of [the gamekeeper's] phallus" [*LCL*, pp. 197–98] is another question.)

Lawrence writes of Chaucer's "natural innocence." He is right in the sense that Chaucer has available to him a language for sex, comic without being coy, down-to-earth without being brutal or demeaning, that was not available in Lawrence's own day and had not been available in literary English for a long time. In Lawrence's mythology, however, Chaucer stands for more than this wistful ideal. He stands for a time before the fall, when the sexual and the excremental retained their opposed polarities, when the excremental taboo had not yet touched the mind with its contagion. To return to Chaucer, to return to innocence, can therefore have two alternative interpretations, between which Lawrence did not always distinguish.

In the first interpretation, to return to Chaucerian innocence means to return to a time before taboos on the representation of sex. It means freedom to call a spade a spade. It means returning to the true names of things, particularly to the "simple and natural" obscene words that have been driven out and now haunt the margins of the imagination.

Strictly speaking, this interpretation is not sustainable. It ignores the complex play of high and low styles, courtly and demotic speech, in Chaucer, attributing to him a language without levels or registers.[15] Oliver Mellors may call a spade a spade, but Geoffrey Chaucer certainly does not. On the contrary, he adverts to it with a great variety of metaphors and metonyms. And if it appears that the slipping and sliding of metaphors and metonyms around body parts, body products, and inter-body acts has accelerated since Chaucer's time, the explanation is in large part simply that linguistic records grow more voluminous as we approach the present.

The second and more interesting interpretation of the figure of Chaucer in Lawrence is that Chaucer stands for an age before the specifically *excremental* taboo touched sex, that is to say, before the names of sexual parts and the naming—and, by contagion, performing—of clean sexual acts had the excremental taboo laid over the traditional taboos, thereby becoming dirty.[16] A return to Chaucer would then require the annihilation of the excremental taboo. Though it is difficult to square this interpretation with all of Lawrence's writings of the period 1928 through 1930 (for instance, with his denunciation of *all* taboos as survivals of savagery), it makes most sense of what Lawrence is up to in *Lady Chatterley's Lover.* From this angle, the episode of anal intercourse in the novel comes to take on central importance.

This scene (*LCL*, pp. 280–81) was the occasion for some rich hermeneutic comedy at the 1960 trial as, without himself calling a spade a spade, prosecuting counsel sought to persuade an uncomprehending jury that something obscenely filthy was going on be-hind the screen of Lawrence's hypermetaphoric prose.[17]

The episode constitutes a rite of initiation for Connie. As the last of "organic shame" is burned from her, she dies a "poignant, marvellous death" and then emerges reborn, "a different woman." The annihilation of shame is achieved by the phallus, which "hunts [shame] out" in "the core of the physical jungle." To her surprise, she finds that what she has in her heart always desired has been the "piercing, consuming, rather awful sensuality" of the act.

Clearly there is a way of reading the episode in line with the account (perhaps the rationalization) Lawrence provides in his es-says of the late 1920s. The excremental taboo is destroyed in its lair. The god-phallus disappears into the labyrinth of the underworld, hunts out the monster, slays it, and emerges triumphant.

But one question remains over which the novel and Lawrence's account of it remain at odds: What is the fate of the monster? In his essays Lawrence argues that, once the power of the excremental taboo has been broken, we can begin to return to a Chaucerian state of linguistic, and ultimately sexual, innocence. In the novel the ar-gument seems to be that, having passed through her rite of passage, Connie has become one of the purified, the reborn, the elect. What do the purified do the night after their initiation, however? Is the piercing sensuality of sodomy lost to them once the taboo (marked by shame) has been destroyed? Do they simply return to the per-formance of the genital rite, a rite now purified of excremental taint? Or may the rite of the hunting and slaying of the monster be performed again and again, night after night, by the god-phallus?

This question can be translated as a question about the durabil-ity of the taboo: Is the taboo annihilated once it has been trans-gressed?[18] Another version of the question might be asked of the act Lawrence claims to be performing in bringing *Lady Chatterley's Lover* into the world, namely, the act of purifying the language of the tribe. Once the tabooed representations have been brought into the light of day, does the taboo die, or is the slaying of the taboo to be acted out again and again, ritually? Does letting *Lady Chat-terley's Lover* go free mean the beginning of the end of dirty books or the beginning of a stream of dirty books?

The answer Lawrence gives in his essays is clear: it means the end of taboos, the end of dirty language, the end of dirty books. But what does *Lady Chatterley's Lover* itself say?

In the reading I give it, *Lady Chatterley's Lover* is a tale about the transgression of boundaries—sexual boundaries and sexualized social boundaries. Its local tensions and dramatic force therefore depend on the continuing viability of taboos. Taboo is a necessary condition of its existence. The sexual economy of the lovers, the dramatic economy of the tale, even the profit or loss of the published book, depend on the vitality of taboos. The book is opened; after long deferrals, after many pages, the lovers are unclothed, their bodies explored, their truth at last told; the book can be closed on them. But the same book waits to be reopened, reexplored. Each time it is reopened, the lovers stand before us again, ready for the prescribed unclothing, the prescribed explorations. Whatever taboos were vanquished in the first traversal of the text are there again, revived. Even bans that have long lost their mandate can reassume, in the pages of certain old books, their shadowy force. The strings of Emma Bovary's corsets whistle like snakes as she disrobes; as long as that moment retains its scandalous power, something has been evoked, something is being transgressed.

Does this reading turn *Lady Chatterley's Lover* into pornography? Is it the reading of a tainted imagination?

"Pornography," said Lawrence, "is the attempt to insult sex, to do dirt on it" (*SLC*, p. 37). "To do dirt on": a euphemism for to shit on. *Pornographer* was a word whose taint Lawrence struggled hard to escape. He invented a creature named Jonathan Swift, "degraded" man in extremis, touched him with the taint of doing dirt on sex, and banished him to a madhouse, from where, like a jackal or hyena, he continued to haunt the margins of Lawrence's imagination. Henry Miller had no doubt that, in denying the transgressiveness of *Lady Chatterley's Lover* and claiming for it an improving moral purpose, Lawrence betrayed the book's proper *mysteria*[19]—in effect, allowed the Swift in himself to do dirt on what he had written after the act.

The trial and acquittal of *Lady Chatterley* is often taken as an emblematic event: a public liberation of trammeled sexual force ushering in the bright new decade of the 1960s. One might ask, however: what exactly was the force that had been trammeled and was now released? Was it the force of the novel Lawrence had written, a novel embroiled in complex ways with, and perhaps even caught in the toils of, taboo; or was it the force of the reading Lawrence had in retrospect given his novel, a reading from whose brisk rationalization and dismissal of taboo the lawyers and expert witnesses at the trial could take their lead in building a case that turned out to be irresistible?

CHAPTER FOUR

The Harms of Pornography: Catharine MacKinnon

THE PORNOGRAPHY INDUSTRY

In the the past decade, a range of sadistically oriented visual pornography has come on to the market; it is particularly widely available in advanced industrial countries. In these countries, even in quarters traditionally opposed to censorship, concern about its effects has been growing. Agitation for controls has been spearheaded by feminists, who argue that consumers of this material—mainly men—not only acquire from it a taste for sexualized violence but pick up techniques of physical sadism. They also claim that, to the degree that representations of women being physically abused or undergoing degrading relationships with men are disseminated in society, women as a class are harmed.

In the sense that it does not invoke prevailing community norms to denounce pornography, the feminist opposition I describe is not conservative in its orientation. Nor is it sympathetically disposed toward the rather abstract preoccupation of liberalism with freedom of speech: in the very emphasis on neutrality in liberal jurisprudence, in fact, it claims to detect one of the disguises of a specifically male point of view.

Of these feminist opponents, the most biting in her onslaught on the new pornography and on the liberal defense of its right to exist has been Catharine MacKinnon.[1] MacKinnon's claims for the pervasiveness of pornography in the United States are probably overstated, and in any event are hardly relevant to most of the rest of the world. Her estimation of the power of pornography may also be excessive: there are in the field of representation forces more insidious and more pervasive in sexualizing human beings and prescribing sexual roles for them. Her comprehension of desire in men strikes one as impoverished to the point of blankness. The interests and desires of human beings are many times more complex, devious, inscrutable, and opaque to their subjects than she seems to allow; the opposition she elaborates between male interests and female interests is simplified to the point of caricature. Nevertheless, it is hard not to be impressed or even carried along by the verve, the sweep, and the sometimes reckless energy of her attack.[2]

MacKinnon directs her criticism almost entirely at the pornography industry of the industrialized countries, with its heavy bias toward visual media (film, video, photo magazines). She has little to say about print pornography. This is understandable. The social reach of the image is greater and its impact more immediate than that of the word. Its cumulative potential for harm (assuming that it causes harm) must therefore be greater.[3]

But MacKinnon privileges visual pornography in another way as well. Rather than approaching film as just one among several media in which erotic-sadistic fantasies may achieve realization, she treats pornographic films and pornographic writing as different in kind. The epistemology implicit in the optics of the camera determines the nature of visual pornography, she argues; but even more determinative of its nature is the fact that living women are indispensable to its manufacture. The involvement of real women in this otherwise male transaction (male pornographers, male viewers) makes the pornographic image *real* in a way that pornographic writing cannot be. I will return to this claim—which I see as central to MacKinnon's critique of pornography—below.

MacKinnon distances herself sharply not only from liberals defending pornography as a means by which people can liberate themselves from timidity and repression ("Sexual liberation in the liberal sense frees male sexual aggression in the feminist sense," [*FU,* p. 149]), but also from the conservative critique of pornography as a poison corrupting society. The feminist critique of pornography is "not a question of good and bad, false or true, edifying or tawdry, but of power and powerlessness." It is part of "a political argument for redistribution and transformation in the terms of power" (*FU*, p. 225). Pornography must be attacked because, along with rape and prostitution, it "institutionalizes the sexuality of male supremacy," which in turn "fuses the erotization of dominance and submission with the social construction of male and female" (*FU*, p. 148).

Seen from this point of view, the connections between pornography and obscenity—against which existing legal sanctions are directed—are fortuitous. The harm of pornography does not lie in the fact that it is offensive but that, at least in developed societies, it is "an industry that mass produces sexual intrusion, access to, possession and use of women by men for profit" (*FT*, p. 195). Whereas obscenity "probably does little harm," pornography "causes attitudes and behaviors of violence and discrimination that define the treatment and status of half the population" (*FU*, p. 147).

The pornography statute drafted by MacKinnon and Andrea Dworkin for the city of Minneapolis in 1983 thus does not turn on a criterion of offensiveness or try to lay down moral norms. Instead it treats pornography politically, as "specifically . . . a harm of gender inequality," a harm that "outweighs any social interest in its protection by recognized First Amendment standards" (standards safeguarding freedom of speech) (*FU*, p. 177). The later statute drafted for Indianapolis specifically addresses civil rights: it affords affected women redress against pornographers under civil-rights legislation and thus belongs to civil law, not criminal law, as MacKinnon is at pains to stress.[4]

Why is a specific proscription of pornography necessary? Despite the categorical difference between pornography and obscenity—the former is political, the latter moral—will a tightening-up of existing laws against obscenity not serve her purposes? MacKinnon claims it will not. She is generally dubious about the readiness of U.S. courts, dominated as they are by men, to use obscenity legislation to advance women's political interests. Mindful of the profitable notoriety accruing to books that have suffered prosecution at law, she is also reluctant to ban material if this will serve only to "eroticize" it for its potential public. On the general issue of censorship she is in fact circumspect to the point of vagueness. She seems reluctant to envisage a fully elaborated system of controls—"Censoring pornography would not delegitimize it; I want to delegitimize it" (*FU*, p. 140)—but does not explain precisely what it means to delegitimize something (one infers that it means something like to create, by whatever means are necessary, a climate of disapprobation surrounding it and the entire class of materials to which it belongs, and to that extent to remove it from the protection of the law) or explore the shadowy area between delegitimizing and censoring. How one would in practice go about delegitimizing something with boundaries as indistinct as those of pornography is, she acknowledges, "unclear" (*FU*, p. 140). Beyond making certain pornography-related harms civilly actionable, extralegal and even violent actions may be required: without spelling out what she has in mind, she invokes examples of liberation movements attacking the presses of the enemy. "In serious movements for human freedom, speech is serious" (*FU*, p. 213).

MacKinnon states her position on censorship most clearly in a 1984 lecture. For women, she says, the urgent issue is not how to prevent government interference with freedom of speech—the dominant concern of liberals—but how to act so as to afford speech to those to whom it has been denied. Applied to pornography, such affirmative action may entail "risks"—again MacKinnon does not spell out what they are, but may have in mind risks to the artistic freedom of writers and filmmakers—but these have to be balanced against "the risks of the status quo" (*FU*, p. 195).

In the 1989 revision of this passage, the word *censorship* is avoided altogether and new language is found to express the same prioritization: "The endless moral debates between good and evil, conservative and liberal, artists and philistines [etc.] . . . would be superseded by the political debate. . . : are women human beings or not? . . . The main question would [then] be: does a practice participate in the subordination of women to men, or is it no part of it?" (*FT*, pp. 247–48).

MacKinnon mistrusts obscenity law as an instrument against pornography not only because it enshrines what she considers to be male-hegemonic sexual standards but because in a deeper sense it serves male sexual interests.[5] In fact, there is a sense in which obscenity law (not obscenity itself) has the same "underlying theme" as pornography.

Superficially both involve morality: rules made and transgressed for purposes of sexual arousal. Actually, both are about power. . . . It seems essential to the kick of pornography that it be to some extent against the rules, but never truly unavailable or truly illegitimate. . . . Obscenity law helps keep pornography sexy. (*FU*, p. 162)

Censorship excites men a lot. (*FU*, p. 143)

Behind the claim that restrictions on obscene exhibitions have behind them a (male) desire to make transgression of these restrictions more exciting lies an analysis of male sexuality and, behind male sexuality, male power. This analysis is discussed in the next section. For the present, let me concentrate on MacKinnon's treatment of works of art.

The harms of pornography, says MacKinnon, ultimately outweigh considerations of free speech. When the law was driven to create a sacrosanct category for works of art, as distinct from works lacking so-called redeeming value, it essentially evaded its obligations (*FT*, p. 200).

Taking the work "as a whole" ignores that which the victims of pornography have long known: legitimate settings diminish the perceptions of injury done to those whose trivialization and objectification they contextualize. Besides . . . if a woman is subjected, why should it matter that the work has other value? Maybe what redeems the work's value is what enhances its injury to women, not to mention that existing standards of literature, art, science, and politics, examined in a feminist light, are remarkably consonant with pornography's mode, meaning, and message. (*FU*, p. 175)

A footnote takes up an instance of child pornography and asks what difference it makes to the child model whether the film of her being abused is art or not (*FU*, p. 269).

Though the target in her essays on pornography is clearly the output of the commercial pornography industry, and though there is no hint that she advocates a general witch-hunt against books and films depicting the sexual subordination of women, MacKinnon clearly regards it as more urgent to address the politics of male hegemony than to affirm the freedom of artists to explore, for instance, the perverse. Her reservations about censorship—on the grounds that it deviously serves the interests of male desire—and her expressed desire to avoid any "chilling effect" on creativity (*FU*,

p. 177) notwithstanding, she clearly stands for limits on representation. To this extent, her heart lies with the censors.

THE TABOO

In MacKinnon's account, men like to create an "aura of danger" around the violation of the powerless. As long as sex is an expression of power, "allowed/not allowed" will remain "the ideological axis along which sexuality is experienced" (*FT*, p. 133). The mechanism for supporting this axis and maintaining an aura of danger around sex is taboo.

Taboos, says Freud, seem to be "self-evident," natural, without origin. They "are not based upon any divine ordinance, but may be said to impose themselves on their own account."[6] MacKinnon treats this seeming self-evidence of taboo as a cunning disguise, uncovering what taboo seeks to censor: that its source is a hypostasized male power. By this means she seeks to move the debate on pornography out of the field of morals (or mores) and into the field of sexual politics.

Pornography relies on the vitality of taboo. As taboos are exposed by feminist analysis to be no more than structural devices upholding (male-created) culture, they lose their grip on people, and the culture of domination that they support is undermined. This explains why resources have to be poured into keeping the idea of the tabooed alive.

> Greater efforts of brutality have become necessary to eroticize the tabooed . . . since the frontier of the tabooed keeps vanishing as one crosses it. Put another way, more and more violence has become necessary to keep the progressively desensitized consumer aroused to the illusion that sex is (and he is) daring and dangerous. (*FU*, p. 151)

The system has no other choice: even though there is something inherently self-defeating in representing what is claimed to be unrepresentable, how, except through escalating extremity, ascending violence, is the taboo that is so essential to the structuring of male desire to be sustained?

Whatever its weakness as history (the logic of escalation described here is not new, but was already faced by Sade), MacKinnon's analysis of the erosion of the grounds of the taboo and the bad faith of narratives that lean heavily upon taboo and the transgression of taboo for their effect is acute.

Keeping the principle of the tabooed alive has a price: an erosion of elementary respect for other people. To trace this process of erosion, MacKinnon turns to the philosopher Bernard Williams. Personhood, says Williams, is defined not from above but among people themselves by mutual respect for one another's most basic wishes, which include the wish not to suffer pain and the wish to preserve self-respect. For torture and debasement to be capable of being eroticized, it is therefore a precondition that personal dignity and freedom from pain must be generally accepted as human values. "Only when self-respect is accepted as human does debasement become sexy and female; only when the avoidance of pain is accepted as human does torture become sexy and female." In other words, the existence of the taboo allows the erotic to occupy the ground of the tabooed. But MacKinnon gives the logic of pornographic desire a further twist. "Exactly what is defined as degrading to a human being, *however* that is socially defined, is exactly what is sexually arousing to the male point of view in pornography, just as the one to whom it is done is the girl regardless of sex" (*FU*, p. 159–60).

In MacKinnon's Manichaean world of male and female, pornography thus serves the ends not of pleasure but of power. It is not a perversion of the erotic (the humanly erotic) in the direction of violence.[7] Pornography cannot see "what eroticism *is* as distinct from the subordination of women. . . . Under male dominance, whatever sexually arouses a man is sex. In pornography the violence *is* the sex. The inequality is the sex" (*FU*, p. 160). Between masters and slaves there can be no common ground of human sexual play and pleasure. Dominance equals violence equals sex.

POWER, SEXUALITY, DESIRE

If we accept that sexual taboos are no more than "guises under which hierarchy is eroticized," then any account of relations between men and women that takes taboos at face value must be naive. "Sexual meaning . . . is made in social relations of power in the world. . . . The fact that male power has power means that the interests of male sexuality construct what sexuality as such means." Sexuality is no more and no less than "the dynamic of control by which male dominance . . . eroticizes and thus defines man and woman, gender identity and sexual pleasure" (*FT*, pp. 135, 137). Male sexual desire is therefore simultaneously created and serviced by male power. As for women's sexuality, this is "largely a construct of male sexuality searching for someplace to happen" (*FT*, p. 152).

The task of feminist criticism is to recognize the master force, male power, operating behind its various conceptual masks. If it fails to do so, it will only assist in "enforcing the hegemony of the social construct 'desire,' hence its product, 'sexuality,' hence its construct 'woman'" (*FT*, p. 129).

In MacKinnon's view of the world—a view that owes much to Michel Foucault and Foucault's elevation of paranoia into the animating principle of historical awareness—male power, as a kind of first principle, creates and uses desire for its own ends. Only once we have understood the genesis of gender, sexuality, and desire—a genesis which power does all it can to obscure—can we fully appreciate the social significance attributed to pornography by MacKinnon: as both an enactment of power realizing itself and a lesson in the modes of epistemological violence through which that realization is achieved. Pornography provides the answer to the question Freud never asked: what do men want? It is the so-called "truth about sex" for men.

> [Pornography] connects the centrality of visual objectification to both male sexual arousal and male models of knowledge and verification, objectivity with objectification. It shows how men see the world, how in seeing it they access and possess it, and how this is an act of dominance over it. (*FT*, p. 138)

MacKinnon identifies objectification of women as the characteristic strategy of male power not only in pornography (where it finds an ally in the objectifying gaze of the camera lens) but in social processes in general. In defining these linkages between male power, objectification, and reification on the one hand, and the camera on the other, MacKinnon is indebted to feminist film criticism and in particular to Laura Mulvey's pioneering essay "Visual Pleasure in Narrative Cinema" (1975), a debt which she acknowledges.

Since Mulvey's contention that the cinema as we know it is a gendered medium is fundamental to MacKinnon's critique of pornographic film, it is worth exploring what Mulvey has to say about objectification, a term which comes to her from psychoanalysis and is thus distinct from objectification in MacKinnon, to whom it has an ethical and political meaning.

Mulvey starts with Freud's notion of scopophilia, a heavy libidinal investment in voyeuristic looking, which "[takes] other people as objects, subjecting them to a controlling and curious gaze."[8] In classic narrative film of the kind perfected by Hollywood, the cinema-spectator's perception is "sutured" together from moment to moment (the term comes from Jacques Lacan) with the on-screen looks orchestrated by the camera and in the editing room. The spectator thus comes to occupy the position of the voyeur, a position historically apportioned (in ways explored by, for instance, John Berger) to the male. As for a putative female look, this, in the Freudian-Lacanian tradition, can come into being only as the castrating stare of the Medusa. Short of looking, the woman can merely see, see herself being seen, see herself seeing herself. Thus seamless suturing of the Hollywood variety achieves the effect of masculinizing the look of the spectator while naturalizing woman as the exhibitionist, the one satisfied to be looked at.

Mulvey relies heavily on Lacan in her theorizing; she does not seem to sense the presence of Jean-Paul Sartre behind or beside Lacan, not only in the linking of the birth of subjectivity to the look through spatialization of the self-image (in Lacan, the so-called mirror phase) but in the analysis of the workings of objectification. Lacan is in no sense a Sartrean. The mirror in Lacan is a real mirror, not the subjectivity of an Other. But Sartre and Lacan share a philosophical lineage (Hegel, Husserl, Heidegger). Lacan criticizes Sartre's account of the gaze, but acknowledges the acuteness with which he captures "the entire phenomenology of shame, of modesty, of prestige, of the specific fear engendered by the gaze," and recommends *Being and Nothingness* as "essential reading for the analyst."[9]

What Lacan very likely has in mind is part 3, chapter 1, section 4 of *Being and Nothingness*, with its extended analysis of the look. Here Sartre seizes on the kind of look, rigid and abstract, that, under the name *Anschauung*, Heidegger associates with spectatorial distance and Greek epistemological ambitions, the look used to discover *(entdecken)* being, and sets it in the arena of Hegel's master-slave dialectic as one of the weapons in the conflict at the heart of all human relations.[10] Sartre emphatically ignores Heidegger's alternative, more primitive kind of look, *Umsicht*, the look of circumspection, ontological rather than epistemological in its bearing, that maintains or cares for what it sees around it in its discovered state *(Entdecktheit)*.[11] The relation between the one who looks and the one looked at is to Sartre fundamentally nonreciprocal because part of a power struggle. The one who looks is subject, the one looked at object. In Sartre, as Martin Jay puts it, "objectification is the telos of the look."[12]

Sartre's hostile account of the look is only one chapter in a critique of the role of vision in Western epistemology that has been an important current in French philosophy in the second half of the twentieth century, broadening in the work of Foucault and Jacques Derrida into an attack on all Western forms of knowledge; indirectly it has also entered the work of Mulvey and other theorists of film and has been used to underpin a feminist critique of the visual representation of women.[13] But Sartre's analysis of looking and being looked at goes further than the identification of looking and objectifying. Through the look, the subjecthood of the Other is also brought about. "The Other . . . is the one who looks at me and at whom I am not yet looking" *(BN, p. 360)*. Before the subjecthood of the Other-who-looks can be realized, however, one must have the experience of being the object of the Other's look. This realization arrives not as an abstract, logical deduction, but in an unbidden moment of transition, experienced as an irruption, from what Sartre calls "non-thetic self-consciousness" to a sense of self he identifies in the first place with *shame*, a shame without a basis in personal history, simply a "recognition of the fact that I am indeed that object which the other is looking at and judging" *(BN, pp. 347, 350)*. (The camera is obviously incapable of entering into relations of looking and recognition such as Sartre describes: when it is not itself looking, it can be looked at only as inert glass and metal. It is, so to speak, an eye rather than a look.)

To put on clothes, Sartre continues, is in effect to claim the privilege of seeing without being seen (*BN*, p. 384), that is, to claim the camera position. But it does not follow that the naked body, when it is looked at, is of necessity a thing, an object. In Sartre's account the looked-at body has an aesthetic dimension. The negative pole of the aesthetic dimension is the obscene, the positive pole the graceful. The obscene extreme is reached when under the assaults of sadistic pain the subjecthood of the Other retreats, annihilated, into the facticity of flesh. The positive extreme is attained when the body moves in a state of freedom, its every next movement unpredictable yet immediately in retrospect recognized as aesthetically necessary (*BN*, pp. 517–23).

In her account of pornographic film as the intersection and mutual reinforcement of two strategies of objectification—the transformation of a woman into a woman's body through the deliberate and intentional act (and enactment) of sadistically unclothing and violating her, and the use of a recording eye incapable of admitting what it sees into subjecthood—MacKinnon thus strikingly, though inadvertently, follows Sartre. Where she does not follow him, where she in effect refuses to follow him, is in conceding the possibility of aesthetic redemption from the objecthood of being filmed naked, filmed even in explicit sex-scenes.[14] Redemption of this kind has clearly been attempted by "serious" filmmakers; it forms the basis of the informal distinction between the erotic and the pornographic.

To MacKinnon, male sexuality is—and indeed is defined by— the possession and consumption of women as sexual objects. Visual pornography caters to male sexuality by creating for it accessible sexual objects, namely images of women. As objects of male desire, women and images of women are not categorically distinct: "Sex in life is no less mediated than it is in art. Men have sex with their image of a woman" (*FT*, p. 199). Through this thoroughly Freudian insight MacKinnon draws into doubt and even collapses the distinction between the reality and the representation. The woman with whom a man has physical relations is only a vehicle through whom he strives to attain the ensemble of representations that make up her image for him.

Female sexuality is a construction of male power. Constructed for her by others, belonging in essence to ideology, female sexuality dictates that a woman's experience of (heterosexual) sex should be of being possessed as an object and consumed. Through the vehicle of the real woman, the man has intercourse with the image-of-the-woman; as for the woman, she experiences herself as a sexualized and therefore sexually constructed being at an equally imaginary level.

This account of desire and sexuality in the service of power, and of power in the hands of men, is totalizing in its ambition. While claiming to repudiate any all-encompassing "objective" worldview as one of the disguises of the male, thereby making truth relative to gender, and to offer itself as only a feminist countertruth, it in fact presents itself as an *undisguised* and therefore an ethically superior truth, shaped by MacKinnon's characteristic rhetoric of forceful certainty.[15] For what may be its own strategic reasons, it does not broach the question of why, if it is in the interests of men to construct and enforce a version of female desire, it should not be in the interests of women to construct and enforce a counterversion of male desire.

In the arena of disputation chosen by MacKinnon, in which all arguments are power moves and power is gendered, let me skirt the most direct form of response, and instead follow the implications of her analysis of desire by imagining a male writer-pornographer who advances the following question to her: "If I were to write an account of power and desire that, unlike yours, does not close the book on desire (by defining its genesis and its ends), but on the contrary sees (but also does not see), in its own desire to know its desire, that which it can never know about itself; if this hypothetical account were further to be offered, not in the discursive terms of 'theory,' but in the form of a representation, an enactment, perhaps in the medium of film; if this representation were to share a thematics with pornography (including perhaps torture, abasement, acts of cruelty), and in other crucial respects as well—its gender politics, for instance—were wide open to bearing the same interpretation as much material classed as pornography—if this project were carried through and offered to the world, what would protect it from suffering the same fate—'delegitimization'—as any work of pornography, except perhaps its *seriousness* (if that were recognized) as a philosophical project?"

Seriousness is, for a certain kind of artist, an imperative uniting the aesthetic and the ethical. It is also deconstructible as a feature of the ideology of so-called high art and the drive to power of the high artist. It is hard to believe that, except on such thoroughly pre-postmodern grounds as its serious intentions, the project I outline above would be saved. But if it were to suffer the fate of being delegitimized, would that be because it is indeed pornography or because it is a critique of the account of power, gender, and desire given by "feminism unmodified," a critique whose radicalism would consist not necessarily in its conceptual power but—if the two could ever be disentangled—in its embrace of the pornographic medium as its own?

The kind of project I outline is not fanciful. To a reader sensitive to their implications, the twists and turns of erotic abasement in the novels of Dostoevsky are far more disturbing than anything likely to be encountered in commercial pornography, no matter what the latter's excesses. Nor is Dostoevsky the only writer one can think of who would run into trouble under strictures on pornography like MacKinnon's. As an object lesson in how the hunter can be turned into the hunted, Harriet Gilbert has given a novel by MacKinnon's collaborator, Andrea Dworkin, a not entirely playful reading as pornography.[16] For someone writing about male-female relations, MacKinnon shows a striking—or perhaps studied—absence of insight into desire as experienced by men. This absence of insight may of course represent a deliberate political decision, or utter lack of sympathy, or principled resistance to the kind of phenomenological projection required, or all of these. Still, because it is essential to MacKinnon's argument to identify male desire as one of the avenues through which male dominance realizes itself, and given the totalizing nature of her project and the strong reserve she expresses about special exemption for artworks, and because male dominance is seen as a fundamental harm—for all these reasons, any assertion of male desire, and the exploration of the nature of that desire—an exploration that can be conducted only under the aegis of desire itself, which will have to be a sexed desire—such as serious erotic art may undertake, must enter the lists in an adversarial relation to MacKinnon's enterprise. There is no reason to expect that, as such, it would not be responded to in the same way that MacKinnon responds to pornography, that is to say, politically.

What is put forward here is not an argument that art (or skeptical philosophy) constitutes a higher good by bringing certitudes of all kinds, political and moral, into doubt, nor is it a plea for the freedom of the individual, including freedom of individual expression, as the highest goal of social evolution. Freedom of expression is desirable; but like all desires (including the pornographer's desire, including the desire that drives MacKinnon, including the desire that drives the present writing) the desire for freedom is devious, does not fully know itself, cannot afford to fully know itself. Neither legal bans on pornographic representation nor the chilling climate of censure or social disapproval of which MacKinnon shows herself well aware will prevent serious writers from exploring the darker areas of human experience.[17] The question is simply: at what cost to them; and do we want to add to that cost?

TRUTH AND REALITY

Through its epistemological instrument (the camera with its objective gaze) and its strategy of reducing persons to objects, says MacKinnon, pornography has the power to "invent" woman, turning its vision of woman into reality. "Men treat women as whom they see women as being. Pornography constructs who that is" (*FT*, pp. 205, 197).

> The harm of pornography is the harm of male supremacy made difficult to see because of its pervasiveness, potency, and success in making the world a pornographic place. Specifically, the harm cannot be discerned from the objective standpoint because it is so much of "what is." Women live in the world pornography creates, live its lie as reality. . . . To the extent pornography succeeds in constructing social reality, it becomes invisible as harm. (*FT*, p. 204)

The scars left on women by pornography may be invisible, but this does not mean that women are not scarred. Sexual oppression cannot be demonstrated, says MacKinnon, as long as empirical standards of truth and empirical methods of demonstration are accepted uncritically. "Male power produces the world before it distorts it." In a world produced by men, "women have little choice but to become persons who then freely choose women's roles." Hence "the reality of women's oppression is, finally, neither demonstrable nor refutable empirically."[18]

There is one arena, however, where violence is done to the woman's body all too visibly: in the pornographic spectacle itself. To MacKinnon, the pornographic harm performed on the woman's body is an emblem of a general and pervasive violation. Thus the suppression of pornographic exhibitions is part of a wider revolution against male hegemony. In this perspective, pornography happens to be a conveniently visible manifestation of a male power that otherwise prefers to veil itself. To put it another way, the ultimate goal of a campaign against pornography is not to make it unprofitable for men to make and exhibit pornographic films (which would be the limited goal of vigorously implemented obscenity legislation) but to defeat pornography itself, the pornography of power. It is only for practical, and perhaps symbolic, reasons that the first target must be pornographic representations themselves.

This may explain why MacKinnon gives so little attention to advertising. Advertising, after all, like pornography, defines and uses female sexuality for its own ends. Its turnover is vastly greater than pornography's, its effects wider and more insidious. It is also open to much the same political critique that MacKinnon launches against pornography. Much of it "fuses the erotization of dominance and submission with the social construction of being." Its harm is likewise "the harm of male supremacy made difficult to see because of its pervasiveness, potency, and [success in transforming the world in its image]." Women "live in the world [it] creates, [living] its lie as reality." To the extent that advertising succeeds in constructing social reality, it too "becomes invisible as harm" (*FU*, pp. 148, 154, 155).[19]

The Greeks barred representations of violence, including mutilation, rape, and death, from the stage. The spirit of visual pornography is deeply anticlassical. Its ontology is the empiricism of naive realism: the real is what we can see.

Death, *pace* Lucretia, is worse than rape. If we are to proscribe pornography for its representations of sexual violence, why not, we may ask, proscribe all violent representations, including those of death? If pornographic films are in their being an offense against womankind, are war films not in their being an offense against humankind? If pornographic films encourage men to commit sexual violence, are not people similarly encouraged to kill by seeing killing on the screen? The case against pornographic exhibitions seems inescapably to entail a wider case against exhibitions that deprave, corrupt, or incite. Why does MacKinnon not make this case, or even hint that it ought to be made?

There are two reasons one can guess at. The first is that, in mainstream cinema, killing is rarely not presented—however casually and spuriously—in a wider framework of law or natural justice, and is rarely not condemned—however insincerely—when done for kicks, to satisfy an appetite; whereas the kind of pornography targeted by MacKinnon presents sexual domination and, in a different way, sensual abasement as exciting and fulfilling. The second follows from a fact on which MacKinnon lays great stress: that, while the violence in violent films is feigned, pornographic films record real sex.

Convincingly realistic portrayals of evil and crime are always unsettling, since their impact on the reader or viewer tends to overpower whatever abstract cautionary frame they may be set in. Hence, for instance, the defense Daniel Defoe feels obliged to offer for publishing the life-story of Moll Flanders: not only (he says) has he moderated the appeal of the adventures of this skillful, courageous, and attractive criminal by setting her story within a frame of moral questioning and self-questioning; he has gone further and written into the action a realistically vivid story of compensatory punishment.

Pornography makes no moral defense of itself. On the contrary, as MacKinnon points out, it is parasitic upon sexual morality, which it fastens upon as a set of taboos to be transgressed in the pursuit of its own ends. Pornography is on every count immoral; it might even be argued that, to the extent that it celebrates a closed universe of exploitation of the weak by the strong, without reparative justice, it is evil.

But MacKinnon treats pornography as a political issue, not a moral one, and in her criticism of it ignores moral grounds. It may be for this reason that she has to claim a special ontological status for pornographic films, the status not of the realistic (that is, the successfully illusionistic) but of the real. Before the gaze of a camera and for the gaze of other men, a male fantasy of power (or a fantasy of male power) is brought to life by actors who indispensably include women acting against their will, or at least against their real and wider interests. The involvement of real women in this otherwise male transaction lends visual pornography a reality transcending realism. Visual pornography is sui generis in that it bears within itself—indeed flaunts—a record of its crime, in the shape of images of real women being abused and degraded. The viewer sees, not only images of women acting women being abused: sometimes he may see women abused into acting women being abused. Indeed, insofar as (to MacKinnon) it is never in the interest of women, as members of a class, to participate in pornographic representations, the viewer is *always* seeing women abused into acting women being abused.

The insistence by MacKinnon on the special status of pornographic film—"In visual media . . . it takes a real person doing each act to make what you see"; "Pornography models are real women to whom something real is being done" (*FU*, pp. 180, 149)—is at first sight puzzling, and certainly worth investigating further.

In pornography we see, or seem to see, acts of violence being carried out upon the bodies of women. Leaving aside films of a special ontological variety—photographic records of real knife-thrusts spilling real blood—in what sense are these acts "something real"?[20] Is their status not, on the contrary, that of the fake: fake acts standing for real acts? The only "real" thing that goes on before the camera in hard-core pornography, the only thing not acted, is the sexual act. The only way to make sense of MacKinnon's "something real is being done" is therefore to translate it as: "Though whatever else goes on before the camera may be acting, the sex is real."

The sex in pornographic movies is a record of something real. But then, so are the kisses in nonpornographic movies: even the chastest of these kisses is a record of real lips touching. The handshakes are real too: real hands touched before the camera's gaze. The seeming acts in film that do not record real acts are small in number—mainly illusions created in the editing room.

So, to distinguish what happens to the actress in pornography (the actress who is not an actor, not the agent of her own acts) from what happens when she is kissed in mainstream film, we have to concretize the meaning of the word *real* even further. What is happening is that her physical integrity is being infringed, and in a way that robs the phrase *infringe someone's physical integrity* of all metaphoric avenues of escape: her body is being penetrated. The penetration of the body is real in its subjective and objective force in a way that the kiss barely is, and the handshake not at all. It is, in fact, numinous.

The penetration of the woman's body in pornographic film is not, of course, an act alone. It is typically part of a narrative scenario that may include the woman's pleasure or the woman's pain or both of these, accompanied by visible emotion. The pleasure and the pain, to say nothing of the emotion, are not real, and in a double sense: the actress does not feel them; and they are acted out for the camera. The feelings are not real, only the intercourse is real. And the intercourse is not real in every respect: to give it the required verisimilitude in the unnatural context of filming, the actress has at some level to recall previous acts of intercourse, real and acted, and reenact them, concealing or forgetting whatever distaste she may really feel.

In the subculture in which pornographic films are made, MacKinnon stresses, the women used as models are often not in charge of their lives. Participation in pornographic films is often forced upon them by means of blackmail or threats. There is thus a further sense in which sex in pornography is real: it is as real as the force by which it is extorted.[21]

What MacKinnon does not say is that such duress is not universal. Actors, both women and men, do wittingly and autonomously enter into contracts to take part in pornographic representations, as is their right.[22] In the entertainment business in general, furthermore, actors routinely perform for public view acts they find personally unpleasant (kissing people they dislike, for instance) or have moral objections to.

Nevertheless, testimony shows that women who have acted in pornographic films, like women who have been raped, may experience what MacKinnon calls "a sense of having lost some irreplaceable integrity" (*FT*, p. 149). How are we to understand this sense of loss? Perhaps by projecting what existential implications for a woman's self-worth and *dignitas* may follow from being physically penetrated—which is as emotionally complex an experience as any that human beings undergo, but certainly includes an instant of loss of power over one's own body—and then having the spectacle of penetration exhibited to a world of unsympathetic and, indeed, hostile strangers.[23] The denial by pornography, as genre, of the existential dimension of loss in the lives of the women it represents, and the denial on the part of the film arm of pornography in particular of the possibility of shock and mourning in the lives of the participants it uses, is its distinguishing lacuna, a redoubled moral blankness.

HONOR AND SHAME

There is an elementary feature of pornographic film on which MacKinnon—surprisingly—lays no stress, namely, that it constitutes a record that can be played over and over. Because the record exists, the abasement of the actress—conceived of as an individual woman, not a representative figure—cannot recede into the past and into the forgotten. Whenever the record is played, the scene is *now*. The pornographic record thus becomes (as some actresses have discovered to their cost) a past they cannot escape from or deny. What has been lost is not easily regained.

Honor, writes Julian Pitt-Rivers,

> is exalted or desecrated through the physical person and through actions related to it which are not merely symbolic representations of a moral state of affairs, but *are* what we might otherwise infer they represent. . . . They are . . . not the bill of goods, but the goods themselves.[24]

Honor and *shame* are not terms MacKinnon uses. Nevertheless, they provide a means of approaching her intuition—an intuition she has trouble finding words for—that there is something unique

in the degradations of pornographic film. The loss of honor under-
gone by the woman when the image of her degradation is fixed on
film is not merely the sign of a moral harm done to or by or
through her (Pitt-Rivers' "moral state of affairs") but "the goods
themselves," the real thing. And the proof of her loss of honor is
not the obscenity of the act itself on some scale of vileness, but the
fact that it can be witnessed endlessly. Though she may never meet
the witnesses, the evidence is irrevocably in the public domain, before the only court of honor that exists: the tribunal of public
opinion.

Pitt-Rivers continues:

> The conflict between honor and legality is a fundamental one which
> persists to this day. For to go to law for redress is to confess publicly
> that you have been wronged and the demonstration of your vulnera-
> bility places your honor in jeopardy, a jeopardy from which the "sat-
> isfaction" of legal compensation at the hands of the secular author-
> ity hardly redeems it. (P. 30)

The ambivalence of rape victims—particularly outside the West—
about seeking redress from the law, and the surprising degree of
suspicion or even hostility with which the public, even in the West,
treats such plaintiffs, indicates that in matters of honor archaic attitudes are far from dead, that is, that the system of justice of the
modern state, based on notions of guilt and innocence, has not entirely supplanted the tribunal of public opinion, based on notions
of honor and shame. The actresses whose testimony rouses Mac-
Kinnon to anger are women who have lost their honor or deeply
feel they have lost their honor (in a regime of honor and shame,
the two are the same);[25] insofar as social solidarities can have a collective honor, women in general have lost honor too; and the legal
system to which, in however a qualified a manner, MacKinnon personally adheres is by its nature unable to address that loss.

An appeal to lost honor is no more absolute or final, however,
than an appeal to harm done: no more and no less. The personal
testimonies that MacKinnon invokes are no doubt sincerely given.
Nevertheless, they are absorbed into what Carol Smart calls the
"rhetorical orchestration" of the larger campaign against pornography, an orchestration learned from nineteenth-century purity and
temperance campaigns.[26] As narratives of repentance and conver-

sion, they are structurally indistinguishable from narratives of religious conversion, and therefore tend to bear a heavy if unspoken moral and even religious freight. Thus, in the end it is hard to be sure whether, instead of yoking the energies of American puritanism to a project in gender politics, MacKinnon has not herself been absorbed into the projects of conservative popular religion.

THE VIEW FROM THE PROVINCES

Pornography may indeed be the master discourse of male oppression, deploying in a paradigmatic way procedures of objectification, constructing the forms that desire may take, and playing out exemplary narratives of domination before our eyes. But it is one thing to say that pornography thereby constitutes the theory of oppression, quite another to say that the oppression of women is the implementation of that theory, or, in MacKinnon's words, that "women live in the world pornography creates" (FU, p. 155). Pornography is simply not as potent or as omnipresent a force in the wider world as it is—or as MacKinnon feels it to be—in the United States. There are a multitude of societies in which rape has long been a practice without pornography ever having been the theory.[27]

The parochialism of MacKinnon's analysis becomes evident as soon as we turn from the United States to, for instance, those Islamic societies where puritanism in public morals is combined with a proprietary attitude toward wives and daughters, or to modern South Africa, a country where strict censorship in the recent past not only rendered a pornography industry impossible but made pornographic materials worthy of the name hard to come by. In such countries, the oppression of women in a variety of more or less violent forms has long flourished. Men have indeed "treat[ed] women as who they see women as being," but "who that is" has to no significant degree been constructed for them by pornography. There are no universals of oppression: in each nation, each culture, oppression has its own historical determinants and its own forms. In pursuing the causes of the quite egregious incidence of sexual violence against women in South Africa, for instance, one must surely start with the trauma of colonial conquest, which fractured the social and customary basis of legality, yet allowed some of the worst features of patriarchalism to survive, including the treatment of unattached (unowned) women as fair game, huntable creatures.

In the past half-century, a large part of the globe has been emerging from the shock of its first historical contact with the West. In the destruction of the cultures of these erstwhile colonies, Western pornography played only the most minor of roles. In such countries, pornography is not a master discourse. If anything, it is simply an exciting picture show that confirms and encourages old predatory attitudes toward women. What is disturbing about the films that disturb MacKinnon, in this wider context, is what is disturbing about modern commerce in general: that, blank as it has ever been about the moral consequences of the goods it handles, it penetrates markets with unexampled speed and, where it fails to find an immediate appetite for its goods, has no trouble in creating one.

CHAPTER FIVE

Erasmus: Madness and Rivalry

1. CHOOSING SIDES

Though he first made his name as a critic of clerical worldliness, Desiderius Erasmus found it hard to commit himself to the side of the Lutheran radicals in their conflict with the Papacy. Sympathetic to many of the ideals of reform, he was nevertheless disturbed by the intolerance and inflexibility of the actual reform movement; generally he tried to maintain a distance between his critique of the Church and Luther's. To the extent that he became involved in the rivalry between the Pope and Luther, his involvement was unwilling. At a personal level he found conflict uncongenial (which is not to say that his reluctance to take sides was merely a matter of temperament: in a deep sense it was political too). Urged by the Pope to denounce Luther's heresies, he replied: "I would rather die than join a faction." Privately he deemed the reform controversy insane in its fanaticism. In his view, the escalating violence of their rivalry made the two sides more and more alike, even as they more and more loudly asserted their difference. "Strange to see how the two factions goad each other on, as if they were in collusion," he writes. But by refusing to choose sides (one should bear in mind here that to choose sides is not always to choose an ally: it is sometimes to choose a foe), by claiming a position from which to judge (or, as he saw it, mediate) the conflict, he only succeeded in drawing the hostility of both factions upon himself. He ended his life isolated and embattled. "King of the Amphibians," Luther called him; "The king of *but*," says Georges Duhamel.[1]

It would be far-fetched to read into *The Praise of Folly*, written on a visit to England in 1509, a premonition of the crisis to come a decade later. Nevertheless, in the monologue of Folly Erasmus rehearses a well-established political role: that of the fool who claims license to criticize all and sundry without reprisal, since his madness defines him as not fully a person and therefore not a political being with political desires and ambitions. *The Praise of Folly* therefore sketches the possibility of a position for the critic of the scene of political rivalry, a position not simply impartial between the rivals but also, by self-definition, off the stage of rivalry altogether, a *non*position. It is a position of this problematic kind that Erasmus himself later tried to take up, with such signal lack of success, between the Pope and Luther.

In the realm of political action, maneuvers such as this, too clever by half, are rarely allowed to prosper: the freedom to criticize both sides while remaining immune from reprisal allows the joker such an advantage in power that the rivals typically unite to suppress him before returning to their quarrels. So in itself the ruse of claiming the privilege of the jester by pretending to embrace madness offers nothing new. However, *The Praise of Folly* is more than simply disingenuous advocacy for the uncommitted, mad-but-really-not-mad position over the committed, rivalrous positions: it is also a highly self-aware reflection on the limitations on any project of speaking on behalf of madness.

In the reading of *The Praise of Folly* offered below in section 4, I focus on Erasmus's analysis—an analysis masked in a form of joking which calls itself madness and which I hesitate to call irony—of the problematics of finding or creating a position in-but-not-in the political dynamic, a position not already given, defined, limited and sanctioned by the game itself. The shape of this analysis emerges in particularly sharp relief if we read *The Praise of Folly* in the light of two projects in our own time, projects comparable with each other in scope and political implication. The one belongs to Michel Foucault: to return authority to madness as a voice counter to the voice of reason. The other is that of Jacques Lacan: to reconceive a science in which the unconscious truly finds its voice. These projects are outlined in section 2.

Erasmus is at his most clear-sighted when he exposes the dynamics of rivalry, and his Folly at her most canny and deft in side-stepping its violent imperatives. In our time, the most extensive account of the vicissitudes of rivalry has been René Girard's. I will accordingly, as well, be reading Erasmus within the framework of Girard's project—sketched in section 3—of giving the phenomenon of rivalry an anthropological, transhistorical sweep. I have no desire to make Erasmus into a Girardian or Foucaultian before the fact, and even less to press Girard or Foucault or Lacan into a putative school of Erasmus. In its etymology, *theory* has to do with seeing. In reading Erasmus "in the light" of theories of our time, I aspire simply to make visible, to bring into sight, features of *The Praise of Folly* that may hitherto have been shadowed.

2. DENOUNCING THE DENUNCIATION OF MADNESS

In the 1960s, an attack was launched from several quarters upon the psychiatric establishment, in the name of madness and of the rights of madness. Among the leaders of this attack were R. D. Laing, Thomas Szasz, and Michel Foucault. Since, of the three, Foucault alone situates his critique of the asylum in a historical and philosophical context, I confine my comments to him.

The essence of Foucault's attack on the privileging of reason over madness in post-Cartesian Europe, and the silencing and exclusion of madness from the commonwealth, is that it is a strategy which does not know itself and is therefore, in its own terms, mad. It does not know itself in that it claims to be based on full self-knowledge, on knowledge of itself as the voice of transcendent reason; whereas it is in fact only the voice of a certain power.

Foucault's denunciation of the denunciation of madness by reason is therefore made in the name of a fuller self-knowledge than reason has. Foucault attempts to reveal the opposition of reason to madness as a merely political opposition, that is, an opposition of rivals on the same plane, one of whom has stifled and silenced the other.

Of Foucault's project of "an archaeology of [the] silence [of madness],"[2] Jacques Derrida wrote as follows in 1963:

Foucault wanted to write a history of madness *itself*, that is madness speaking on the basis of its own experience and under its own authority, and not a history of madness described from within the language of reason, the language of psychiatry *on* madness.

It is a question, therefore, of escaping the trap or objectivist naiveté that would consist in writing a history of untamed madness. . . . from within the very language of classical reason itself. . . . Foucault's determination to avoid this trap is constant. It is the most audacious and seductive aspect of his venture. . . . But it is also, with all seriousness, the *maddest* aspect of his project.[3]

Foucault was not unaware of the paradoxical nature of his project. In the preface to the original French edition of *Madness and Civilization* he wrote: "The perception which seeks to seize [the words of madness] in their natural state belongs necessarily to a world which has already captured them."[4] But what specifically is it that Derrida finds "mad" in the project?

Would not the archeology of silence be the most efficacious and subtle restoration, the *repetition* . . . of the act perpetrated against madness—and be so at the very moment when this act is denounced? Without taking into account that all the signs which allegedly serve as indices of the origin of this silence and of this stifled speech, and as indices of everything that has made madness an interrupted and forbidden, that is, arrested, discourse—all these signs and documents are borrowed, without exception, from the juridical province of interdiction. (*WD*, p. 35)

There are thus two strands to Derrida's criticism: (a) the discourse of Foucault's archaeology belongs to reason and cannot belong elsewhere; (b) the procedure of Foucault's investigation consists in rereading the historical record—largely (Derrida says "without exception") a juridical record—in which madness is denounced: madness speaking in its own right goes unheard.

Nothing within this language [the language of reason], and *no one* among those who speak it, can escape the historical guilt . . . which Foucault apparently wishes to put on trial. But such a trial may be impossible, for by the simple fact of their articulation the proceedings and the verdict unceasingly reiterate the crime. (*WD*, p. 35)

And Derrida sadly concludes the general phase of his critique of *Madness and Civilization* as follows:

The misfortune of the mad . . . is that their best spokesmen are those who betray them best; which is to say that when one attempts to convey their silence *itself,* one has already passed over to the side of the enemy, the side of order. (*WD,* p. 36)

Much of the rest of the critique is devoted to demonstrating that the relation of mutual exclusion that obtains between discourse and madness does not have a definable point of historical origin—for instance, in Descartes—but instead itself has the function of defining the economy of discourse. In the words of Shoshana Felman, whose commentary I follow closely:

The very status of language is that of a break with madness. . . . With respect to "madness itself," language is always *somewhere else.* The difficulty of Foucault's task is thus not contingent, but fundamental. Far from being a historical accident, the exclusion of madness is the general condition and the constitutive foundation of the very enterprise of speech. (*WM,* p. 44)

In his 1972 response to Derrida, Foucault concedes that the philosopher trying to enter madness *inside* of thought can do so only as a fictional project.[5] But the question then arises: would such a fiction lie inside philosophy? Felman comments:

To state, as does Foucault, that the mad subject cannot situate himself within his fiction, that, *inside* literature, he knows no longer *where* he is, is to imply indeed that fiction may not exactly be located "*inside of* thought," that literature cannot be properly enclosed *within* philosophy, present, that is, to itself and at the same time present *to* philosophy: that the fiction is not always where we think, or where it thinks it is. . . . In the play of forces underlying the relationship between philosophy and fiction, literature and madness, the crucial problem is that of the subject's *place,* of his *position* with respect to the delusion. And the position of the subject is not defined by *what* he says, nor by what he talks *about,* but by the place— unknown to him—*from which* he speaks. (*WM,* p. 50)

One result of the campaign to liberate madness is thus to invert the positions of madness and poetry (or writing): whereas poetry had been inside culture and madness outside, now madness is welcomed inside and poetry takes up the place of the unspoken, the repressed. But in that case, what matters more: whatever it is that occupies the outsider position—poetry or madness—or the position itself? Derrida observes:

> Everything transpires as if Foucault *knew* what "madness" means. . . . In fact, however, it could be demonstrated that as Foucault intends it . . . the concept of madness overlaps everything that can be put under the rubric of *negativity.* (*WD*, p. 41)

Inside and outside constitute an economy, but an economy with a difference. For the position outside the inside, the position to which Derrida gives the generic name of negativity, cannot be occupied knowingly, cannot be occupied by reason. To philosophize used to be to speak from the inside, after expelling and forgetting madness (and therefore forgetting oneself). Today, however, to philosophize is to philosophize "in *terror,* . . . in the *confessed* terror of going mad." The outside, today, is an ever-present shadow on the edge of consciousness, a penumbra. Yet even this shift does not change the nature of the economy of inside and outside. While the articulation of the shadow's presence does expose what had not been exposed before, this articulation remains a form of protection: in the same movement that it unveils it also forgets; and therefore, as much as the putting up of barriers against madness had earlier created an economy, it too creates or permits an economy (*WD*, p. 62).

What kind of knowledge is accessible from a position outside, a position that does not know itself? Felman reformulates this as a question about the unconscious: What kind of knowledge can the subject hope for via psychoanalysis of the unconscious? Her answer: "A knowledge that does not allow for knowing that one knows" (*WM*, p. 121).

This is not a knowledge accessible to reason. In classical psychoanalysis, it can be reached only via dreams, slips of the tongue, jokes—in other words, mistakes. What then can psychoanalysis be but a theory of mistakes? But if so, from what position can a theory of mistakes be constructed that is not itself mistaken? To call for a theory of mistakes is surely to fall into the same paradox as Foucault in speaking the silence of madness from the position of reason. As it is not possible to speak madness, so it ought not to be possible to speak the unconscious without betraying it and oneself—"not possible to free oneself from [the] fundamental function [of the unconscious] as deception in order to enunciate, without deceiving oneself, the absolute law of deception" (*WM*, p. 124).

Faced with this impossibility, Lacan's response is to cut the knot by collapsing, at least momentarily, the distance between the subject speaking unheard from outside the inside and the subject speaking for him, Lacan or "Lacan," in his name, from inside—the distance, so to speak, between the silent madman and the archaeologist of his silence. "Retain at least what this text . . . bears witness to: my enterprise does not go beyond the act in which it is caught, and therefore, its only chance lies in its error—in its misprision [*méprise*]."[6]

Lacan, then, gives up the position of "the subject supposed to know" [*le sujet supposé savoir*] in the hope of finding himself in a position of knowledge, a knowledge supposed to be a subject [*le savoir supposé sujet*]. This latter he proposes as a formula defining *writing*. Felman comments:

> [This formula] suggests that what is at stake in writing is precisely a reversal, a subversion of subjective knowledge [i.e., of that knowledge which believes it knows itself], a subversion of the self and its self-knowledge. Writing's knowledge . . . is nothing other in effect than the textual knowledge of what links the signifiers in the text [and not the signifieds] to one another: *knowledge that escapes* the subject but through which the subject is precisely constituted as the one who *knows how to escape*—by means of signifiers—his own self-presence. (*WM*, p. 132)

And she goes on to quote from one of Lacan's seminars:

> As Plato pointed out . . . it is not at all necessary that the poet know what he is doing, in fact, it is preferable that he not know. That is what gives a primordial value to what he does. We can only bow our heads before it. . . . Freud always repudiated . . . the interpretation of art; what is called "psychoanalysis of art" is to be avoided even more than the famous "psychology of art" which is itself an insane notion. (*WM*, p. 133)

Of course, it is not all of poetry (or, in Lacan's version, all of writing) that is betrayed when it is given the voice of philosophizing discourse: only that poetry whose difference is taken away when philosophy speaks it. Nor is it all poetry that is banished to the outside in the name of reason. Here is the *locus classicus* of that banishment in Plato's *Republic:*

> Socrates: You will know that the only poetry that should be allowed in a state is hymns to the gods and paeans in praise of good men; once you go beyond that and admit the sweet lyric or epic muse, pleasure and pain become your rulers instead of law *[anti nomou]* and the principles *[logou]* commonly accepted as best.
> Glaucon: Quite true.
> Socrates: Our defence, then, when we are reminded that we banished poetry from our state, must be that reason demands it.[7]

But the Plato of the *Republic* is not the only Plato to whom Lacan refers. Lacan also speaks for the Plato who acknowledges the madness in which poetry is composed. It is not necessary, he says (following Plato), that the poet know what he is doing. In fact, it is preferable that he not know—that is what gives a primordial value to what he does. Are Lacan's two Platos then compatible? If the first Plato speaks from the position of the subject who does not know, from where does the second speak but from the position of the subject supposed to know, a position that Lacan doubles in his own voice? To the second Plato, poetry is desirable-while-undesirable; and, despite the gesture Lacan makes of *not* incorporating poetry and thereby betraying it by giving it the blessing of reason, of the desirable ("We can only bow our heads before it"), he is in fact no more silent before it than Foucault is silent before madness: he *speaks* the silence he claims.

3. MIMETIC VIOLENCE

When Foucault gives a voice to madness, he does not do so, of course, in the court that condemned madness to exclusion in the first place. The enterprise of *Madness and Civilization* is to reveal the Reason of the Age of Reason as a mere power hiding behind a certain discourse, and thus to deny the authority (in universal reason) by which it claimed to sit in judgment on madness. In the reading that René Girard gives to Foucault, Foucault belongs to an age in which the law has lost its mystery; he tries to make up for the death of the law, says Girard, by substituting for the corpse an intangible, omnipresent, and omniscient Power.[8] But, without abandoning Girard's metaphorics, we can bring Foucault and Erasmus into closer conjunction by seeing Foucault, in *Madness and Civilization,* as politicizing madness: reducing reason and madness to the status of warring twins. In this perspective, each of the twins sees the other as possessing an overmastering prestige (a prestige perhaps no different from the power that Girard sees Foucault hypostatizing) which it must at all costs have for itself. This in turn may help us to see why it is that the actions of reason come to look more and more like madness, just as madness, and particularly the madness of paranoia, looks like an excess of reason: because each is imitating the other.[9]

Let me briefly rehearse the Girardian scheme of mimetic violence. (Since the outline that follows emphasizes features of Girard's thought important to my reading of Erasmus, it gives a certain bias to the Girardian corpus, as well as attributing to it a degree of unity that it does not possess.)

In a series of books and essays going back to 1961, Girard has built up an apocalyptic anthropology intended to do no less than explain the origins of religion, account for historical conflict, and prophesy the destiny of man. His scheme is based on an account of human desire that goes back not to Freud but to Sartre and, behind Sartre, to Hegel, in the reading given to Hegel by Alexandre Kojève.[10] Desire does not involve only a desiring subject and a desired object: the object acquires its desirable value through the mediating glance of an Other whose desire serves as a model for the subject's imitation. The clearest examples of such mimetic desire are to be found in novels: Quixote's desires, for instance, are mediated by Amadis of Gaul, Emma Bovary's by heroines of romantic fiction (*DDN*, pp. 84–85).

Desire, then, does not know itself. It proceeds from a lack. What the desiring subject lacks, and ultimately desires, is fullness of being. The model is adopted as model because it appears endowed with superior being. Imitating the desires of the model is a way of gaining being (*VS*, p. 146).

Because the desires of subject and model by definition coincide, rivalry over the object is from the start built into imitative desire. It is not, however, in the interest of the model to bring this inherent contradiction into the open—namely, the contradiction that the injunction "Imitate me!" is invariably accompanied by the parallel injunction "Do not appropriate my object!" (*VS*, pp. 146–47).

Model becomes rival, rival becomes obstacle. In fact, a spiraling dynamic is set in train: the more model transforms itself into obstacle, the more desire tends to transform obstacle into model (*DBB*, p. 39). It is because of this dynamic, rather than because the desires in play are necessarily powerful, that the clash of desires will escalate into violence. Desire is mimetic—that is to say, it seeks models for itself. Once it is let loose, it cannot therefore but turn into "a search for, and if need be a creation of, the insurmountable obstacle." If no such obstacle is at hand, "indifference itself can be turned into the most invincible obstacle" (*DBB*, p. 73).

It is thus loss of difference rather than difference itself that leads to conflict. Primitive religion and classical tragedy were aware of this.

> Order, peace and fecundity depend on cultural distinctions; it is not these distinctions but the loss of them that gives birth to fierce rivalries and sets members of the same family or social group at one another's throats. (*VS*, p. 49)

From loss of difference emerges rivalry. Once rivalry begins to grow, "each [of the rivals] wishes to prevent the other from incarnating the irresistible violence he wishes to incarnate himself" (*TH*, pp. 304–5). Rivals who fight for no more than intangible prestige or *kudos* (which Girard, following Benveniste, defines as "a talisman of supremacy" [*VS*, p. 152]) are in the deepest sense fighting for nothing. For to possess *kudos* is to be possessed by it, to be convinced that one's own violence is irresistible: there is no option for the rival but to exert himself further to break the enchantment and take the talisman away.

As differences dwindle and mimetic violence mounts, there is ultimately nothing done or felt by one protagonist that is not done or felt by the other. There is no way of differentiating them: the protagonists become doubles. The appearance of doubles is a sign that the mimetic process has been carried to its ultimate reaches: the whole of culture, based on the principle of difference, has revealed itself as arbitrary.[11]

The creation of an impersonal judicial system results from the efforts of primitive societies to move beyond the reciprocal violence of the vendetta. Though the judicial system is in fact based on the principle of retribution, the system tends to function best when this basis is denied and loyalty to a principle of abstract justice is invoked. The veil that used to hide the institution of sacrifice is now used to cover the machinery of law. Justice protects society against a return to the warring confusion of doubles only as long as the last word is granted to it, that is, as long as it does not reveal itself as part of a dynamic of retribution. When its claim to transcendental sanction is called into doubt as mere priestly mystification, the system begins to disintegrate (*VS*, pp. 135, 23).

The archetypal figure of nondifference is the twin. Twins *represent* nondifference. Yet at the same time, because they are unusual, their appearance on the scene manifests difference, monstrosity. "With enemy brothers, as with twins, the sign cannot fail to betray the thing signified because that 'thing' is the destruction of all signification." This is the most astute, or at least the most complex, twist in Girard's argument. The process of violent reciprocity, which destroys all differences, *itself resists representation*, since language is made up of differences. This explains the blindness of philosophy, to date, to what Girard has had the insight to see.[12]

4. *THE PRAISE OF FOLLY*

Madness, says Erasmus's Folly, is of two kinds. One kind manifests itself in bloodlust, greed, illicit passion; "the other kind is far different from this. It comes, you see, from me; and of all things is most to be desired."[13] To the first kind belongs the madness of those who, certain of their own rightness, give themselves to unbounded rivalry. As for the other kind of madness, its status is problematic from the start, since it is distinguished as a separate species on the authority only of Folly, Moria, herself.

What kind of authority can folly have? "Veracity," says Moria, "is disliked by kings." Yet from fools

> not only true things, but even sharp reproaches, will be listened to. . . . [A] statement which, . . . from a wise man's mouth, might be

a capital offence, coming from a fool gives rise to incredible delight [*voluptatem*]. Veracity . . . has a certain authentic power of giving pleasure [*delectandi*], if nothing offensive goes with it: but this the gods have granted only to fools. (P. 50/67)

It is not, then, in the content or substance of folly that its difference from truth lies, but in where it comes from. It comes not from "the wise man's mouth" but from the mouth of the subject assumed *not* to know and speak the truth. It is the knowledge of a Saint Peter, who "received the keys . . . and yet I doubt that he ever understood . . . that a person who did not have knowledge could have the key to knowledge" (p. 80). *The Praise of Folly* antedates that welling up of theological strife with which the Reformation announced itself. Yet, however indirectly, it projects an imaginary way out of a dilemma that Erasmus would confront and be unable to resolve in real life, namely the problem of how to *position* himself as critic of both sides. In essence, this problem is no different from the problem of critics of classical Reason, like Foucault, trying to define a position outside both madness and rationality from which to address both. Such a position, says Folly, is not created simply by declaring oneself outside the fray. It becomes available only to the subject who declares himself outside the discourse commanded by, and commanding, the fray, that is, outside reason, that is, inside a certain kind of folly. It is in this sense that the initial question about the difference between the two species of madness resolves itself as a question of position. The first madness positions itself inside reason, the second outside. Of course, neither is really where it claims to be. The madness of the first madness is that it does not know where it is. As for the claim of the second to be distinguished by knowing where it truly is (namely outside both reason and madness), this knowledge is the knowledge of folly, and therefore constitutionally suspect.

Moria goes on: the truth spoken by folly, because it is not rivalrous truth (not the mark of an intolerable prestige or *kudos* in the rival), but issues from outside the scene of imitative violence, gives rise to an "incredible delight" that is felt all the more keenly by "[those] more inclined to pleasure [*ad voluptatem . . . natura propensiores*]."

What is the connection enunciated here between pleasure

(voluptas) and wayward, masterless, gratuitous, "foolish" truth? For an answer, we must turn to the discussion of love and madness later in the book.

According to Plato, says Moria, the madness of lovers is the happiest state of all. The more perfect the love, the greater the madness. What can then the future life be but a life of full knowledge, perfect love, perfect madness? In heaven,

> the whole man will be outside of himself *[extra se]*, nor will he be happy for any other reason than that, so placed outside of himself, he shall have some ineffable portion of [the] *summum bonum.* . . . Hence those who are permitted to have a foretaste of this . . . suffer something very like to madness. They say things that are not quite coherent . . .; they weep, then laugh, and then sigh; in brief, they are truly outside themselves. (Pp. 123–24/188)

It is not only in *The Praise of Folly* that Erasmus brings together madness and mystical Christian theolepsy ("The Christian religion on the whole seems to have a kinship *[cognationem]* with some sort of folly, while it has no alliance whatever with wisdom," p. 118/ 180): the theme is present in all his works, even emerging in his annotations to the New Testament.[14] Madness of the second type, then, is a kind of *ek-stasis*, a being outside oneself, being beside oneself, a state in which truth is known (and spoken) from a position that does not know itself to be the position of truth. "For my part," says Moria, "it has always been most satisfactory *[gratissimum]* to speak 'whatever pops into my head'"—that is, to speak from the unconscious.[15] Such speech, in which the linear propulsive force of reason gives way to the unpredictable metamorphosis of figure into figure, yields a bliss that is the object of the desire of those most open to the promptings of desire; and the first manifestation of such bliss is of course laughter, an anarchic convulsion of the body that marks the defeat of the defenses of the censor.[16]

Madness of the second kind is therefore unsocialized, *rudis*, rude. "I do not feign one thing in my face while I hold something else in my heart," says Folly:

> I am in all points so like myself *[mei undique simillima]* that even those who . . . [call themselves] wise men cannot conceal me. Let them carry it as cunningly as you could ask, the protruding *[prominentes]* ears betray the Midas. . . . [Yet] although they are wholly of

my party, in public they are so ashamed of my name that they toss it up at others as a great reproach! (Pp. 10/6–7)

What is this unreasonable thing that even reasonable men have, that keeps protruding willy-nilly, that they refuse to name as their own but project upon others, that is so identical to itself in all points that it cannot be made to stand for anything else? The phallus, clearly (or less than clearly), but what species of phallus? It cannot be the phallus of the first species, the "big" phallus, the pillar of the law behind which the reasonable man stands; it can only (provisionally, hypothetically, dubiously) be a phallus of a second species, naked, ridiculous, without robes and crown and orb and sceptre, without grandeur, the "little" phallus that speaks for/of Moria: not the transcendental signifier but a *thing* of sport, of free play, of carefree dissemination rather than patrilinearity.

To whom is "the beginning and first principle of life" owed but to this *other* phallus, says Folly?

> Not the spear of "potent-fathered" [Gk. *obrimopatres*] Pallas, not the shield of "cloud-compelling" Jove, procreates the children of men. . . . Even he, the father of gods and king of men . . . is obliged to lay aside his three-pronged thunder and . . . Titanic aspect . . . and assume another character in the slavish manner of an actor, if he wishes to do what he never refrains from doing, that is to say, to beget children [Gk. *paidopoiein,* make a child]. . . . In fine, the wise man must send for me [namely, Folly] . . . if he ever wishes to become a father. And why not speak to you still more frankly . . . ? I beg to inquire whether the head, whether the face, the breast, the hand, or the ear . . . generates gods and men? I judge not; nay, rather that foolish, even silly [*stulta adeoque ridicula*] part which cannot be named without laughter, is the propagator [*propagatrix*] of the human race. This is at last the sacred spring from which all things derive existence. (Pp. 14/13–14)

The first principle, the *propagatrix* (feminine in gender: Erasmus does not call on the masculine form *propagator*), says Moria, is not the three-pronged thunderbolt of the patriarchal phallus but the thing of laughter; all living beings derive their existence from a "spring" which is as feminine as masculine in its ambivalent symbolism. And Moria presses further her originary claims. With the help of her attendant powers, she says, "I bring every sort of thing under my rule, maintaining my empire even over emperors."

Venus herself would not deny that without the addition of my presence her strength would be enfeebled and ineffectual. So it is that from this brisk and silly little game *[temulento ridiculoque lusu]* of mine come forth the haughty philosophers . . . and kings . . ., priests . . ., popes; also, finally, [the] assembly of the gods. (Pp. 13, 15/15)

How is it that Moria, with such pretensions to ultimate power, does not evoke the hostility of these philosophers, kings, priests, and popes? The obvious answer is that, not being made from within a discourse that matters, from a position that knows itself, such pretensions can be smiled at and dismissed by those who know better. Yet it is not as simple as that. Moria speaks:

Just as, according to the proverb of the Greeks, "an ape is always an ape, though dressed in scarlet," so a woman is always a woman— that is, a fool—whatever part she may have chosen to play. And yet I do not suppose the female sex is so foolish as to become incensed at me for this, that I, a woman and Folly as well, attribute folly to women. (P. 24)

One is tempted to comment: The irony is complex. Yet to say this is precisely to betray Moria. To attribute irony to her, to call her *o eiron,* the dissembler, is to put her back in the position of the subject supposed to know, the position she (foolishly) claims not to occupy. To put the point in another way: to attribute irony to her is to attribute the big phallus to her in the face of her claim to be the god/dess of the little phallus; where the markers *big* and *little,* like the markers *first* and *second* distinguishing species of madness, are endlessly provisional, endlessly subject to interchange.[17] Moria need not be taken seriously because, as she says, she is a woman. Why should a cardinal in his scarlet robes be incensed by a proverb about an ape, and coming from a woman at that?

Since even tyrants will take anything from their jesters, and laugh, and think it unmannerly to be offended by any pleasantries, it seems extraordinary that these people (it doesn't matter who they are) cannot bear to hear anything from the very lips of Folly—as if anything that was said about vice must immediately apply to themselves.[18]

If there is rage at Folly, on the part of of cardinals or even on the part of women, it can be attributed only to delusions of reference. Such anger is unmotivated, out of all proportion to its occasion, to words that just "pop into [the] head" of "a woman and Folly as well." It is mad. Again and again the point is made: to take as a rival and aim violence at someone who declares him/herself outside reason, *hors de combat*, is a symptom of unreason; and the rage that the spuriousness of this argument evokes (how could the argument be other than spurious?—it is the argument of unreason) only provides further proof of unreason.

It should be clear by now that the entire project of Erasmus to create for himself a position from which to speak without being drawn into a dynamic of rivalry (Erasmus adopted Terminus, Roman god of boundaries, as his personal emblem) depends on a massive elaboration of the Cretan liar paradox, an elaboration whose very dazzling complexity—to say nothing of the monological form of its *declamatio* (no one but Moria gets a word in edgewise)—threatens a discursive power which cannot but be taken as an object of envy and hence cannot but make of its exponent a model and rival.

It is to the inherent self-defeatingness of this essay in power, this project of drawing a boundary around a subject defined as inviolable because powerless, that Erasmus responds, I believe, in the best-known section of *The Praise of Folly*, the pages on the *theatrum mundi*. All human affairs, says Moria, are played out in disguise. Nothing is what it seems at first sight. But,

> if a person were to try stripping the disguises from actors while they play a scene . . . showing to the audience their real looks . . . would not such a one spoil the whole play *[fabulam]*? . . . Destroy the illusion and any play is ruined. . . . All things are presented by shadows; yet this play is put on in no other way *[haec fabula non aliter agitur]*.

Without social fictions there is no society. It is madness of the first—not the second—kind to *seriously* try to destroy these fictions. Suppose that "some wise man who has dropped down from the sky" should attempt it—

> what would he get by it, except to be considered by everyone as insane and raving *[demens ac furiosus]*? As nothing is more foolish than wisdom out of place, so nothing is more imprudent than unseasonable *[perverse]* prudence. And he is unseasonable who does not accommodate himself to things as they are. . . . The part of a truly

prudent man . . . is . . . not to aspire to wisdom beyond his station and either . . . [to] pretend not to notice anything, or affably and companionably [to] be deceived *[vel connivere libenter, vel comiter errare]*. (Pp. 37–38/48–50)

Glossing this passage, Ernesto Grassi comments: If the essence of wisdom were to be insight *(theoria)*, then it might be supposed that the task of the scholar would be to unmask the actors and destroy the spectacle. But this would be pure insanity. "The worst thing . . . is not the *deception that is suffered* by folly in human history as it happens to those who know": on the contrary, not to be deceived is to be most miserable of all *[falli . . . miserum est. Imo non falli, miserrimum]*. "The wish not to be deceived any more destroys life. . . . Knowledge, as the highest form of folly, of human aspiration, is equivalent to 'insanity.'"[19]

Side by side with *The Praise of Folly* Grassi sets Leon Battista Alberti's *Momus*. In the face of the madness of history, Grassi says, "we can affirm folly as Erasmus did as *ratio vivendi* out of the recognition that otherwise life . . . would have no meaning" or alternatively take Alberti's position: when we see that masks serve only to hide, to withdraw from their illusory world. "That is, we should no longer play with the others. It is the attitude of the 'last game' that no longer believes in the divinity of the holy fire."[20]

Both Erasmus and Alberti address a moment in history when the metaphysical sanction of the law seems to have withdrawn. (At first sight it may seem hard to maintain this as a reading of Erasmus the Christian. Yet it is of the essence of his half-suppressed conception of Christ as holy fool that faith in him should be irrational, absurd.) If all of life is a play *(fabula)* of contending forces which functions as a play only by keeping alive fictions of community, then law, too, is merely a force. What, in times like these, is the position of the scholar, the man of *theoria* who sees behind the masks to the dynamic that truly runs the play? What is the position of an Erasmus, an Alberti, but also of a Girard seeing behind the various masks the only play in town, the play of warring twins? Of the three, it is only Erasmus who, instead of giving his answer to the question, complicates it by asking in return: What is *to take a position*? Is there a position which is not a position, a position of *ek-stasis* in which one knows without knowing, sees without seeing? *The Praise of Folly* marks out such a "position," prudently disarming itself in advance, keeping its phallus the size of the woman's, steering clear of the play of power, clear of politics.

But, of course, the very mark of the success of the paradoxical project of embracing the position of the fool, the eunuch, the woman, is that as, to the surprise of all, the power of that position reveals itself, the paradox dissolves and the rivalrousness of the project is revealed. The claims of the little phallus to dubiousness and provisionality dissolve: the little phallus grows, threatens the big phallus, threatens to become a figure of law itself. The more of a success *The Praise of Folly* becomes, the more Erasmus has to disown or play at disowning it: his friend Thomas More egged him on to write it, he protests, it is out of keeping with his own real character, it is anyhow a silly book.[21] His attempts fail, or succeed, it is hard knowing which: the more the book amuses some, the more it angers others; the more it is condemned, the more it is read; the more successful Erasmus is at defining a position from which he can comment on power from the outside, the more he is caught up in the play of resentful powers.

The failure of Erasmus to define a position outside the dynamic of rivalry extended beyond his lifetime; that is to say, the Erasmian text itself (and the Erasmian biography too) became absorbed into other rivalries. As soon as Erasmus's oeuvre had been placed on the Index Librorum Prohibitorum in 1559, and thereby effectively closed off to Catholic printers, it was exploited for its consequent notoriety by Protestant printers.[22] Efforts to enlist Erasmus in the rivalries of the day were still being made four centuries later. I conclude by pointing to two instances in Europe of the 1930s, lurching toward war.

5. ERASMUS AS MODEL

The first case is of the Dutch historian Johannes Huizinga. "Our confused times require strong stimuli," writes Huizinga, summing up, not without regret, his case against Erasmus. "Our interest is in a piety that is ardent, our admiration is for extremes." What is needed in the twentieth century, as it was needed in the sixteenth, is "the oaken strength of Luther . . ., the steely sharpness of Calvin, the fiery heat of Loyola; not the velvet softness of Erasmus." Erasmus was "an utterly unpolitical spirit" who "from moment he saw that the conflict [of the Reformation] would lead to bitter strife, . . . wanted to be no more than a spectator."[23]

In the context of the failure of European intellectuals to provide political direction to their countries in the 1920s—a failure as marked as anywhere in the Netherlands—we can read Huizinga's judgment on Erasmus as a judgment on his own peers. The key term of his judgment is, of course, "unpolitical" [onpolitisch]. It assimilates Erasmus to a gallery of political types, one of which is the unpolitical, the type that has no competence in, but also a fastidious aversion for, politics. How just is this characterization? *The Praise of Folly* (which, with the *Colloquia*, is in Huizinga's view the only work of Erasmus's that still deserves to be read) is a complex reflection upon the notion of the political as a totalizing category and an outline of the possibility of a stance outside politics— namely, a stance of not aspiring to wisdom beyond one's station, but rather pretending not to notice anything or "affably and companionably" being deceived—whose feasibility is nevertheless skeptically regarded. This is far from the merely reactive playing out of the consequences of a personal temperament that Huizinga diagnoses: indeed, we might say that in the figure of the play that "can be put on in no other way" Erasmus foresees the powerlessness of his own discourse to resist being swallowed by Huizinga's, that is to say, foresees how in times of violence differences (boundaries, *termini*) are erased.

Writing in 1934, Stefan Zweig reads Erasmus—the Erasmian text and the Erasmian figure—in another light. A citizen less of Austria than of a cosmopolitan republic of letters whose origins go back to the Enlightenment and, further back, to Erasmian humanism, antipathetic to notions of racial and national destiny, Zweig finds Europe of the interwar years alarmingly similar to Europe of the Reformation. "From every side the individual is attacked by the overwhelming force of the masses, and there is no means of protection, no means of salvation from the collective madness." "The demon of war [is] let loose." "The average man is under the spell of hatred."[24]

In such times "a supranational and panhuman ideal such as Erasmism," the teaching of "the most unfanatical, the most anti-fanatical of men," in which "there is no room for the passion of hatred," unfortunately lacks "the elementary attraction which a mettlesome encounter with the foe who lives across a frontier, speaks another tongue, and holds another creed invariably exercises" (*ERH*, pp. 8, 7).

Yet, says Zweig, Erasmus still provides a model for the age. "[When] neutrality is stigmatized as a crime . . . , [when] the world insists upon a clear Yes or No," Erasmus refuses to choose sides. He quotes Erasmus: "I would rather suffer things to remain as they are than that through my intervention fresh unrest should arise" (*ERH*, p. 120).

The madness Zweig refers to is in the first place the madness of warring nationalisms, led by resurgent xenophobic German nationalism. In this context Erasmus stands for the transcendence of nationalism in pan-European humanism. But we should by now be alert to the complexity that the notion of *standing for* holds in Erasmus's thinking. Erasmus does not stand for pan-Europeanism *as against* nationalism, as he clearly says in the very words Zweig quotes. To stand for one or the other would be madness of the first species, the madness of the one who locates himself within reason: it would be to set up pan-Europeanism as a rival to nationalism and to further rivalrous conflict.

Huizinga, pondering Erasmus of Deventer as a model for the European intellectual of the 1930s, finds him too soft. Zweig, on the other hand, finds much to imitate. Indeed, as Klaus Heydemann has shown, Zweig in his book on Erasmus not only encoded the plight of Erasmus as his own plight, but saw Erasmus in *The Praise of Folly* as writing a comparably esoteric text about the plight of the intellectual in times of madness.[25]

But how Erasmian is Zweig's *Imitatio Erasmi*? The average man is under the spell of hatred, Zweig writes, whereas in Erasmism there is no room for hatred. The "unfanatical" Erasmian is "menaced [from outside] by irrational passion," by "a torrent of unreason" (*ERH*, p. 8). "The individual is attacked by the overwhelming force of the masses," by their "collective madness." It is not Zweig's Erasmian, then, who is beside himself, *extra se*. On the contrary, the Erasmian possesses himself in certainty: he is the one who knows. The self-certainty of the masses, on the other hand, is a deluded certainty: they are in the grip of madness. One might ask: does the certainty of being right make Zweig's Erasmian individual and Zweig's fanatic nationalist-collectivist more or less alike? Does it turn them into opposites or into twins?

A comment of Zweig's on Calvin—the type, to him, of the fanatic convinced of his own rightness—points to a blindness in Zweig's own eye. "Throughout life this man, who in other respects showed clearsightedness, was never able to doubt that he alone was competent to interpret the word of God, and that he alone possessed the truth" (*ERH*, p. 202). The blindness of Calvin to the possibility that he was wrong marks him as a madman of the first species. But from what position can such a judgment on Calvin be made? Either it is a judgment based on a conviction of certainty characteristic of Erasmus's wise man, the man who is "uniquely sane" (*Praise of Folly*, p. 39) and therefore more than likely to be touched with the first madness, or it is the judgment of Folly, that knows it is folly but does not therefore drop its mask, for it also knows that "the play is put on in no other way."

As Zweig and Huizinga try to make of Erasmus a figure in their own political quarrels, what I try to bring forward is an extraordinary resistance in the Erasmian text to being read into and made part of another discourse. We are dealing here with a text in confrontation with powers of interpretation that mean to bend it to their own meaning (though we should warily note that in the very use of the word "bend" one begins to set up a certain field of rivalry and align oneself within it). The discourse of Erasmus's Protean Folly ("shape-changer," in Stephen Dedalus's phrase) is only by the most strenuous effort wrestled on to the field of politics: Erasmus virtually disarms anyone (like Zweig) who passionately decides to take up the Erasmian cause by elevating him in advance to the status of *one who knows*. Instead, the power of the text lies in its weakness—its jocoserious abnegation of big-phallus status, its evasive (non)position inside/outside the play—just as its weakness lies in its power to grow, to propagate itself, to beget Erasmians.

CHAPTER SIX

Osip Mandelstam and the Stalin Ode

MANDELSTAM AND STALIN

In November 1933, Osip Mandelstam composed a brief poem on Stalin which ends (in the Raffel/Burago translation):

> He forges decrees like horseshoes—decrees and decrees:
> This one gets it in the balls, that one in the forehead,
>   him right between the eyes.
>
> Whenever he's got a victim, he glows like a broadchested
> Georgian munching a raspberry.[1]

The poem was never written down, but was recited to a small gathering of friends. In May of 1934 the security police searched Mandelstam's apartment; it is generally assumed that they were looking for a copy of the poem. Arrest, interrogation, incarceration, and eventually exile to the city of Voronezh followed. In Voronezh, isolated, spied upon, in poor health, unable to earn a living, Mandelstam yielded to pressure and wrote an ode to Stalin.[2] The Ode did not save him from rearrest as the Terror mounted or from death in a Siberian camp in 1938, though it may have saved his wife.[3]

For long it was accepted that the Ode had not survived. In 1975, however, a truncated version supplied by an anonymous contributor appeared in an American journal.[4] A full version was published in 1976. Together with the full Ode came evidence—again from sources who did not wish to be named—that Mandelstam had not been ashamed of the Ode, as Anna Akhmatova and Nadezhda Mandelstam had claimed, but on the contrary had several times read it to gatherings.[5]

The prehistory and history of the composition of the Ode, together with its textual history and the history of its interpretation, therefore constitute an unusually complex case of control over the word, spoken and written. The forces at work included: a state censorship apparatus that made unapproved publication impossible, and a security apparatus operating beyond the bounds of legality which made not only the publication but the very composition of oppositional literature, even literature amenable to an oppositional construal, dangerous;[6] pressure on all writers not only to declare their *partiinost* (Party-spiritedness) but to evince it in their work (in a time of a rampant cult of personality, this amounted to pressure that they evince devotion to Stalin in their work); and, later on, as the record of Mandelstam's life and oeuvre began to be assembled, subtler pressures from a variety of sources for the suppression of the Stalin Ode, and indeed for suppression of discussion of the Ode and its existence.

The third kind of pressure is less well-attested than the others, but is easy enough to understand. No Soviet writer had withstood demands to declare him/herself for Stalin ("Which of us [would be] immune to the blandishments of trying to go on living?" asks Clarence Brown rhetorically.)[7] After Stalin's death there was a natural enough desire to set aside such work produced under duress. Nadezhda Mandelstam admits that she and Anna Akhmatova destroyed at least one such "glib" poem of Mandelstam's (*HaH*, p. 46). Clarence Brown acknowledges that before making his researches into the Ode public he asked himself whether what he had written would not be "discreditable" to Mandelstam.[8] Reviewing the 1980 Paris edition of the Collected Works, the politically liberal scholar and critic Efim Etkind asks whether, as a matter of editorial policy, the Ode should not have been printed in small type and set among the Notes, rather than in the body of the text.[9]

A critical crisis of a kind therefore develops around the status of the Ode in the Mandelstam corpus, centering on the question, not of its authenticity, which is undoubted, but of the spirit in which it was written, and in particular of whether Mandelstam stood behind the poem, whether he sincerely meant what he wrote. Only at the price of retreating into a rigid formalism can the issue of Mandelstam's sincerity, with its political as well as its moral implications, be evaded.

To Stalin and those members of the apparatus concerned with surveillance of the literary intelligentsia, what mattered was that every writer should make public obeisance to the great man and thus have both his pride and his power broken; in what spirit the praise-songs were sung was immaterial, as was the question of whether they constituted good or bad literature, as long as they did not carry discernible traces of insincerity—that is to say, traces of disobedience or even mockery. For those concerned with the integrity of Mandelstam's reputation it has therefore been important, for the honor not only of the poet but of poetry in general, that his praise of Stalin should not only be accepted as insincere, but should bear actual signs of not coming from his true self.

Before the text of the Ode resurfaced it was taken as self-evident that the Ode had to have been inauthentic work, what Jennifer Baines calls "tainted water."[10] Critics took their lead from Nadezhda Mandelstam's account of the composition of the poem. In order to compose the Ode, she wrote, Mandelstam

> deliberately [gave] way to the general hypnosis and [put himself] under the spell of the liturgy which in those days blotted out all human voices. . . . Working himself up into the state needed to write the "Ode," he was in effect deliberately upsetting the balance of his own mind. (*HaH*, p. 203)

In other words, Mandelstam's praise of Stalin was not sincere; if it seems sincere, that is because it came not from the poet Mandelstam but from another voice (a voice of madness, the voice of a people driven to madness) speaking through him.

Once the Ode had been published, and readers were able to make their own judgments, the focus of critical attention shifted, though it remained within the moral sphere. Thus Gregory Freidin, for instance, having acknowledged a "tone of profound sincerity" in the Ode, pursues the implications of this recognition for our valuation of Mandelstam as man and poet.[11]

There are ways of bypassing the debate over Mandelstam's sincerity—for instance, by historicizing the notion of sincerity itself and treating it as no more than a feature of Romantic style. But if sincerity and the poet's truth constituted a real issue to Nadezhda Mandelstam, there is every reason to think they constituted a real issue to her husband. If there were urgent reasons why marks of insincerity could not have been encoded in the poem (and there are plenty of such reasons, the most forceful of which would be that such marks mean nothing unless they can be detected, and no one is more skillful at such detection than the paranoid and therefore overdetecting censor), if what Nadezhda calls "madness" has to be invoked as an explanation, then it does most credit to both the Mandelstams that it should be a madness like Hamlet's, a madness that knows itself, rather than a madness that is, in the old phrase, an alienation: an alienation of the self from the self. The critical task in reading Mandelstam's Ode should not, then, be one of searching it for an ineffable sincerity or insincerity, but of seeking the nature of its madness and, perhaps more importantly, seeking for signs of reflection within the Ode upon the Ode's own madness. That is to say, our eyes should be open not to the representation of *Stalin* in the Ode but to the *representation* of Stalin, that is, to the representation of the project of representation itself.

Although, as anyone who reads his "Conversation about Dante" (1933) can confirm, Mandelstam was perfectly *au courant* with the terms of Formalist criticism and in particular with the advocacy—associated with Viktor Shklovsky—of *priëm ostranenija*, the device of making-strange,[12] *ostranenie* is not characteristic of Mandelstam's poetry before the Ode. Mandelstam typically writes poetry of direct address of the subject; the act of address itself is not framed or estranged. Yet not only is the Ode in large part *about* the act of representing Stalin, it is also about the addressing of the project of writing an ode as something that may or may not be brought off, something of which one may or may not be capable.[13]

> Were I to take up the charcoal for the sake of
>   supreme praise—
> For the sake of the eternal joy of drawing—
> I would divide the air into clever angles

> Both carefully and anxiously.
> To make the present echo in his features
> (My art bordering on audacity),
> I would speak about him who has shifted the world's
>   axis. . .[14]

Thus begins the Ode, in a hypothetical-conditional mode: *Kogda b ya . . . vzyal,* "If I were to take up." This mode of the verb persists in the second stanza (of seven). In the third, the poet-artist with the charcoal in his hand is apostrophized as someone out there, separate from the I who speaks: "Artist, cherish and guard the warrior [i.e., Stalin]." In the fourth stanza we are still in the hypothetical mode: "I would like to mark [*ya xotel by . . . ukazat'*] with an arrow / The firmness of his mouth." In the fifth stanza the verb becomes definite in time-reference, but the time-reference is *future* (*iskroshu,* "I crumble," perfective with future meaning):

> Grasping the charcoal, the focus of everything, . . .
> I shall make the coal crumble, searching out his features.
> I am learning from him, but learning not for my own
>   sake,
> I am learning from him to be merciless to myself.

How is this *present* process of learning achieved? Not through having *completed* the artwork but in the first place from preparing for that labor, from girding the loins for the labor, so to speak, and subsequently in the imagined process of *following* with the charcoal the outline of the features. In fact, the Ode as a whole is about being daunted by the project of the ode but of learning dauntlessness from its dauntless subject, Stalin; even definite—as opposed to hypothetical—representation of the act of representation itself is elided; and the final stanza of the poem presents the poet-self in the vanishing perspective of a rapidly receding present-becoming-past:

> The hillocks of people's heads are growing more distant:
> I am diminishing in them, won't even be noticed,
> But in tender books and in children's games,
> I shall be resurrected. . .

Thus we have a future in which the ode is contemplated and a further future in which the ode has been achieved; in between the two we have to imagine the presence (present-ness) of the ode; but of the ode itself we really see only a kind of residue, an aftereffect of the contemplation, forward and backward, of the idea of an ode.

This is of course by no means the whole story. The content of the 84 lines, abstracted from its framing in the mode of the hypothetical, is what has caused the critical, moral, and political crisis among commentators. This content includes fulsome adulation typical of the peak years of the cult of personality, the late 1930s, when the myth of Stalin as father of the Russian people was being sedulously fostered by the propaganda organs.[15] It is only the present-day reader, familiar with his widow's memoirs, who can have an inkling of what private meaning Mandelstam gave to some of these stock phrases and images: for instance, the image of "hillocks of heads" in stanza 4, which, though it refers in the first place to a newsreel of Lenin addressing a crowd—"a prototype for many a Lenin poster," as Freidin observes—also summons up, in Mandelstam's personal repertoire of images from history, Gengis Khan and the mounds of heads he left outside the gates of cities that resisted his armies.[16]

So to think of the Ode as a sly piece of work guarded by an irony invisible to its subject, as an insult masquerading as a tribute, would be quite mistaken. Not only is there no insincerity written into and readable out of the poem, there is even a certain fervor or at least feverishness detectable. The general account of the composition of the poem given by Nadezhda Mandelstam, and confirmed by the painstaking analysis of all the other poems of the period 16 January to 9 February 1937 carried out by Clarence Brown, is thoroughly convincing. Mandelstam did indeed circle around and around the subject of an ode to the tyrant, descending deeper and deeper into a whirlpool that Nadezhda called madness but for which a better name would be alienation, one of the translations of *ostranenie:* an alienation effect, but also an alienation of Mandelstam from himself under the gravitational pull of Stalin.

Thus we have two forces leaving their traces in the poem: a force of alienation and a force of identification. Identification centers on the mysterious image of the twin (*blizn'ets*, from *bliz*, near, close) in stanza 2:

> . . .In the friendship of his [Stalin's] wise eyes, I shall
> find for the twin
> (I won't say who he is) that expression, drawing close to
> Which, to him—you suddenly recognize the father
> And gasp. . .

Representing the father—drawing his features with the charcoal—thus turns out not to be something that can be done directly. It is as though representation must be done at a remove, in two stages: first turning one's attention to a dummy or mock-up of the subject, and then, in the light of the subject's eyes/expression, filling in the dummy until all at once it becomes the twin of the subject: the same but different (the confusing double prepositional phrase "to which, to him," imitated in Freidin's translation from Mandelstam's Russian, mimes this instant of confused double identification).

The first pair of twins mentioned in the poem is the pair Stalin-Dzhugashvili (stanza 2):

> I want to thank the hills
> That have shaped this bone and this hand:
> He was born in the mountains and knew the bitterness of
> jail.
> I want to call him, not Stalin,—Dzhugashvili!

This twin-pair is strange in that, though they are in one sense brothers, there is also a sense in which Dzhugashvili is the antecedent of Stalin, and a further sense in which Stalin is the older man, Dzhugashvili the younger, forever frozen in the youth in which he was left behind. So an unresolved question of primacy is already in the air.

The second pair, constituting a mythic substrate to the poem, is Prometheus, bearer of the glowing (char)coal *(ugol')*, bringer of fire to man, forever punished for that deed by the all-father Zeus (stanza 1), and Christ, drinker of the cup of gall (stanza 5), both figures of the suffering son/artist, one belonging to the old pantheon and the old dispensation, the other to the new.

Insofar as the Ode constitutes a submission and a plea to Stalin,

Mandelstam is here putting forward two alternative modes of fatherly behavior: the eternal vengefulness of Zeus, and the mercifulness of the Christian God which will issue in the resurrection of the son (see stanza 7). He is also clearly pleading for the merciful alternative.

However, locating the figures of writer and tyrant, son and father, in its mythic substrate does not exhaust the puzzling issues of representation in the poem. Why must Stalin be represented by his twin, whether Dzhugashvili or the one unnamed ("I won't say who he is")? Why must drawing Stalin be so difficult? Why must drawing become drawing (drawing upon) a millionfold representation of Stalin ("His eyelid, sculpted, complicated and abrupt, / Projects, verily, out of a million frames")? Why must the language of address in the poem be so unlike Mandelstam's own language and be instead a displaced language, the language of other people's address ("absorb[ing] contemporary official rhetoric," as Freidin says, "with all its maniacal verbosity," *CMC*, p. 263)? Is what is being evaded here by Mandelstam not the dark side of representation, namely, the aspiration (which is also a threat) of the son (as likeness of the father) to usurp his progenitor? What can Mandelstam's reason be for making the resurrection looked forward to at the end of the poem not a glorious resurrection in which the son ascends the father's throne, but a far-off, harmless resurrection back into eternal and submissive childhood, except that the son's growing up menaces the father and the father's being-menaced even more menaces the son?

> The hillocks of people's heads are growing more distant:
> I am diminishing in them, won't even be noticed,
> But in tender books and in children's games,
> I shall be resurrected to say that the sun—shines.

Portraiture by its nature creates an Oedipal structure and Oedipal tensions between subject and artist. The account Pasternak gave of his telephone conversation with Stalin after Mandelstam's first arrest in 1934 makes it clear that Stalin's anxiety was about whether Mandelstam was a mere versifier (in which case it would not matter what happened to him), or a great poet, a *master*, one whose fame *and whose representation of Stalin* might outlast Stalin himself.[17] Max Hayward reminds us that, with the exception of Mandelstam, none of the great poets of Stalin's day was killed or even imprisoned; there is even an argument to be made that the arrest and deportation of Mandelstam in 1937 may have been the work of an over-zealous underling. Stalin had "a kind of superstitious appreciation of the supreme worth [of great poets]," Hayward suggests.[18] In any event, what is striking about the Ode is Mandelstam's preternatural sensitivity to the Oedipal threat that a *great* poem about Stalin holds, and the lengths to which he is prepared to go—self-abasing obsequiousness, cloying concern for Stalin's happiness—to mask the threat. This sensitivity in turn not only attests to Stalin's sensitivity on the question of usurpation—a sensitivity all too well known to every Russian—but also, perhaps, to the power of usurpatory urges in Mandelstam himself.[19]

NADEZHDA MANDELSTAM AND THE STALIN ODE

Not only did Nadezhda Mandelstam play an important role by acting as her husband's editor and explicator to a wider world: in her widely-read memoir, *Hope against Hope*, she also encouraged a myth of Mandelstam as the sacrificed artist-hero, Prometheus and Christ. In a very real sense it was she who kept alive both the memory of Mandelstam and the Mandelstam corpus; in her books she resurrects Mandelstam as a myth for our times.

I have referred above to Nadezhda's explanation of how the Ode came to be written: Mandelstam "deliberately gave way to the general hypnosis..., [putting himself] under the spell of the liturgy which in those days blotted out all human voices." In her account, Osip was therefore *not himself* when he wrote the Ode. The Ode is extracanonical.

Her account goes further, however: it sets out the wider significance of the composition of the Ode. Stalin's most darkly cunning strategy against the writers of her husband's generation was, in her words, that

> their tongues were cut out and with the stump that remained they were forced to glorify the tyrant.... Among all those who contin-

ued to play the role of writers in those years, none have come forth
[since] as witnesses. They can never . . . say anything with the
stumps of their tongues. (*HaH*, p. 202)

This is a fable about poetic castration: poets who yielded and did
the bidding of the tyrant lost for good their power as truth-bearers,
bringers of fire—in fact, their creative power. The fable is one that
Mandelstam himself had resorted to: in the *Fourth Prose* (1929–30)
he uses the metaphor of "priests of [the] tribe" who appear before
him armed with the knife of circumcision/castration to stand for
the literary-bureaucratic apparatus with its powers of commanding
and forbidding.[20] Stalin and his apparatus castrated a generation of
writers, robbing it not only of its generative power but of its power
of historical witness and therefore of its political power. By the
wounds he inflicted, Stalin in effect ensured that he could not be
repudiated even after his death; by this means he intended to guarantee himself a backhand immortality.

Nadezhda Mandelstam insists that the contest between artist
and despot is a struggle over power, a struggle in which—surprisingly—the artist starts with a built-in advantage. This paradox is
already detectable in the anecdote she retells from Pasternak, where
the question of who will outlast whom and the question of whose
version or representation of whom will have the power to prevail
are intertwined. In the following passage from *Hope against Hope*
the issue of power emerges nakedly:

> "Poetry is power," [Mandelstam] once said to Akhmatova in Voro-
> nezh, and she bowed her head on its slender neck. Banished, sick,
> penniless and hounded, they still would not give up their power.
> [Mandelstam] behaved like a man conscious of his power, and this
> only egged on those who wanted to destroy him. For them power
> was expressed in guns, agencies of repression, the distribution
> of everything—including fame—by coupons, the possibility of
> commissioning their portraits from any artist they chose. But [Man-
> delstam] stubbornly maintained that if they killed people for poetry,
> then they must fear and respect it—in other words, that it too was
> a power in the land. (P. 170)

All the themes I have touched on are present in this passage: the
lowly, persecuted, Christ-like poet who is yet a figure of mysterious
power; the question of fame or reputation and of who is its true

author; the question of who will control representations; and finally, the power-rivalry of poet and despot.

"In this country," Nadezhda Mandelstam writes, "all real poetry
is outrageous" (*HaH*, p. 92). It is outrageous because it affronts
power, contests power. But why is poetry an affront to power? Two
provocative statements by Osip Mandelstam, from earlier and less
menaced days, give a clue:

> Social differences and class antagonisms pale before the new division
> of people into friends and enemies of the word: literally, sheep and
> goats. I sense an almost physically unclean goat-breath emanating
> from the enemies of the word. ("The Word and Culture" [1921], in
> *P&L*, p. 113)
>
> I divide all of world literature into authorized and unauthorized
> works. The former are all trash; the latter—stolen air. I want to spit
> in the face of every writer who first obtains permission and then
> writes. ("Fourth Prose" [1929–30], in *P&L*, p. 316)

Though statements like these speak on behalf of "the word,"
they are not themselves "the word" in any real sense. They belong,
instead, to the polemic of rivalry, and specifically to the rivalry of
writer and censor. They are reactive moves whose provocativeness
consists in asserting a wholly different dichotomy from the overwhelming dichotomy in whose terms the word was censored. The
state asserted a distinction between progressive literature and reac-
tionary literature, authorizing the first (by the same act asserting
the power of its own *secondary* authorship) and denying the second; it included in the category of the unauthorized the saving
Word for which Mandelstam as poet spent his life waiting. Mandelstam's response is to invert the categories authorized/unauthorized,
claiming the latter as the positive pole, and then to deny the primacy of the progressive/reactionary distinction by asserting (he-
retically) that "social differences and class antagonisms" are not
fundamental.

The stake is thus deliberately and provocatively raised (at a time
in Soviet history, admittedly, when such a move did not entail the
ultimate penalty). Whereas in the first confrontation between poet
and state, the issue is simply freedom to publish, what is at stake
now becomes the truth of Marxism. An alternative allegiance, an
alternative patriotism is proclaimed, and all who do not give them-

selves to the new order are consigned to darkness *(goats . . . I spit in their face)*. Mandelstam himself, or at least Nadezhda's Mandelstam, had recognized the *madness* of patriotism,[21] and in other contexts recognized the power of the state to drive its citizens into paranoia (*HaH*, pp. 33–34), but there is no sign that Mandelstam recognizes the spiral of madness here, as the reactions of the state drive him into megalomaniac rivalry. This rivalry and this megalomania are clearly spelled out:

> There is nothing hungrier than the contemporary State, and a hungry State is more terrifying than a hungry man. To show compassion for the State which denies the word shall be the contemporary poet's social obligation and heroic feat. ("Word and Culture" [1921], in *P&L*, p. 115)

Compassion for the state: heroic perhaps, on the part of the poet; to the state, however, it can hardly but sound *de haut en bas*.

Osip Mandelstam, says Nadezhda, despite being mutilated and afterwards slain, has been reborn in the fullness of his power, while his persecutor and killer has been consigned to darkness. But how did little Osip survive big Iosif (the names are cognates) when, in her own account, so many of his brothers were robbed of their power forever by writing to order? The answer is: by not being there, by not being himself, by being beside himself when the knife struck. Who wielded the mutilating knife? In each case, she insists, it was the poet himself. The sentence on the poet was diabolical, extraordinary even in the long annals of censorship: to pick up the tool of Oedipal menace and mutilate himself by using it to write, upon his own body or corpus, the words of the father's dictate.

Nadezhda's allegory thus confirms that if Mandelstam's poem to Stalin is about anything, it is about *not* wielding the tool. Instead, it is about all that would be entailed by taking up the tool of obedient representation (representation as repetition), all that would be entailed by speaking the father's language as the father's.[22] The act itself (the act of self-mutilation) is not there. It is somewhere at the center of the poem, the poem spins around it, but only as a painting spins around the vanishing-point of perspective: it is absent, not represented. Mandelstam's performance, achieved through what I call alienation and his wife called madness, is a desperate one: to fabricate the body of an Ode without actually inhabiting it. In the chess game of power that Stalin played not only with Mandelstam but with all those masters of the word to whom it would fall to pronounce the last word on him and his times—a game in which Stalin cannily sought to preempt their verdict by demanding their best last words there and then—we may think of Mandelstam, in his own ode, as playing for a draw. Not an equal draw (that would be too much of a provocation), not even a draw too actively *played for:* rather, one of those technical draws that a weaker player can sometimes *slip into* without seeming to *slip it over* his opponent, emerging with a lucky half-point, outgunned but not disgraced.

CHAPTER SEVEN

Censorship and Polemic: Solzhenitsyn

WRITER AND CENSOR

In the account that follows of the skirmishes between Aleksandr Solzhenitsyn and the powers of the Soviet state in the years leading up to Solzhenitsyn's involuntary departure from the Soviet Union in 1974, I will not be attempting to breathe life back into issues of Cold War literary politics, though most of the writers, critics, historians, and commentators who feature in the account disposed themselves, or found themselves disposed, on one side or the other of the Cold War divide. My interest is more general: in the belligerence that tends to be generated in any field ruled over by censorship, and that in this case swirled around the figure of Solzhenitsyn. While I am certainly not impartial between the belligerents, the Soviet literary bureaucracy on the one hand, certain Soviet writers on the other, I try to steer a course between what I see as a Scylla and Charybdis before me: the Scylla of denouncing either the house of the censors or the house of Solzhenitsyn, or indeed, in the name of "intelligence" as opposed to "stupidity," both houses together; and the Charybdis of denouncing denunciation itself and the rhetoric of the denunciatory mode.

Out of our quarrels with others, said Yeats, we make rhetoric. I resurrect old quarrels between writers and censors of the Soviet era in order to pursue a suspicion that these clashes, primitive in their force, vehement in the escalating passion of their rhetoric, rarely spelled out what truly animated them. Following the lead of René Girard, I explore a dynamic always threatening to overtake controversies over censorship, a destructuring dynamic of escalation in which the rivals, writer and censor, become less and less clearly distinguishable.

What I take over from Girard is not the anthropological scheme at the heart of his enterprise or his counter-Freudian psychology, but the outline of a politics of desire. Specifically, I use Girard's account of imitative desire leading to rivalrous conflict and loss of difference not as a theory to be confirmed or disconfirmed by the Solzhenitsyn case study but as a heuristic framework within which to describe the structural dynamic—or, on Girardian lines, the destructuring dynamic—of a sequence of historical events centering on Solzhenitsyn.[1]

In describing writer and censor as carried on waves of polemic toward identity or twinship, I implicitly grant them equivalent stature. With relief I therefore pass by two tired images of the writer under censorship: the moral giant under attack from hordes of moral pygmies and the helpless innocent persecuted by a mighty state apparatus. In abandoning David-and-Goliath models I in effect question Oedipal conflict as the natural framework within which to see contests between writers and the state. I do so principally because the Oedipus myth takes as given what Girard puts at issue: primacy. Beneath the conflicts described in this chapter lie two irreconcilable assumptions of a political order: on the one hand, that the writer is born into the state and is no different from any other citizen in this respect; on the other, that the state is a superimposition over a human community out of which and for which the writer speaks. These are assumptions about priority and hence about legitimacy, right, and the origin of the law. Inasmuch as they are rival assumptions, they also imply different founding myths and translate the struggle between writer and state into a struggle over which myth shall prevail. In asserting the myth of a higher-order state, and doing what it can to impose and internalize it, all the while covering the traces of its operations and generally controlling the terms of the discourse, the state-as-father already asserts a prior right to make the rules, speak the law. The challenge that a Tolstoy or a Solzhenitsyn chooses to issue to the state, on the other hand, is: Who truly speaks for the people and who is the pretender?—a question framed in terms of representation, not of priority.

There is no *getting behind* the contending myths of father-son and brother-brother. There is thus an undeniable component of willfulness in my turn to the anti-Oedipal Girardian model, as indeed there is in my framing of the conflict between models as a conflict between equal rivals. I am in this respect in no more tenable a position than Girard is in reading the elevation of the Oedipus story to centrality as a strategy on Freud's part for masking his own professional rivalries, a reading that implicitly constructs (or masks) Girard's own attack on Freud as not Oedipal (Freudian) but rivalrous (Girardian). No more tenable, but also no less.[2]

SOURCES

The field I describe is the USSR in the period 1956 to 1974, which largely overlaps the career as writer of Aleksandr Solzhenitsyn before he departed into exile. Many of the sources of my information have the inherent weakness of being contaminated by the very biliousness that is one of the objects of my scrutiny. I refer particularly to: (1) commentaries by dissident internal Soviet intellectuals, by their nature partisan; (2) records of the pronouncements of Party ideologists and bureaucratic administrators of culture, in the form quoted by their enemies; and (3) the works of Sovietologists (for instance, Swayze, Johnson, Rothberg, Spechler) and émigrés (for instance, Etkind, Turchin, Glazov), all in one degree or another involved in the rivalry of the Cold War or having rivalrous motives of their own.

The only way of to some extent transcending or at least not being taken over by the biases and rancors of these sources is to absorb them into the field of discourse I analyze, namely, the discourse of censorship. I follow this course where I can.

As for the place of Solzhenitsyn in this account, I treat him, at least in the first instance, as a formidable polemicist and political in-fighter. That he could be this and also a great Russian-humanist novelist is clearly what his aggrieved ex-colleagues—sometimes, perhaps, disingenuously—found hard to comprehend. They accused him of making use of them for his own ends. The truth is very likely that Solzhenitsyn would have made use of anyone in what he conceived of as the higher cause of furthering his own vision of Russian history. The conclusion one should be wary of settling for takes the form: Solzhenitsyn the man may be an unpleasant character, treacherous, in many ways crazy, but in the end all that matters is the quality of his work; the work can be separated from the character. The work, I would argue instead, includes a project of understanding the immoral deposits of the Stalinist past—including unpleasantness, treachery, and craziness—within the character, and so of replacing a dialectic of violence by one of healing.

THE IMPERIAL BACKGROUND

Surveillance and control of writing in the Soviet Union built upon certain Tsarist precedents and inherited certain Tsarist structures, which it is worth outlining. Tsarist surveillance dates from the creation by Alexander I of a secret police force to report on the activities of political opponents, intercept mails, oversee the issuing of passports, and supervise press and theater censorship. But the institutionalization and bureaucratization of surveillance belongs to the second quarter of the nineteenth century and the reign of Nicholas I, who, in response to the Decembrist uprising of 1825 and the European revolutions of 1830, created a body—the Third Section of the Imperial Chancery—responsible directly to him and charged, inter alia, with "[providing] information concerning all events, without exception."[3]

Though it did not perform day-to-day censorship, the Third Section routinely checked on the censors in the Ministry of the Interior until, as part of the post-1848 repressions, Nicholas brought into being a special body for that task. As Nicholas felt more and more threatened, a process of proliferating bureaucraticization took place in which censors sat over censors, decisions were made more and more in secret, and paranoia—evoked by the paranoia of the state—swept the land. In his diary, the censor Aleksandr Nikitenko wrote: "Terror gripped everyone who thought or wrote. Secret denunciations and spying complicated the situation even more. People began to fear for each day of their existence."[4]

Many of the characteristic moves of Soviet censorship and many of the responses by writers to these moves are foreshadowed in the Tsarist era. In 1836, for instance, in the first of his "Philosophical Letters," Pyotr Yakovlevich Chaadayev described Russia as lacking the most basic feature of a great European state: a history. His letter caused an uproar: on the recommendation of the Third Section, Chaadayev was declared of unsound mind and placed under supervision amounting to house arrest. "The Russian people have at once comprehended that such an article could not have been written by a compatriot . . . fully in possession of his mind," wrote its Director.[5] Thus was established the practice of branding offending writers as mad.

Another instance. Starting with Belinsky and Chernyshevsky, writers began to evade the censor by disguising political comment as literary criticism. The task of the censor suddenly took on an Augean aspect: a work that had passed scrutiny, or indeed a classic, might be given (or, in the censor's opinion, have foisted upon it) a new interpretation critical of the regime. Control had to be extended to literary criticism; a censorship not only of texts but of readings had to be instituted.

Yet the reign of Nicholas I was in some ways a flowering-time for Russian literature. The Third Section was not simply a force for philistinism.[6] The actions it took against writers and publishers were generally limited to reprimands, warnings, fines, or periods of exile. Even the treatment of Chaadayev can be seen as a way of avoiding more extreme measures. Nevertheless, the censorship did fulfil its larger aim of creating a divide between literature and philosophy on the one hand and politics on the other. In the process it fomented insecurity and mutual estrangement among the intelligentsia while encouraging what Sidney Monas calls a literature of "noninstrumental values": tenderness, capacity for love, compassion—in fact, the literature of the Turgenev school.[7]

The demand made on the printed word by Nicholas's imperial successors remained, broadly, that it should advance the aims of the regime and preserve social and religious standards. Alexander II began his reign by relaxing censorship. Prepublication censorship was abolished for full-length books (though not for the "thick" journals in which novels usually first appeared). Censors could be required to give grounds for their bans—a crucial innovation. This often led to public derision directed at the censors. But Alexander abandoned further liberalization after the attempt on his life in 1866. Successive Ministers of the Interior gave closer and closer instructions to the censors, the most significant being that they should not confine their scrutiny to the words on the page but should see beyond them to the "ruling view" or "tendency" of the whole. This concept allowed the censors to define an author's intention on the basis of the presumed effect of his work on some putative reader. In practice, the worst possible intention on the writer's part was assumed: David Balmuth rightly calls the elevation of tendency above textual detail "a recipe for suspicion, . . . a formula for arbitrariness."[8]

Because the system seemed immovable, writers and publishers generally cooperated to the extent of staying within the bounds laid down. The system was, however, resented and despised.[9] Cooperation retained a pro forma character. The intelligentsia, unable to defeat the system, responded by closing ranks and enforcing its own conformity. No one who supported the system had any chance of being accepted as an *intelligent.* Such people, says Monas, were "socially snubbed and in a semi-organized way made to feel like pariahs." (In this enforcement of a code of correctness on its members, Monas acutely detects the roots of the intolerance and inflexibility of a Soviet literary establishment that inherited not not only the structures and practices of an autocratic system of censorship but the habits of thought of an embattled intelligentsia.)[10]

For their part, rank-and-file censors drawn from the intelligentsia were not necessarily, or did not wish to seem, tools of reaction; indeed, says Balmuth, some "considered themselves to be silent partners with writers and journalists in the task of enlightening the Russian public." Persuasion rather than punishment was the mode they preferred.

> Censors were neither blind nor fools; . . . they were often as well equipped as other members of educated society to "read between the lines." . . . The censorship, despite its sometimes harsh words about writers, did not consider itself to be at war with writers. . . . Censors

and writers were enemies but enemies did not destroy each other; they merely fought each other, carefully observing rules for limited warfare.

Writers grew "expert at the use of elliptical language, at innuendo and allusion, at the art of not saying explicitly what they meant and not meaning exactly what they said."[11] "Allegorical modes, Aesopean language, and implicit references abounded. A difficult and complex style became a badge of honor."[12] As for the censors, they had many reasons for avoiding confrontation, among them the Machiavellian consideration that they could best keep track of subversive ideas by permitting them to be voiced in restricted form. Organs of "legitimate" radicalism and "legitimate" liberalism were therefore allowed to exist and express muted criticism of government.

Periods of uneasy equilibrium in which the authorities refrain from using the full force of the law so long as writers operate within tacit boundaries are by no means rare in the annals of censorship: the hostile and resentful accommodation achieved in Russia is, for instance, surprisingly similar to the accommodation described by Annabel Patterson in Tudor and Stuart England.[13]

SOVIET CENSORSHIP

The Tsarist censorship apparatus was liquidated after the revolution of 1905. Within five years of coming to power, however, the Soviets had resurrected it in the form of Glavlit, the Central Administration for Literary Affairs and Publishing.[14] In their everyday practice, both imperial censorship and Soviet censorship were highly arbitrary. But between imperial arbitrariness and Soviet arbitrariness there were notable differences. The justification given for the control of publishing and distribution in prerevolutionary Russia was essentially pragmatic: a flood of subversive foreign doctrine had to be stopped at the gates, its spread within Russian society cut short. No theory of the censorable was called for, merely a capacity to sniff out contagion. In particular, no aesthetic theory was required. No aesthetic forms were inherently suspect: if a work was condemned, it was condemned on the basis of content or tendency.

Censorship in the Soviet Union, on the other hand, rested on a body of theory that, whether or not it truly followed Marx, claimed to be Marxist. Basing itself on a certain evolutionary historical scheme and a certain sociology of knowledge, this theory asserted that true and objective knowledge of reality must be associated with a particular class position, that of the proletariat. The question of whether, even from a proletarian position, there could be more than one route to knowledge, was effectively pushed aside by Party ideologists taking their lead from Lenin's verdict that bourgeois freedom was only a disguised dependence, that a truly free literature will be "*openly* bound to the proletariat," a "Party literature" exhibiting *partiinost*, a word that originally meant "partisanship" but that under Lenin's influence came to mean "Party-spiritedness."[15]

The demand for *partiinost* came together with a demand for *ideinost* (ideological consciousness) and *narodnost* (awareness of the people). The demand for *narodnost* was used to justify the requirement that art should not be unintelligible to the masses. In practice, however, since the Party both determined ideology and represented the people, *partiinost* swallowed up *ideinost* and *narodnost*. Further, since, in terms of the Marxist-Leninist theory of ideology, ideas serve and reflect class interests, ideas that diverged from Party ideas could only serve interests "alien to the proletariat" (Karl Radek, 1934). Ideas whose origin was "alien" could therefore not serve the interests of the proletariat: by a trick of logic, foreign aesthetic movements like Modernism were discredited.[16]

Thus, in the Soviet era the bureaucracy of control built up under the Tsars was not only massively extended—by the time the bureaucracy reached its fullest extent in the 1960s a new work had to pass the scrutiny of no fewer than twelve distinct committees, editors with political responsibilities, and other gatekeepers before it could emerge into the light of day[17]—but also given a new Marxist-Leninist theoretical underpinning. The result was a system that, in the eyes of the novelist Vasily Aksyonov, made the old system look "primitive." "What in the West is called Soviet censorship is nothing less than the Soviet air that one breathes."[18] Nevertheless, when the Party that defined the theory was under the sway of a dominating personality like Stalin's, or even a tone-setting personality like Khrushchev's or Brezhnev's, the everyday conseqences were no more predictable than under the Empire.

AFTER STALIN

Prescription

Most systems of censorship lay down, with varying degrees of clarity, limits that shall not be transgressed, and are in this sense proscriptive. But Soviet censorship had a strong prescriptive bent as well. The demand that literature should exhibit *partiinost, ideinost,* and *narodnost* received numerous elaborations—for instance by Commissar of Culture Andrei Zhdanov at the First Congress of the Union of Soviet Writers in 1934: Soviet writing should be "tendentious, . . . optimistic, heroic, serve the cause of socialist construction, and draw its heroes and heroines from [among] working men and women"; further, it should be guided by the methods of socialist realism, "in which truthfulness and historical concreteness must be combined with the ideological remolding and re-education of workers in the spirit of socialism." *Meshchanstvo,* a petty concern with private life and private feelings, was denounced.[19]

Self-Censorship

The more closely a system of censorship succeeds in defining its rules, and the more rigorously and visibly it polices infringements, the easier it becomes to administer. Once censorship has established itself as a regime of writing and reading, writers can be expected either to regulate themselves or, by rejecting the rules, to place themselves outside the law. Self-regulation via what Isaac Babel called "the genre of silence" or via writing for the desk drawer were widespread in Stalin's USSR but had venerable Russian precedents.[20] The system finally became self-ordering and invisible when no one spoke openly of it. Gayle Durham writes of a "grey belt" of activities "that the law [did] not specifically forbid but that [were] in fact prohibited by the authorities." One such de facto prohibition was on the duplication of manuscripts.[21] When what is prohibited is for all practical purposes defined by the desire of authority, and when attempts to bring that desire into the open are taken as attacks on authority, it may be prudent for the writer who is not prepared to internalize the system—which is what the system desires above all—not merely to write for the desk drawer (or, in the case of Solzhenitsyn, for the glass jar buried in the garden), but to deny being a writer.[22]

Criticism and Self-Criticism

Just as utopian communism looked forward to the withering away of the state, Soviet authority dreamed of a censorship that would wither away as its desires were internalized by writers. Hence the emphasis on the couple *kritika-samokritika*—criticism and self-criticism—in the regulation of Soviet writing. The censoring/censuring of the writer from above had to be answered by a response on the part of the writer accepting criticism and recognizing the error of his ways. As a therapy for *meshchanstvo*, *samokritika* is reminiscent of a form of psychotherapy popular in nineteenth-century France: dousing the patient with cold water until the patient confessed to madness. "Madness as a reality [that is to say, as a real affliction] disappears when the patient asserts the truth and says he is mad," comments Michel Foucault drily.[23]

What did *samokritika* involve? In 1957, Margarita Aliger made two confessions before assemblies of the Writers' Union. In the second, she said:

> I can now, without any evasion or qualification, without any false fear of losing my sense of personal worth, say frankly and firmly to my comrades that it is all true that I really committed those mistakes about which Comrade Khrushchev speaks. I committed them, I persisted in them, but I have [now] understood and admitted them deliberately and consciously. . . . I spoke of this at a similar meeting . . . three months ago. However, since that time . . . I have succeeded in understanding more profoundly the causes of those mistakes. . . . I must now be much more exacting with myself, free myself of an inclination toward abstract thinking, more rigorously [correct my views] . . . in short, do what Comrade Khrushchev teaches and urges in his speeches.[24]

The emphasis in this confession (a satisfactory confession after a first, unsatisfactory confession in which Aliger had merely bowed to the rod) falls on explicit denial of any reservation and on a spontaneous undertaking to reform the self. Any later retraction, based on the claim that the confession was insincere because made under duress, is robbed of its force beforehand by the fact that the confession addresses unambiguously the question of its own sincerity.

Aliger made her confession during the clampdown that followed the 1956 uprising in Hungary. In the *samokritika* of the freeze of 1963, in contrast, we can see, behind the exhausted shuffling of codified phrases, distinct gestures toward the baton of authority dictating the terms of *kritika*, and thus, implicitly, toward the contestational nature of *samokritika* sessions. I quote from the confessions of the two (then) young writers Vasily Aksyonov and Andrei Voznesensky.

> Aksyonov: At [the] plenary session [of the Writers' Union] there was stern criticism of the incorrect behaviour and thoughtlessness of Yevtushenko, Voznesensky, and me. I believe this criticism was correct. . . . I must think over many things and I must do a great deal of studying. I must learn about the various sides of the life of the people, I must overcome the one-sidedness of my observations, . . . go more deeply into the guiding ideas of our times and express them to the best of my ability in my work. Of course, this is difficult, but it is in this that one finds the happiness of creativity.

> Voznesensky: I have been told that I must not forget Nikita Sergeyevich [Khrushchev's] stern and severe words. I will never forget them. I will not forget either these severe words or the advice that Nikita Sergeyevich addressed to me. He said: "Work." This word is a program for me. I shall work, I am now working, I am thinking a lot, I have understood a lot of . . . what has been said. I understand my tremendous responsibility to the people, to the times, to the Communist Party. For me this is a most precious understanding. I am not justifying myself now; I simply want to say: The main thing for me now is to work, work, and work, and this work will show what my attitude is to the country and to communism, will show my nature.[25]

Here one finds, besides a (studied) emphasis on the fatherliness of the *kritika*, a strong if courteous emphasis on the unfinishedness and perhaps even the hesitancy of the *samokritika*: criticism has been accepted, the two writers say, but in a properly critical spirit, and therefore perhaps selectively, with reserve. Furthermore, they

seem to say between the lines, these reports of ours are only provisional: where our *samokritika* will ultimately lead cannot yet be
foretold.

These instances of *samokritika* illustrate a general point: that,
while in its highly repressive phase up to 1956 Soviet censorship
had been able to censor out reference to its own workings, the first
outlines that began to emerge—or to be forced into the open—
when the rigor of the system was relaxed were the outlines of the
system itself: authority on the one side, and the subject on the
other, not strong enough to actually resist, but asserting nevertheless, in terms no matter how veiled, a claim to independence.

Permitted Dissent

The desire of censorship to include its own workings among its
erasures (one of the most jealously guarded books in the Soviet
Union was the so-called Talmud, the Glavlit index of forbidden top-
ics, names, facts, etc.)[26] does much to explain *permitted dissent* in
the USSR. In her study of this paradoxical phenomenon, Dina
Spechler focuses on the literary journal *Novy Mir,* from the death
of Stalin in 1953 to 1970, tracing in detail the relations between the
dissentient opinions it published and the twists and turns of Soviet
political life.[27] Since it was *Novy Mir* that in 1962 published Solzhenitsyn's first novel, *A Day in the Life of Ivan Denisovich,* doing
so after intensive consultation extending to Khrushchev's office,[28]
it will be useful to follow Spechler's analysis in some detail.

The pages of *Novy Mir,* in Spechler's account, provided a testing-
ground for mutations of ideology in the 1960s. The use by the authorities of a literary journal for such purposes was not as strange
as it may at first seem. As I have pointed out, the practice of embed-
ding social criticism in literary commentary—a practice fostered
by censorship—had a long history in Russia. Furthermore, the
whole of Soviet education emphasized the interrelatedness of the
sociopolitical and the aesthetic.

Khrushchev, in Spechler's eyes, was an "ambitious reformer"
who, meeting with nagging resistance from Party and bureaucracy,
used *Novy Mir* as a vehicle to "expose and dramatize problems and
reveal facts that demonstrated . . . the necessity of the changes he
proposed." In his struggle with Party and bureaucracy, Khrushchev

recognized the importance of winning the support of both "moral humanist" and "historical revisionist" (i.e., anti-Stalinist) intellectuals. Party and bureaucracy, for their part, were prepared to believe that *Novy Mir* constituted a convenient escape-valve for the grievances of intellectuals, an escape-valve more easily controlled than the underground press. Furthermore, because of widespread suspicion of intellectuals among the working class and peasantry, they were sure that whatever grouping formed around *Novy Mir* would represent no political challenge.[29]

As for *Novy Mir*, its editors followed "a carefully calculated strategy of restraint, flexibility, and avoidance of gratuitous provocation." Aleksandr Tvardovsky, the chief editor, never openly urged the elimination of literary censorship (though he did make such a plea in private meetings). Following the accommodationist precedent of the nineteenth century, *Novy Mir* imposed in-house restraints on what it published.

> However intensely [the editors] disliked the Zhdanovite criteria, . . . they kept these criteria firmly in mind. They encouraged criticism and violation of them but only up to a point. When contributors passed that point . . . the editors became censors and either rejected. . . manuscripts . . . or demanded revisions.

The editors also "adjusted the quantity and boldness of the dissent they published" in response to variations in the political climate (pp. 253–57).

To the Soviet leadership, as events surrounding the publication of *Ivan Denisovich* would prove, the degree to which dissent should be permitted was decided not on principle but on the basis that at any given time benefits should outweigh costs. In 1954, 1957, 1958, and 1963, when cost seemed to outweigh benefit, *Novy Mir* was curbed. But by 1969, Spechler suggests, the tactic of tightening and slackening the reins on the journal was no longer effective as a signal to regulate the level of public dissent. A counterculture, "a culture of dissent," had by then evolved, at least among the youth of the major cities, for whose "nihilism" *Novy Mir* was increasingly held to blame. Furthermore, criticism of Stalinism in the pages of the journal had begun to threaten those office-holders with a Stalinist past. Since the policies of Brezhnev, unlike those of

Khrushchev, did not involve bringing public pressure to bear on power-wielding cliques within the establishment—with which Brezhnev had no quarrel—there was little reason to retain the journal. Tvardovsky was accordingly forced to resign and *Novy Mir* was silenced (pp. 258–63).

It is not far-fetched to blame *Novy Mir*, at least in part, for the growth of "nihilism" among Soviet youth. Under a regime of censorship, censored texts are read with extraordinary attention. The censor may cut out what he wishes, but every text has a context: the absence of the censored stays behind not only as a scar on the context but as a mark of the censor's wish, readily picked out by the eye obsessed with seeing what it wants to see.

In accommodations between authorities and writers (and here I include Tvardovsky among the writers) there is always a degree of disingenuousness. Unless they are wholeheartedly entered into, agreements can never cover intentions. Contracts, unlike novels, have no unspoken "tendency." What is not "in" the text can always be denied to be there; the letter of the agreement can be followed at the same time that its spirit is broken. What was agreed to in the case of *Novy Mir* was agreed to a great deal less than wholeheartedly: a limited freedom to operate in exchange for agreement that the limits to this freedom should be tacit, i.e., that the authorities should not have to define these limits *and* that the question of what they were should be under erasure, i.e., that from the public point of view the limits should be invisible (Tvardovsky played by the rules in not bringing the issue of censorship into the open).

In Spechler's account, the initiative in the contest between *Novy Mir* and the Party lay always with the Party, and the fate of *Novy Mir* was therefore always subject to political whim. But there is another way of regarding the affair. Given that the sanctions faced by writers and editors were no longer draconian, *Novy Mir* elected to play a game of showing and hiding its meaning in which, if only because it commanded the necessary skills, it held the initiative. The authorities were always doomed to play a reactive role, falling back as a last resort on force. The so-called culture of dissent for whose growth magazines like *Novy Mir* were in no small part responsible was in time to become a political factor to be reckoned with.

Transgression and the Law

The treatment of offending writers under law reveals a telling anxiety in the Soviet state about staging trials as contests of equals. In the trial of Joseph Brodsky in 1964, the principal charge was that, not being regularly employed, Brodsky was a social parasite (the sign outside the courtroom on the day of the hearing already read "Hearing of the Parasite Brodsky"). A second charge was that he had written anti-Soviet verse. But in the trial the judge refused to allow Brodsky's lawyer to test the latter charge by quoting the relevant poems, thus silencing the offending texts even within the arena of their prosecution. Nor did she allow Brodsky's response, "I write poetry," to the question, "What work do you do?"[30]

Not allowing dissidents to contest charges on equal ground was a common feature of trials in the 1960s and 1970s. Defense lawyers, claims Frederick Barghoorn, were pushed into "virtual collusion with the prosecution" in in a project of "reeducating" the defendant. The purposes of the trial were deemed to have been fulfilled only if the accused admitted guilt and expressed repentance. "Authorities view[ed] with extreme disfavor a vigorous rebuttal of charges."[31] Pavel Litvinov was warned by a KGB officer that if he made public his transcripts of the proceedings of trials of dissidents, he himself would be put on trial, even though making transcripts was technically within the law. In other trials defendants were declared legally irresponsible and remanded to psychiatric hospitals.

Counterauthority

Shortly after Khrushchev's secret speech to the Twentieth Party Congress making public some of Stalin's crimes, Aleksandr Fadeyev, one-time Secetary-General of the Writers' Union, committed suicide. Fadeyev had once remarked, "I am afraid of two people—my mother and Stalin. I fear [them]—and I love [them]."[32] A mixture of fear and love for a figure to whom Fadeyev's words metonymically point as a father was sedulously fostered during the Stalin era.

Arrested preparatory to being forcibly deported in 1974, Solzhenitsyn issued a brief statement: "I shall take no part either in your investigation or in your trial."[33] Speaking with the felt authority of a Nobel Prize–winner, rejecting the jurisdiction of Soviet courts, Solzhenitsyn in effect denied Soviet law any basis except in force, and reduced the state from the symbolic status of father to that of rival.

Between the poles represented by Fadeyev and Solzhenitsyn an epoch may be said to have passed. The strategy of the dissidents of the 1960s of trying to make their voices heard by challenging authority in the protected space of the lawcourts was simply by-passed by Solzhenitsyn. In identifying the law with the censor and refusing to play the game of either, he is in one respect closer to the absolutist spirit of Stalinism than were the dissidents, with their faith in the notion of a fair hearing and therefore in the idea of fairness or justice itself. Whether we take his unacknowledged rival/model to be the Tsar or the later Tolstoy (whose status as the most famous man in Russia made him rival to the Tsar), Solzhenit-syn betrays leanings as rivalrous as they are authoritarian.[34]

SOVIET LANGUAGE

Of the purges of the 1930s, Isaac Deutscher writes: "The lie of the Moscow trials was so huge, so fantastic and so all-pervading that it was well-nigh unanswerable. It had the quality of something as immovable, as persistent and as powerful as reality itself."[35] The falsifications paraded in the trials were so complete, so monolithic, that the truth was literally remade. But beyond the nightmare of the reconstruction of history exhibited here lies the nightmare of the reconstruction of thought itself via the reconstitution of language. This is what lies behind George Orwell's fable of a Newspeak whose purpose is "to make thoughtcrime . . . impossible, because there will be no words in which to express it."[36]

The bizarreries of the language that grew up under Stalin have often been satirized. It is in the nature of satire to give a view from the outside, not the inside. In the case of Stalinist Newspeak there could be no view from the inside, since the language did not allow for critical self-reflection. Those morally substantial analyses that we possess therefore come from people inside Soviet Russia but outside Soviet language. Such a position was more widespread than one might think. Yuri Glazov describes a "behavioral bilingualism" in which the Soviet citizen spoke in a mode of absolute conformism in public, yet expressed radically opposite viewpoints in private. Far from regarding the survival of opposition in the private sphere as a stubborn relic of bourgeois thought needing to be crushed, Glazov suggests, the Soviet state encouraged this impotent, "schizoid" doubleness. The soul unable to survive in the USSR was not the schizoid soul—Dmitri Shostakovich is a good example of a soul surviving by splitting itself—but the soul that could not accept the alternatives of bilingualism or death: Pasternak's poet Zhivago.[37]

Valentin Turchin confirms this "bilingualism" when he writes of the double sense in which certain socially crucial words were used: a "theoretical," official sense and a "practical" sense quite opposite in meaning but more accurately reflecting reality.[38] As a matter of course the Soviet citizen became adept at reading for the "practical" sense between the lines.[39]

It is in the context of this pervasive doublethought, in a society where not only the public record but history itself was dictated from above, that we should see the contestation staged by Solzhenitsyn, in his Nobel Prize acceptance speech, between Soviet language and the language of the individual writer:

> The simple act of an ordinary brave man is not to participate in lies. . . . But it is within the power of writers and artists to do much more: *to defeat the lie!* For in the struggle with lies art has always triumphed and shall always triumph! . . . Lies can prevail against much in this world, but never against art.[40]

DENUNCIATION: IMITATION AND ESCALATION

The Collapsing of Distinctions

A. Kemp-Welch describes as follows the kind of argumentation practiced by Soviet ideologists of the Stalin period:

> Their methodology was one of dogmatic orthodoxy, culled from a superficial reading of the "classics": Marx, Engels, Lenin and Stalin. . . . Argument itself was reduced to the elementary juxtaposition of opposite extremes, with the abolition of distinctions or intermediate positions. Such characteristics made them at once the originators and the bearers of the Stalinist intellectual order.[41]

Polemical in style, this passage denounces a denunciatory polemical style and serves to alert us to a continuing pattern of crudely confrontational argumentation in the generation after Stalin, a pattern occurring not only among the heirs of the Stalinist intellectual order but on the other side of the fence too. Nor was it confined to Cold Warriors. To some citizens of Brezhnev's Russia, "whether applied to a pair of socks or a new ballet, the adjective 'Soviet' [became] a sneering pejorative. Everything 'Sov' (to use the hip short form) repel[led] them."[42] In the preface to Efim Etkind's memoir of how he was expelled from his university position, Etkind's translator suggests that the episode should be conceived of as a struggle between the *intelligentnost* of Etkind—"a combination of education, decency, taste, love of ideas and language, sense of duty towards moral and cultural values"—and the *khamstvo*—"a sort of aggressive philistinism"—of his academic-bureaucratic opponents.[43]

As for "the abolition of distinctions or intermediate positions" in the thinking of the Soviet authorities, this barely needs attesting. "A standard weapon in the Stalinist arsenal of abuse and intimidation" against writers, writes Rothberg, was routinely to hold them responsible for how "enemies of the State" used their work. In the prosecution of dissidents, writes Marshall Shatz, expression was given to an "obsessive patriotism, verging on xenophobia, which attempt[ed] to brand any critic of the Soviet government or Soviet conditions as an agent of foreign enemies."[44]

These observations have their own polemical intent and stridency of tone, as though Rothberg and Shatz have been drawn to imitate the style of denunciation they oppose. (Indeed, does the present writing escape these forces?)

The Escalation of Denunciation and Abuse

There is a certain idiom of outrage and vituperation that belongs to levels of escalation at which debate is no longer possible. The annals of Soviet censorship are full of such language. In the wake of the award of the 1958 Nobel Prize to Boris Pasternak, mainly for his novel *Doctor Zhivago*, V. Semichastny, First Secretary of the Komsomol, compared the author to "[a pig] who fouled the spot where

he ate and cast filth on those by whose labor he lives and breathes."
After reading *Zhivago,* the writer K. L. Zelinsky reported: "I felt as
though I had literally been spat upon. The whole of my life seemed
to be defiled."[45]

Imagery of excretion and expectoration (in which there is all too
plausibly an element of displaced aggression) was a feature, too, of
the notorious utterances of Khrushchev about the exhibition of
new paintings he viewed in Moscow in 1962. It was as though "a
child had done his business on the canvas," he said, "and then
spread it around with his hands." "We aren't going to spend a ko-
peck on this dog shit. . . . The people and government have taken a
lot of trouble with you [artists], and you pay them back with this
shit. . . . Your paintings just give a person constipation." (The other
recurring theme of Khrushchev's fulminations was that the artists
were "pederasts".)[46]

It is not the *khamstvo* of this language but its belligerence that
is to the point. A counter-belligerence, couched less formulaically,
is apparent in the responses of Soviet intellectuals. In the exchanges
that followed the sentencing of Yuli Daniel and Andrei Sinyavsky
in 1966 for anti-Soviet propaganda, for instance, we find a rapid
escalation of invective between their supporters and Mikhail Sholokhov, who not only endorsed the court's verdict but called for a
heavier sentence. Thus in an open letter Lydia Chukovskaya wrote
to Sholokhov *ad hominem:* "Literature will take its own vengeance. . . . It has condemned you to the worst sentence to which an
artist can be condemned—creative sterility."[47] Among his academic
censors, Efim Etkind describes "a woman . . . who looked like a cross
between a fish-wife and a Mother Superior . . . [and spoke] in a
lifeless, desperately boring and rather illiterate way."[48] Through the
means of provocative insult, the monologic ground of official denunciation is redefined (somewhat magically, in Etkind's case, since
his memoir was not published in the Soviet Union) as the dialogic
ground of polemical strife, that is to say, redefined as a ground on
which it is possible for the opposing voice to *win.* An analogous
redefinition of the ground occurs in the tussle between the psychiatrists intent on committing Zhores Medvedev to a mental hospital,
and Medvedev's writer-friends: Andrei Sakharov quite clearly used

the threat of leaking the story to the Western press—i.e., taking the controversy off disadvantageous Soviet ground—as a way of raising the stakes against his psychiatric foes.[49]

In all three of these cases writers responded to an erasure of writing by the authorities (Medvedev was called in for a psychiatric examination on the basis of a book he had written) with speech that both denounced the erasure and doubled the wager. Since the second round of speech would certainly find no public outlet in the Soviet Union, other means of making it public were used or threatened: Chukovskaya's open letter (which, though never published in the Soviet Union, was spread by word of mouth), Etkind's memoir published in France, Sakharov's threat of going to the Western press.

Foreseeing the uses that foreign propaganda would make of stories put out by dissidents, Soviet propaganda agencies sought to preempt the effect of these stories by denouncing them in anticipation. Domestic radio countered foreign broadcasts by "mount[ing] a broad counterpropaganda [effort] earlier than the bourgeois radio stations and at the same time prepar[ing] listeners for a critical reception of falsified materials broadcast by them."[50]

SOLZHENITSYN

The case of Aleksandr Solzhenitsyn, a writer embattled in controversy from the time he brought the manuscript of *A Day in the Life of Ivan Denisovich* into the open, illustrates particularly well the dynamic of spiraling mimetic violence precipitated by a collapsing of distinctions.

It is striking how conscious Solzhenitsyn was, at times, of his potential not only for provoking but also for falling into this dynamic. In the wake of the fame brought to him by *Ivan Denisovich*, he was questioned by Western newsmen. He records:

> I said not a single word. . . , although there was nothing to stop me from saying a very great deal, very boldly, and the thunderstruck newsmen would have splashed it to the ends of the earth. I was afraid that if I once started answering Western correspondents, I would be asked questions by Soviet newsmen too, questions that would predetermine my response: either an immediate act of rebellion or

a life of cheerless conformity. Not wishing to lie, and not daring to rebel, I preferred silence.[51]

The earlier phase of Solzhenitsyn's career, before he won the Nobel Prize and thereby acquired a degree of invulnerability, can be seen as a time of strategic silence, of self-control. What most dismayed his associates and protectors on the editorial board of *Novy Mir*, in retrospect, was that he had never confided in them that a form of authorial self-suppression over and above the prudent editorial suppression they themselves practiced was being applied—indeed, that there was anything written by Solzhenitsyn that warranted self-suppression. Thus Solzhenitsyn never revealed to Tvardovsky that there were lengthy passages of an unquestionably anti-Soviet nature in the original *First Circle*—the version Solzhenitsyn had completed in 1964—passages that would have undermined Tvardovsky's defense of the novel as an ultimately patriotic work had they been made public. (These passages were worked back into the text of the full, 96-chapter Russian-language edition published in France in 1978.)[52] A retrospective memoir by Vladimir Lakshin, a fellow-editor of Tvardovsky's on *Novy Mir*, contains some bitter reflections on Solzhenitsyn, in whom Lakshin diagnoses the propensity for counter- or imitative violence that Solzhenitsyn had earlier detected in himself.

Where did this propensity come from? Lakshin suggests that Solzhenitsyn absorbed and never shed the psychology of the prison inmate:

If you sense danger, anticipate the blow and strike first; pity no one; tell lies with ease and wriggle out of trouble; throw up a smoke screen to escape an awkward situation. . . ; finally, adopt the habit of always believing the worst of others.

"Having been rightly schooled in hatred of Stalinism," Lakshin continues, "without realizing it Solzhenitsyn also imbibed the poisons of Stalinism."[53]

But the mythic fluid for which Lakshin is groping here is not a poison, for poison, once imbibed, kills. The fluid that makes one person take on the life of another is blood. Having denounced Solzhenitsyn as blood-kin to Stalin, to the enemy, as a camp wolf in disguise, no friend to Tvardovsky, Lakshin ranges himself, Tvardovsky's friend, as Solzhenitsyn's enemy, and escalates the violence of his counter-language accordingly.

Solzhenitsyn himself showed an acute sense of the reciprocal self-definition that the structure of *enemies* allows (his necessary blind spot was that he could not see to what a degree it dictated his self-definition). In an open letter to his opponents in the Writers' Union, he wrote: "What would you do without 'enemies'? You could not live without 'enemies.'"[54] Having responded to the KGB's denunciations of him with his own public denunciation of Semichastny, head of the KGB, Solzhenitsyn afterwards recorded: "In a loud voice, and with a feeling of triumph and simple joy, I . . . *paid him back.*"[55] Michael Scammell, Solzhenitsyn's biographer, acknowledges that in certain of the plottings and counterplottings between Solzhenitsyn and the authorities there may be an appearance of symmetry, but calls this appearance "fraudulent" on the grounds that the "stature[s]" of the antagonists were incommensurable.[56] One might respond that, as long as the rivals see each other as rivals, their objective statures are irrelevant; also that Solzhenitsyn rarely carried a plot through to its conclusion unless he stood a good chance of winning.

The Solzhenitsyn affair, an affair less of events than of multiplying texts, proceeded with a confusing escalation of accusations, denunciations, and abuse from both hostile and friendly camps, from which I extract the following five illustrative moments.

1. After keeping a rendezvous that included elaborate precautions against being photographed or tape-recorded by KGB agents, Solzhenitsyn's first wife, Reshetovskaya, came to the conclusion that Solzhenitsyn had lost touch with reality, and accused him of being a "fanatic." Of the episode, Scammell writes:

> She had her own anxieties and fears to contend with, and her own conspiracy theory: "Somebody is deceiving you [Solzhenitsyn], inflaming your suspicions, practising some terrible emotional blackmail on you." But the very fact that Solzhenitsyn treated her as an emissary [of the KGB] . . . testified to a highly colored vision of reality [on his part], if not symptoms of genuine paranoia.[57]

Besides the mutual suspiciousness of Solzhenitsyn and Reshetovskaya, and the way in which the projection of another woman envenoming Solzhenitsyn against her provokes Reshetovskaya to her own venomous abuse, the rhetorical disposition of Scammell's account, climaxing in an accusation of paranoia against Solzhenitsyn, is worthy of note.

2. In the wake of the publication abroad of *The Gulag Archipelago* in 1974, a campaign of vilification of Solzhenitsyn was set in train in the Soviet media. Starting with an article in *Pravda* calling Solzhenitsyn anti-patriotic, anti-Russian and pro-German, and claiming that he was "literally choking with hatred" for the Soviet Union, the campaign continued with a piece in *Literaturnaya Gazeta* diagnosing in him "an overly bestial hatred for everything Soviet" and likening him to a reptile. This attack sparked anonymous abusive and threatening telephone calls. Soon headlines in the press were routinely calling Solzhenitsyn a renegade, a traitor, a Judas, a blasphemer, a counterrevolutionary.[58]

It would not be accurate to label this a *whipped-up* campaign, for there is no reason to believe that the abuse against Solzhenitsyn did not come from the heart. A better metaphor would be one of unleashing, of letting loose a chained fury of language. Furthermore, what characterizes language in the upper reaches of the spiral of violence is not an artificial (whipped-up) quality, but a quality of nakedness in which the writer loses control over the repressive process that normally allows him to disguise not only the violent impulse behind his writing but the degree to which it imitates its object. Thus language choking with hatred accuses its object of inspiring this choking by choking with hatred itself, that is, by exhibiting the sympathetic effects of witchcraft. A hatred that expels its object from humanity does so by accusing its object of a hatred such as only something outside humanity can feel. (One wonders, though, whether reptiles truly feel hatred.)

3. As noted above, Vladimir Lakshin tries to explain the coexistence in Solzhenitsyn of a lofty humanity with spitefulness and vengefulness by suggesting that he was permanently marked by the prison camps, that his psychology remained that of a "prison-camp wolf":

> Solzhenitsyn himself, it seems, does not realize quite how much of his prison-camp education, of which he is so proud, is the purely *Stalinist* element of the camp ethos. . .: indifference to means, the psychology of the preventive strike, cruelty, and lying. Having been

rightly schooled in hatred of Stalinism, without realizing it, Solzhenitsyn also imbibed the poisons of Stalinism; is that not surely
the reason why his book [*The Oak and the Calf*] contains so much
intolerance, malice, deviousness, and ingratitude? . . . While loudly
condemning all forms of violence, Solzhenitsyn does not seem to
notice that he himself is fostering the idea of a war to the death,
ridiculously aping his antagonists even in their predilection for military phraseology.[59]

This comment is extraordinary both in its violence and in its
insight. Presenting itself as a polemical response to Solzhenitsyn's
polemic against Tvardovsky and the editors of *Novy Mir*, it attempts to close off any response by accusing Solzhenitsyn of being
a secret Stalinist, that is, of being his own enemy, rival, twin. Furthermore, it lays bare, if only as a move in its own rhetorical strategy, the mechanism of imitative violence ("aping"), thereby exhibiting Solzhenitsyn as an actor in a dynamic over which he has no
control.

4. Discourses that label the rival mad seek to cut short the chain
of imitative violence—and claim victory—by invalidating his
response in advance. This move was routinely played against
Solzhenitsyn. In an unpublished speech in 1967, the editor of
Pravda explained why Solzhenitsyn could not be published in the
Soviet Union: he was "not in his right mind, . . . psychologically
unbalanced. . . , a schizophrenic."[60]

5. Responding to a 1968 attack on Solzhenitsyn in *Literaturnaya
Gazeta*, the writer V. F. Turchin wrote to the editor-in-chief:

> Of course, you may disagree with [Solzhenitsyn's] vision and inter-
> pretation of truth. . . . But . . . you are afraid of truth, truth as such,
> in any interpretation. . . . Yes, you are afraid even of your own inter-
> pretation of truth! You have grown so accustomed to masquerading
> that you regard writing what you think as nothing short of indecent.

And Turchin followed this accusation by accusing the editor of not
believing in his own lies about Solzhenitsyn.[61] The essence of this
ploy is again to invalidate a response before it is made. In this respect it is much like an accusation of self-alienation, of madness.

What did Solzhenitsyn himself have to say about truth, lies, and
the violence of literary polemic?

1. Expelled from the Writers' Union in 1969, Solzhenitsyn wrote a letter condemning the Union's decision and prophesying that "the day is near when every one of you will try to find out how you can scrape your signatures off today's resolution. The blind lead the blind." Why, he asks, does the Union deliberate in secret. "'The enemy is listening.' That's your answer. Those eternal enemies are the basis of your existence. What would you do without your enemies? You would not be able to live without [them]."[62]

Here Solzhenitsyn is not only jeering at the Union, claiming that it does not understand itself ("the blind leading the blind"), calling it mad (paranoid): he is pointing to a structure of reciprocal paranoid definition of which Cold War antagonism was the overwhelming example in his lifetime (as it was, indeed, in the lifetime of his contemporary René Girard, diagnostician of reciprocally defining antagonisms). It hardly needs to be pointed out, in addition, that the postures Solzhenitsyn takes up in his letter are those of diagnostician and prophet but not of antagonist: antagonism, he implies, is a play of shadows, and the antagonists are shadows themselves.

The initial moves in this stage of the war between the Union hierarchy and Solzhenitsyn—the former declaring the latter outside writing, the latter declaring the former outside reason—were followed by a widening of the polemic, predictable in view of Solzhenitsyn's eminence, to the international arena. An open letter from thirty-one prominent Western intellectuals called the Soviet treatment of Solzhenitsyn "an international scandal, . . . a crime against civilization."[63] There is no record of demurral on Solzhenitsyn's part at this rhetorical escalation.

2. In his Nobel Prize speech, Solzhenitsyn addressed the interrelations of violence and lies.

> Violence does not and cannot exist by itself: it is invariably intertwined with *the lie*. They are linked in the most intimate, most organic and profound fashion: violence cannot conceal itself behind anything except lies, and lies have nothing to maintain them save violence. Anyone who has once proclaimed violence as his *method* must inexorably choose the lie as his *principle*. At birth, violence acts openly and even takes pride in itself. But as soon as it gains

strength and becomes firmly established, . . . it can no longer exist without veiling itself in a mist of lies.[64]

Solzhenitsyn here takes up a position close to that of Girard (and Nietzsche): the origin of legality lies in violence; in order to flourish, a legality needs to veil its violent origins, that is to say, write its own history, impose its own originary myth. Where Solzhenitsyn differs from Girard is that his perspective is not anthropological and indeed, in Girard's terms, not even religious. It is, specifically, at this stage of Solzhenitsyn's career, political and perhaps merely anti-Soviet. A certain politically inspired blindness, either unpremeditated or calculated, takes over, at least in Solzhenitsyn's public utterances: he no longer presents himself and his own interventions as part of the historical process he uncovers, but speaks from the rostrum as history personified.

In a speech given on his first visit to the United States in 1976, Solzhenitsyn likened the study of Russian history to the archaeological study of prehistory, an era that can no longer speak for itself. "The spine of [Russia's] history has been fractured, its memory has failed, it has lost the power of speech."[65] In this figure we get a more considered indication of the position that Solzhenitsyn believes he has adopted for himself. Modern Russia is without memory, without speech: he remembers for it, speaks for it, speaks against the violence that has destroyed its memory and the lies that have supplanted its speech. Underlying the figure are the opposites of a true (old) Russia, into which Solzhenitsyn inscribes himself, and a false (Soviet) Russia, against whose all-prevailing violence and lies he will do battle. It is no less than a schema of warring brothers/sisters.

ATTRIBUTING MADNESS

The Madness of Dissidence

In 1962, at a meeting between Party leaders and creative artists, Leonid Ilyichev, chairman of the Ideological Commission of the Central Committee, delivered a lengthy speech (according to some accounts, ten hours long) in which dissident writers came under attack. Aleksandr Yesenin-Volpin was singled out for publishing (abroad) a book of "misanthropic anti-Soviet doggerel, the ravings of a mental case."

This attack exhibits a contradiction characteristic of much of the condemnation of dissidents. On the one hand the offending artist is dismissed as insignificant ("This rogue [Yesenin-Volpin] represents no one. He is nothing more than a poisonous mushroom"). On the other he is deemed worthy of extended *kritika*. The contradiction reaches its apogee in the diagnosis of the offender as mad ("a mental case"), since it defines him as both outside the law and unable to comprehend the judgment pronounced on him.[66]

Solzhenitsyn did not escape this fate. In 1967, speaking to journalists, the editor-in-chief of *Pravda* called him "a psychologically unbalanced person, a schizophrenic." As Theodore Friedgut points out, such labeling evoked prejudices widespread among the Soviet public, who had shown a tendency to shun dissidents for fear they were *beshenye*, "possessed."[67]

The best-known case of the use of psychiatric confinement against political transgressions—what Vladimir Bukovsky called "crimes from the point of view of the authorities . . . which do not exist as crimes from the point of view of the law"—was that of the scientist Zhores Medvedev. The psychiatric intervention against him was replete with double-bind logic ("If you feel so marvelous [i.e., not mad], why do you think we [psychiatrists] have turned up here [at Medvedev's home] today?" . . . "[If] you are so sure you are perfectly well, [then] you have nothing to fear from an examination"). The attentions of the authorities had been provoked not by Medvedev's behavior but by his writings: "I read his manuscript *Biology and the Cult of Personality* and began to have doubts about the sanity of the person who had written it," said the investigating psychiatrist. Similarly, when the writer Leonid Plyushch was confined to a psychiatric hospital, and his wife asked what symptoms in her husband required treatment, the attending physician replied: "His views and convictions."[68]

The effect of such reports—as indeed of comparable satiric accounts of psychiatry in the West—is to present the psychiatrist as mad and the patient as the victim of a crazy discourse backed by brute power. But one must bear in mind that turning the tables on the psychiatric world is itself achieved via a discursive power. *A*

Question of Madness can be read as an exemplarily repressive book in which the Medvedev brothers organize and constrain the utterances of the psychiatric community in such a way that, as symptomatic speech, it continually *betrays* its users.

Instances can be multiplied in which the rhetorical armamentarium of the writer is used to gain the upper hand over an official discourse that tries to label deviancy as mad. Solzhenitsyn's own intervention in the case of Zhores Medvedev is characteristically hyperbolic:

> The incarceration of free-thinking people in madhouses is *spiritual murder*, it is a variation on the gas chamber, but is even more cruel: the torments of those done to death in this way are more evil and protracted.[69]

Yet madness was not an identity rejected out of hand by the dissident. Hamlet using madness as a strategy of prudent self-disguise has been a model for Russian freethinkers from Pushkin onwards. In his translation of Shakespeare's play, Boris Pasternak brings to the fore his vision of Hamlet as "judge of his own time and servant of the future," a role with which not only Pasternak himself but Solzhenitsyn could identify. What Pasternak's famous phrase does not point to is that Hamlet's is a yet-to-be-revealed identity, veiled by what preserves him for the future: his "madness."[70]

The Madness of Authority

The strategy of table-turning I have described consists in the counterattribution of madness to the repressive state. Stalin in particular has suffered this fate. Discussing *The First Circle,* Western scholars have often picked on this feature of Solzhenitsyn's Stalin. I quote three instances.

1. "Stalin emerges not as a demon but as a sick, fearful, psychologically identifiable individual."[71]

2. "Such a mind [as Stalin's] . . . has no foundation."[72]

3. "[Stalin's] symptoms fall into seven clinical clusters: paranoia, hyperdeveloped narcissism, megalomania, agoraphobia, obsessive power hunger, sadism (with associated masochism), and defective conscience (underdeveloped superego)."[73]

Solzhenitsyn acknowledged that he was ignorant of many of the details of Stalin's life. However, he argued, this was Stalin's fault rather than his own, since Stalin was the one who had chosen to lead a secretive life. Hence, he concluded (speciously but revealingly), he—or anyone else—"was entitled to write about [Stalin] as he saw fit."[74] The Stalin Solzhenitsyn created is petty, vain and murderous; the coexistence in him of these traits, together with entire lack of self-scrutiny or remorse, defines him as perhaps mad, but certainly evil. The judgment on Stalin that emerges from Solzhenitsyn's chapters is above all moral and spiritual. In the comments quoted above, however, we see not moral or spiritual judgment but psychiatric diagnosis. It is not that the commentators I quote wish to pronounce a judgment any less severe than the author's. As readers of Solzhenitsyn, they want to get to the truth of Solzhenitsyn's Stalin, that is, to uncover Solzhenitsyn's meaning. But in addition, like Solzhenitsyn, who employs a narrative mode in which the most intimate (fictional) ruminations of the dictator are revealed, they wish to get from the character in the book to the man behind the character, from "Stalin" to Stalin. They are after the truth of Stalin himself. What they uncover is a creature who belongs in an asylum for the criminally insane; this they present as Solzhenitsyn's truth, the novelist's insight into and report on the real.

A psychiatric casting out of this kind may be the *ne plus ultra* of judgment for secular Westerners. Yet what is Solzhenitsyn doing in these chapters but, by a meticulous process of detail-by-detail admission of Stalin (into his novel, into life in all its ordinariness), establishing both his own likeness to Stalin yet at a higher level his difference from Stalin? (Is that not one of the essential functions of character-creation: to define the self by defining what the self is not but is no longer afraid to entertain the possibility of being?) If literary life under censorship breeds polemic and the destruction of difference, Solzhenitsyn's life in art is the painstaking, healing rebuilding of the possibility of difference (we underestimate Solzhenitsyn if we think he is blind to the degree to which Stalin's terror and Stalin's camps formed him). For Solzhenitsyn, Stalin has to be declared sane before he can be judged and given his sentence; whereas Solzhenitsyn's interpreters, speaking for their author, find

Stalin insane and render judgment impossible. One may ask: do they not thereby associate themselves more closely with Solzhenitsyn the polemicist, and with the Soviet Marxist enemies of that polemicist, including those whose crowning polemical move was to condemn their enemies to the madhouse, than with Solzhenitsyn the novelist? Which is the true antagonist pair: Aleksandr Solzhenitsyn and the murderous pseudo father, pretender to the throne of the Tsars, dead but settled upon him like an incubus; or the Russian Solzhenitsyn, heir of Christian Russian civilization, and the Soviet Solzhenitsyn, creature of the camps? And how is this antagonism to be resolved: by killing the bad father in one version, killing the bad, Soviet self in the other; or by taming them, imagining a way of living with them, living with difference?

Before he began his major literary work, Solzhenitsyn spent a long period of linguistic study during which he gradually cast out the Soviet Russian he had learned and recreated the language for himself from its Old Russian etymological roots.[75] The remaking of Russia in Solzhenitsyn goes on at all levels. Of Solzhenitsyn's language, the theologian Alexander Schmemann writes:

> For me, the miracle of Solzhenitsyn is that this Soviet language, which more than anything else had expressed and embodied the fall not only of literature, but of Russia herself, which was corrupted and corroded by the unctuous Soviet deceit, intrusiveness, and lies, and the alteration and subversion of all meanings; that this language became in Solzhenitsyn for the first time so clearly and so completely the language of *truth*. If we were to use a religious image, we could say that Solzhenitsyn *exorcised* the language.[76]

The domestication of the Soviet language, the restoration of continuity with language before 1917, the achievement that will ensure Solzhenitsyn a place in history (domesticate: to bring into the home), is described by Schmemann in triumphalist terms as a victory over evil spirits. Yet in making of him their polemical spokesman, playing out through him their rivalrous fantasies, do not Schmemann and other of Solzhenitsyn's allies ultimately betray their champion?

CHAPTER EIGHT

Zbigniew Herbert and the Figure of the Censor

Under pressure at the 1934 Soviet Writers' Congress to embrace socialist realism, Isaac Babel announced that he would prefer to practice "the genre of silence."[1] As a form of resistance to ideological prescription, the genre of silence was obdurately followed by a handful of Russia's leading writers. Widely interpreted as a refusal to accommodate their art to the demands of the state, their silence had an enduring moral and even political impact.

Until Stalin's death in 1953, and for a few years thereafter, writers in the Soviet Union and its satellite states had what Stanislaw Baranczak calls a "complex system of terrors, baits, lies and sophistic rationalizations" deployed against them.[2] After 1956 the component of outright terrorization in this mixture diminished. Of the Hungarian variant of the new and more manipulative censorship that evolved, Miklos Haraszti wrote:

> Traditional censorship presupposes the inherent opposition of creators and censors; the new censorship strives to eliminate this antagonism. The artist and the censor—two faces of official culture—diligently and cheerfully cultivate the gardens of art together.

The decommissioning of the iron fist did not thus of itself entail a slackening of control. On the contrary, Haraszti suggests, by internalizing the censoring function, the individual writer became assimilated into the system. Cooperating with the censor who controlled him, he had in a sense become a prototype of the "new individual" that Communism sought to create.[3]

In Poland, censorship underwent its own phases of thaw and

freeze, some taking their cue from the Soviet Union, others responding to developments within Poland itself. During the 1970s control was particularly rigid, the censors making some 10,000 interventions a year. The degree to which not only cultural life but the everyday flow of information was controlled from above came to light in 1977, when one of the employees of the apparatus smuggled a batch of ministerial directives out of the country. From these documents—later made public as the so-called Black Book—it emerged that cultural figures of whom the regime disapproved were treated according to closely defined rules. In the most extreme cases—like that of the philosopher Leszek Kolakowski—no mention of the offender's name was allowed, nor any favorable comment on his or her work. In a second category (in which Czeslaw Milosz and Aleksandr Wat figured) no mention might be made without prior and specific approval of the ministry; in the popular media (radio, television, the press) the ban was to be total. A third and more lenient category limited mention to scholarly publications. In 1976, Zbigniew Herbert, along with thirty-six other intellectuals who had protested against amendments to the constitution, was blacklisted: his name was not to be mentioned without approval from head office.[4]

The existence of a censorship apparatus was itself treated as classified information. Instructions in the Black Book were marked as for the eyes of the censors alone, "not [to] be revealed or referred to as a reason for censorship to anyone."[5] But as the contents of the Black Book became widely known, censorship developed into a hot political issue. Relaxation of censorship was high on the list of demands of the Gdansk strikers in 1980.[6]

While the system was in control, censorship was part of the writer's professional but also psychical environment. Its operations were complicated by ties between writers and fellow-intellectuals who for reasons of their own, some bad, some less bad, might have been part of the apparatus. Managing a relationship with the censors, inner and outer, became not only a preoccupation but a persistent if veiled theme of Polish writing. Baranczak writes:

> The author used to make a show before the censor, pretending that he had really intended to write a novel about the Borgias; at the

same time he used to wink at the reader, pretending that in fact he had written a novel about Stalinism. The reader in turn used to wink back, pretending that he understood the allusion, and the censor did the same, pretending that he did not notice it.[7]

Ultimately, however, Baranczak concludes, this web of deception and self-deception produced a "sterile" literature. The novelist Tadeusz Konwicki confirms this judgment. Censorship may indeed "mobilize a writer to create ways of by-passing censorship, [forcing] the writer to employ metaphors which raise the piece of writing to a higher level."[8] Yet in time the hypersubtle forms born out of the game with the censor themselves become conventions. "The secret language becomes public, and the censor will ban it too. So new, more subtle forms are devised. And so it goes, on and on, the literature becoming increasingly more obscure, eventually losing all traces of life."[9]

The play of collusion, connivance, and mutual deception between authors and intellectuals did not limit itself to the field of the text, but reproduced itself in cultural life in general, where it developed on a dynamic of its own and led to unexpected results. "The very system set up to propagate socialist art," says Jeffrey Goldfarb, "[promoted] an unanticipated critical cultural life. The battle with rigid editors, censors, officials [led] to estrangement of artists, so that 'cultural dissidents' [were] reproduced by the system itself."[10]

Zbigniew Herbert was 24 years old when the communists took power in Poland. When it became apparent—as it soon did—that the Party expected writers to be, in Stalin's phrase, "engineers of human souls," Herbert resigned from the Writers' Union and retreated into silence.

Of the Stalinist repression—or, as the revisionist locution had it, "the period of errors and distortions"—Herbert has observed: "I believed that [it] would last until the end of my life. I was absolutely sure. . . . One had to choose internal emigration. . . . When I was still a member of the Writers' Union I told myself that I would never write anything according to party directions. I simply won't." For this refusal he has claimed no heroic motive. "Can someone who feels no attraction to women be called ascetic? . . . Is it a virtue, or is it invalidism?"[11]

Herbert's first book of poems appeared in 1956. As his reputation grew, he was able to travel outside Poland. During the period 1965 to 1971, and then again during the harsh years from 1976 to 1980, he lived abroad. By the 1970s his international reputation had grown too secure for blacklisting at home to harm him. His relationship with the censors was thus in some respects untypical. Nonetheless, writing under a regime of censorship in a language spoken in only one country remains a qualititatively different fate from writing in a world language for an open market. The censor's office creates a force field that affects all those working in proximity to it, whether or not they try to ignore it: what varies from case to case is how the force makes itself felt, how it is internally transformed.

There is a further dimension as well. A work brought out under censorship has a different mode of existence from a work brought out in unrestricted circumstances. In the former case, publication is an act with a different and heightened social meaning, while reading is a more complex, more suspicious, and perhaps more alert activity. Whatever Herbert's efforts to block out or ignore the censorship, his poems could not seclude themselves from the environment in which they were destined to be read.

It is within this complex of forces, internal and external, that I turn to Herbert's poems, reading them less as responses to the Polish censorship as that censorship responded to and embodied specific moments in Poland's postwar history, than as instances of the complex general problem of writing within a regime of censorship.

I start with a poem that has every appearance of being an anti-Soviet statement cloaked in allegory to deceive the dull-witted censor. The dramatic situation in "To Marcus Aurelius" is a familiar one in Herbert. The speaker, representative of a dying order awaiting the invasion of the barbarians ("terror continuous dark terror / against the fragile human land"), addresses Marcus Aurelius: "give me your hand across the dark," he says.[12] The poem is thus about solidarity, and specifically evokes the solidarity of comrades facing extinction. In the obvious allegorical reading, Marcus Aurelius and the poet who stretches out a hand to him from Poland across the centuries stand for the values of Western civilization, the threatening hordes for the Russians.

Yet to uncloak the poem in this way, to propose that uncloaking the allegory constitutes a reading, does far less than justice to it. For, in the same motion that it invites uncloaking, the poem invites a question: In the face of the pressure for an allegorical reading created by the realities of Poland's historical situation and indeed by the paranoia of censorship itself—which, constitutionally opposed to innocent readings, spreads its habits of overreading through the whole of the reading community—how would it be possible to write a poem genuinely about Marcus Aurelius?

This question, which at its heart is the question of the genuine itself—What is the genuine? Is it possible to write the genuine in a regime of overreading?—is addressed less obliquely in "Why the Classics."[13] This poem arises out of an autobiographical passage in *The Peloponnesian War* in which, without trying to excuse himself, Thucydides describes his single failure of generalship in the war, a failure for which he paid with lifelong exile. Herbert's poem ends as follows, drawing an explicit moral:

> if art for its subject
> will have a broken jar
> a small broken soul
> with a great self-pity
>
> what will remain after us
> will be like lovers' weeping
> in a small dirty hotel
> when wall-paper dawns

The answer to the question proposed by the title—Why the classics?—is thus: The classics because they provide models of response to misfortune that, unlike the self-pity of the lovers, will outlast us; the classics because the classics give an answer to our appeal for a model of how to become classic, that is, how to endure. (Again in the poem "The Old Masters" Herbert will write: "I call on you Old Masters / in my moments of doubt.")[14]

It is quite possible to push the reading of "Why the Classics" further, making its disguised addressee the Polish artist or intellectual facing lifelong exile from the Western culture to which he feels he belongs. Nevertheless, the first reading cannot be submerged beneath the second: no less than it is about how to outlast the conqueror, this is a poem about how to outlast all-conquering Time. On the other hand, as a poem about time and mortality, it is hard to see how it could not invoke a past—the classical past—that has succeeded in lasting into the present, and thereby lay itself open to being read between the lines as a poem about how to make the unreconstructed past-in-the-present (what survives of the West in Poland) last into the future.

Writing between the lines is of course a familiar strategy, one whose ingenuity is that it places the censor, himself quite as capable of reading between the lines as the writer is of writing between them, at a tactical disadvantage: unless he can somehow demonstrate the presence of a something where there seems to be a nothing, a blank, he risks ridicule. Under the paternalistic post-Stalinist censorship, however, even the space between the lines had been colonized. Writing of Hungary in the early 1980s, Haraszti observes:

> Debates between the lines are an acceptable launching ground for trial balloons. . . . The opinions expressed there are not alien to the state but are perhaps simply premature. This is the true function of this space: it is the repository of loyal digressions that, for one reason or another, cannot now be openly expressed.[15]

When writers and censors have reached the level of accommodation Haraszti describes and the between-the-lines has been established as a privileged channel for esoteric communications, the honorable writer may prefer not use it.

I am closer now to defining the warp in the plane on which Herbert operates, a warp that originates squarely with the censor-reader and not with the poet. It is that Herbert's genuine field of reference and genuine mode of operation heavily overlap the field of reference and mode of operation of a writer writing with an anxious eye to the censor. Herbert is an allusive and ironic poet not because he uses allusiveness and irony as devices to evade the censor's red pencil, not even because the history of his times has made him wary and indirect by temperament, but because allusiveness is for him a mode of humanistic affirmation, and irony an ethical value.[16]

Consider in this light "Three Studies on the Subject of Realism."[17] The poem is in three parts, each describing (as if describing a painting) a different historical style of realism: classicist realism, romantic realism, socialist realism. Socialist realism uses "only two colors / color yes and color no" and employs a well-worn iconography of clenched fists, etc. ("Later," says its apologist, "when we get installed in the fruits of our labor / we will use the subtle color 'perhaps.'") The poem is thus "about" the grace of the seventeenth century, the color and variety (but also heaviness) of the nineteenth, the drabness of the twentieth; but these characterizations are set out not as judgments on historical reality but as accounts of historically conditioned modes of representation, that is, of realisms. The poem may read to the censoring eye as if it has set out to disguise a judgment on life under socialism as a judgment on art; but in its firm logic the poem reprimands such a reading for confusing reality with its representations.

In this poem, somewhat labored despite its gestures toward lightness, it is hard to avoid the impression that, in the force-field created by the institution of censorship, Herbert is conducting a didactic demonstration of how the censor can be shepherded into performing a misreading, mistaking the secondary referent for the primary. (If the censor, seeing through the game that is being played with him, tries to sidestep the lesson by taking the poem at face value, he runs the risk of seeming naive, of revealing himself as unable to see through disguises as he is paid to do, of failing to embody the paranoia of the state. Lacking any guiding principle, he can only fall back on the politically most opportune reading—as Goldfarb acutely observes.)[18]

All of which is not to say that Herbert never adopts the Aesopian mode. There are poems—more often than not prose poems—which, in their very form, proclaim a parabolic intent: "Emperor," "The Emperor's Dream," "A Russian Tale," "A Description of the King," for instance. In these pieces Stalin is the unmistakable if veiled first subject.[19]

"The Return of the Proconsul" is, at first glance, another poem of unambiguous ambiguity: the court of the emperor to which the proconsul nervously returns from the remote outreaches of the empire can be no other than the court of Stalin (or of one of Stalin's petty imitators), and the fate that awaits him there will be no other than the liquidation that befell so many of Stalin's lieutenants.[20]

The fatalism of Stalin's victims, even their paralysis in the face of extinction, has often been commented on. Insofar as the poem invites a reading as a Browningesque dramatization of the self-deception by which such fatalism justifies itself to itself, the following lines belong to that psychology of self-deception:

> besides the emperor likes courage of convictions
> to a certain extent to a certain reasonable extent
> he is after all a man like everyone else

These lines are about second-guessing the tyrant, about presenting a face not of abject fear but of "courage of convictions," to an appropriate degree, as a strategy of survival, doing so to put a distance between oneself and the other candidates for liquidation. Insofar as it is no longer a value in itself but a means to a calculated end, the version of courage the proconsul plans to employ is therefore inauthentic.

It is at this point that "Return of the Proconsul" invites another level of questioning. Does the poem present its own true convictions to the gaze of authority? If it does, and if those convictions are courageous, is their courage not perhaps inauthentic, the result of a calculation, an attempt to second-guess him? In such a reading the harshness or leniency of the tyrant is of no consequence (that is to say, it does not matter whether or not he is a Stalin). The poem is about the relation between the self and authority in conditions of absolutism, and specifically about the impossibility of being "genuine," of expressing the authentic self, under threat (threat of death, threat of censorship)—that is to say, about the impossibility of being sure the self is authentically presenting itself.

It is in the light of questions like these that I turn to one of Herbert's Mr. Cogito series, "The Monster of Mr. Cogito."[21] Whereas the looming dark of the earlier Marcus Aurelius poem is the definable (if all-destroying) darkness of barbarism, what "monster" it is that threatens Mr. Cogito is hard to pin down:

> it is spread out like low pressure
> hanging over the country

you can't touch it
with a pen
or with a spear

were it not for its suffocating weight
and the death it sends down
one would think
it is an abstraction
of the type *informel*

but it exists
for certain it exists

like carbon monoxide
it enters all the windows
poisons the wells
covers bread with mold

the proof of the monster
is its victims
it is not direct proof
but sufficient

Stanislaw Baranczak points out the shift in focus in Herbert's later poems, including this one, toward

> the widespread dissolution of value systems, the banalization of evil, the fading of threshold situations in which contemporary man could define himself in moral terms, and the lack of transcendental mainstays toward which he could orient himself. Emptiness . . . acquires new appearances and meanings.[22]

In a sense, the suffocating low pressure system against which Mr. Cogito rides out is a metaphor for the set of losses or absences that Baranczak describes. Yet to say that it "is" a metaphor is precisely to minimize Mr. Cogito's problem. The "low pressure system" "is" not there: rather, it is a lack standing for a lack: it looks like a metaphor but has only the form, not the body, of a metaphor; nor "has" it the form: it "has" nothing; it is "of the type *informel*."

The task of Mr. Cogito, quixotic knight of the pen, is therefore not so much to slay the monster as to track it down. His strategy is to "offend the monster / provoke the monster" in the hope that it will show itself

before there will be
a fall from inertia

an ordinary death without glory
suffocation from formlessness

It is clear that the monster will never come, clear that Mr. Cogito is doomed to pace the suburban streets with his lance/pen, calling into the fog (or whatever it is), till the neighbors and other "reasonable people" who believe that "we can live together / with the monster" coax him home to be cured of his folly.

What is it that ruins the life of Mr. Cogito? One kind of answer, the kind of answer Baranczak gives in the passage quoted above, is that it is a pervasive moral inertia, an entropy of civilization: it is something that has befallen the modern world, a collapse into meaningless. An alternative version of this kind of answer would be that it is the dead weight of socialism in Eastern Europe, exhausted of all belief in itself but not as yet prepared to die.

Why, then, is Mr. Cogito a figure of absurdity? What qualifies him for the irony with which he is treated? It is not that he has decided that the "transcendental mainstays" are gone, or that Polish socialism has turned old and deathly: most intelligent people, even most "reasonable people," would agree. It is, rather, that Mr. Cogito believes in the existence of a monster, the only proof of whose existence is that the wells are poisoned, the bread is covered with mold, and there are victims everywhere. Like Don Quixote, he does not appreciate how second-order representations (which include metaphors) work. He does not appreciate that "dragon" stands for a certain set of abstractions (such as those above), whose effect happens to be fatal. Were he to read, Mr. Cogito would almost certainly show himself to be as naive a reader as Quixote.

Herbert's great poem "The Envoy of Mr. Cogito"[23] ends:

> go because only in this way will you be admitted to the
>   company of cold skulls
> to the company of your ancestors: Gilgamesh Hector Roland
> the defenders of the kingdom without limit and the city of
>   ashes
>
> Be faithful Go

The dominant mode of "The Envoy" is, for a change, not irony but tragic paradox. That is why Quixote is not numbered among

"the defenders of the kingdom without limit and the city of ashes."
For among the other charges addressed to his creature Mr. Cogito
by Zbigniew Herbert, speaking in the voices of François Villon and
numerous other ghostly avatars, is the charge that he

> repeat old incantations of humanity fables and legends
> because this is how you will attain the good you will not attain
> repeat great words repeat them stubbornly
> like those crossing the desert who perished in the sand

The hero is not a decoder of second-level significations but a naive
reader who takes stories at their face value. The allegiance of "The
Envoy" is at an ethical level to fidelity in and for itself, and at an
aesthetic level to "great words" in and for themselves. The allegiance of "The Monster of Mr. Cogito" is to the fidelity of its comic
hero to his knightly duty; its aesthetic allegiance is to a naive reading in which "monster" stands for monster.[24]

Five men are to be executed by firing squad ("Five Men").[25] In
such terrible times, the relevance of poetry must be questioned,
even by the poet. Why, in these times, "have I been writing / unimportant poems on flowers"? Herbert postpones his reply till he has
asked and answered an apparently slighter question: What did the
five men talk of the night before their execution?

> of prophetic dreams
> of an escapade in a brothel
> of automobile parts
> of a sea voyage
> of how when he had spades
> he ought not to have opened
> of how vodka is best
> after wine you get a headache
> of girls
> of fruit
> of life

Without transition he now returns to and answers the original
question:

> thus one can use in poetry
> names of Greek shepherds
> one can attempt to catch the color of morning sky
> write of love

and also
once again
in dead earnest
offer to the betrayed world
a rose

What is the logic that allows the word "thus" to come out so decisively? One answer, the answer the reader perhaps infers: *because* the five men had not occupied their last night in being heroes, because they had not acted as if upon the stage of history but had instead gone on being their ordinary human selves, *therefore* poetry can (Herbert's careful word: not *must*) give to the world something of what ordinary people fumble towards in their hopes and longings: a vision of an ideal world. The poem then has something to do with the precious, with what should be held on to from the story of these five lives and five deaths.

Nevertheless, the move from the *because* to the *therefore* belongs not to logic but to rhetoric: it is meant to convince, but its capacity to convince comes specifically from the breathtaking leap it makes across the abyss of the non sequitur. Virtually anything could occur after the words "thus one can use in poetry," including the clarion calls to action that would likely be favored by the questioner behind the question, "Why write unimportant poems on flowers?"—as long as whatever comes after "thus" comes equipped with sufficient rhetorical firepower.

"Five Men" may seem to be a poem defending the autonomy of art against attempts to prescribe a certain social role for it, but that is not quite the truth of the matter. Rather, "Five Men" is an attempt to enact in poetry the power of art to validate itself. The poem does not *conduct* an argument—as an argument it literally has a hole in its middle—but *is* an argument. If it is about anything, therefore, it is about power: about its own power to compel a logic upon art and history, but also, by implication, about the power that would be required to compel a rival logic upon art and history. In this sense it sets itself up not only against questioners who attack "unimportant poems" but against interpretation, any interpretation, that tries to subject and defeat it. When Herbert pits himself against those questioners and interpreters—who include the socialist censor ready to condemn aestheticism or solipsism—

the test he proposes is ultimately the most violent of all: the power to withstand the battering of time, the test of endurance, the test of the classic.

In his study of Herbert, Baranczak suggests that the framework of Herbert's poetry is constituted by the polarities East versus West, past versus present, mythic versus empiric. These polarities can on occasion coalesce, he goes on, into the syncretic polarity heritage versus disinheritance, where the heritage is a European and classical one, and the disinheritance dates, symbolically at least, from 1944. In none of these polarizations does a particular pole prevail for long: instead, opposites hold each other in "dynamic equilibrium."

Thus far Baranczak describes only what we might think of as the aesthetic structure of prototypical New Criticism poetry. But he goes on: "The basic structural pattern in Herbert's poetry is not only . . . incessant confrontation . . . but the *mutual unmasking* of the two sets of antinomical values and two types of reality: the reality of heritage and the reality of disinheritance."[26] In Baranczak's reading, Herbert's irony is therefore quite different in nature from the irony held in esteem by the New Criticism, which is a kind of magnetic field in which the poem as verbal icon hangs suspended. Herbert's irony is ontologically more fundamental: on the one hand, it says, the story of the past told by the great European tradition may present itself as reality, but contemporary experience unmasks it as no more than a collection of consoling fictions; on the other hand the world in its brute empirical presence claims to be reality, but the classics reveal that a tissue of familiar old myths move behind it and animate it. (Finally, "From Mythology" unmasks the god of irony himself: "Then came the barbarians. They too valued highly the little god of irony. They would crush it under their heels and add it to their dishes.")[27]

If even irony can be crushed, domesticated, and used as a condiment, what is left that can stand up to the barbarian? Is there indeed an absolute in Herbert's poetry? Is that absolute the nihilism of the Longobards, the newly arrived appropriators of the civilized world, who "flock into the valley / shouting their protracted nothing nothing nothing"?[28]

I turn to two of Herbert's poems that in any *interpretation* must be about barbarism: "At the Gate of the Valley," in which the angels dividing mankind into the saved and the damned resemble nothing so much as SS soldiers dividing convoys of prisoners into those who will live and those who will die; and "Apollo and Marsyas," in which Apollo, god of rationality, guardian of Olympian order, is also the barbaric torturer of Marsyas.[29]

What links the conquering Longobards to Olympian gods and heavenly angels, and to those functionaries of the Inquisition who interrogated, tortured, and executed the Albigensians and Knights Templar—atrocities that Herbert recounts at length in *Barbarian in the Garden*—is their absolutism. They all believe in the tyranny of system; they tolerate no exceptions.

Side by side with these poems we may set "The Seventh Angel," in which Shemkel, the seventh angel, black and nervous, by his imperfection humanizes (so to speak) the heavenly heptad; and "Report from Paradise," a report from a "real" paradise where things are better, though only a little better, than on earth (a thirty-hour work week, for instance). In this latter paradise, heavenly perfection does not, alas, reign: someone forget that the resurrection would take place in the flesh; and when flesh was admitted into paradise, the human, the imperfect—the spirit of imperfection, in fact—was admitted too.[30]

What do such poems as the latter two, of which the best characterization is perhaps *sly*, imply for the order of interpretation?

Herbert's poems present us with a gallery of absolutists who believe that the universe we presently have is an imperfect form of another, ideal order—an imperfect form of paradise, for instance, or of the classless society, or of the perfectly ductile kind of society created by totalitarian terror. The language of the ideal order preferred by these absolutists is a language perfectly abstracted from human language, which is an imperfect medium born of an imperfect world. Unfortunately for utopians, the language that people, real people, stubbornly desire to speak and hear is not perfect and other-worldly: it remains the imperfect, this-worldly language of the flesh. The only expedient through which the language of the flesh can be redeemed for the ideal is by interpreting it, abstracting it. As this process is performed, as the flesh is flayed off it, the skeleton of the ideal, it is hoped, will begin to gleam through.

Interpretation is therefore the road absolutists take to the truth behind poetry. The censor is a figure of the absolutist reader: he reads the poem in order to know what it *really* means, to know its truth.

Herbert offers two kinds of reflection on truth and interpretation. On the one hand, he offers credos like "Five Men" or "Eschatological Forebodings of Mr. Cogito,"[31] in the latter of which the Mr. Cogito persona explicitly muses on whether he might not be permitted to forgo paradise and remain in service of the world. On the other hand, Herbert offers fables about interpretation.

What the interpreter/censor desires from Herbert and looks for in him is second-order writing (metaphor, allegory) that will open itself to interpretation—to interpretation as belief in a heavenly, abstract order of one or other variety, for instance. What he looks for is therefore a certain faith. But an underpinning, foundational faith in a second order of representation, a faith that by its nature would sanction some revelation of itself, however devious, some opening of itself to interpretation, is stubbornly not there. Herbert's fidelity remains to the first-order language, the language of the flesh.

The reading I have given to Herbert, therefore—a project not without its own ironies, considering the resistances detectable in Herbert to being given a reading at all—makes of the censor a generalized yet highly problematic figure. Herbert's real-life situation may have robbed the censor of much of his prohibitory and inhibitory power. Nevertheless, the censor remains the emblematic tyrannical second-order reader, whether his tyranny is the tyranny of political absolutism or of rationalistic reduction. On the one hand he stands in relation to Herbert as a necessary resistance, a marker for a limit beyond which the poem exceeds itself and begins to act out ambitions to partake in an ideal order. On the other, as interpreter par excellence of a poetry which is much of the time occupied in reflecting on its distance from all interpretations of itself, he is a figure of absurdity.

The present reading is directed at Herbert's more powerful and intellectually scrupulous poetry. It does not try to embrace all of his work. There are certainly poems in which the tactics of second-order representation are employed unreflectively and without qualification. Read in isolation, such poems may indeed support Paul Coates's judgment that "the calculated art of outwitting the censor [has] muted some aspect of [Herbert's] sensibility (and that of his entire generation), a constant resort to classical allusion filtering out direct feeling in a manner that comes perilously close to aestheticism."[32] Nevertheless, the body of Herbert's poetry rests on one great secret that the censor does not know: the secret of what makes a classic. Whatever popular opinion may say, whatever the classics themselves may claim, the classic does not belong to an ideal order, nor is it attained by adhering to one set of ideas or another. On the contrary, the classic is the human; or, at least, it is what survives of the human.

CHAPTER NINE

Apartheid Thinking

APARTHEID

If there is an orthodoxy among historians of apartheid today, it is that apartheid was not different in nature from the policies and practices of segregation that preceded it; furthermore, that apartheid legislation was a by no means irrational response to social developments which threatened the expectations of Afrikaners and the privilege of white South Africans in general. White liberals who diagnosed apartheid as a form of hubris or madness, and by denouncing it as such distanced themselves from it, were ultimately, in this reading, attempting little more than to distract attention from their continuing material complicity in the exploitation of black labor.

But to call apartheid mad is by no means to imply that the liberal-capitalist segregationism that preceded it was sane. It makes sense of a kind, indeed, to argue that both were mad. Rationality and economic (or "real") self-interest do not have to be the same thing; the logic that takes apartheid to be sane because rational, rational because governed by self-interest, deserves to be questioned. How short-sighted does self-interest have to be before it ceases to be sane, and how much more short-sighted before it begins to be crazy? The theorists of apartheid justified their doctrine on the grounds that it was in the long-term interest of whites; apartheid demanded sacrifices, they said, but in the long term such sacrifices would pay off. Like Poe's detective turning to the most obvious place for the hidden letter, we ought at least to entertain the possibility that what animated these worthies may have been, not the altruism they claimed, but on the contrary the crassest absorption in their own passions and appetites, and that their justificatory utterances may have been no more than a cover for the deepest indifference to the fate of their descendants.

The notion I will explore here is that the men who invented and installed apartheid—or at least some of the men, some of the time—were possessed by demons. Pinning the blame for apartheid on demons is, I realize, pinning it nowhere at all. Nevertheless, if madness has a place in life, it has a place in history too. The indifference of South African historiography to the question of madness, and the tacit consensus in the social sciences that while madness—like what used to be called the "illegal Bantu"—may be conceded to have a place in society, this is ontologically a place apart, a *non*place that does not entitle madness to a part in history, should arouse nothing but mistrust, and make us redouble rather than abate our efforts to call up and interrogate the demons of the past.

As an episode in historical time, apartheid was causally overdetermined. It did indeed flower out of self-interest and greed, but also out of desire, and the denial of desire. In its greed, it demanded black bodies in all their physicality in order to burn up their energy as labor. In its anxiety about black bodies, it also made laws to banish them from sight. Apartheid did not understand itself and could not afford to understand itself. Its essence from the beginning was confusion, a confusion it displaced wildly all around itself.

Contemporary historical scholarship on apartheid suffers from a self-imposed limitation: it approaches apartheid from the outside, treating only its workings in the world. Churchmen called apartheid a sin, not because it was a crime of huge dimensions (the notion of crime has an inbuilt weakness: crimes are defined by the victors, and apartheid was not a victor), but because it set for itself the task of reforming—that is to say, deforming and hardening—the human heart. Apartheid will remain a mystery as long as it is not approached in the lair of the heart. If we want to understand it, we cannot ignore those passages of its testament that reach us in the heart-speech of autobiography and confession.

It is in this spirit that I approach the writings of Geoffrey Cronjé. I treat them as a confession: not as repentant confession—far from it—but as a confession of belief, a credo all the more revealing for being full of ignorance and madness. In what now seems old-fashioned innocence, Cronjé falls into a delirium of writing with a lack of reserve, a lack of prudent self-censorship, quite foreign to his successors in the academic-bureaucratic castle he helped to build. In that delirium we catch glimpses of apartheid nakedly occupied in thinking itself out. But we can share these glimpses only if we read the texts, follow the ravings, from inside, if we inhabit with part of ourselves Cronjé's position as writing subject. In reading him, we must make an effort of projection, entering his language, listening closely to what he says, and even more closely to what he does not say, is afraid of saying.

What Cronjé does not address in his text, what he turns away from, is the desire for mixture. Yet to mixture his mind obsessively returns. What does mixture mean to him? Rather than try to pin it down, I prefer to allow the concept to float in its endlessly attractive yet repulsive allure, itself a self-contradiction, itself a mixture. It is mixture and the desire for mixture that is the secret enemy of Geoffrey Cronjé and his fellow-knights of apartheid, the baffling force that must be thwarted, imprisoned, shut away. Apartheid is a dream of purity, but an impure dream. It is many things, a mixture of things; one of the things it is, is a set of barriers that will make it impossible for the desire to mix to find fulfillment.

My concern is thus less with Geoffrey Cronjé himself—a man of no great historical importance—than with his madness, and with the question of how madness spreads itself or is made to spread through a social body. More generally, it is with the reinsertion of madness into history.

GEOFFREY CRONJÉ: CAREER AND REPUTATION

Geoffrey Cronjé (1907–1992) graduated from the University of Stellenbosch in 1929, then, like other nationalistically inclined young Afrikaner intellectuals of his generation, continued his studies in Germany and the Netherlands, whence he returned full of enthusiasm for the goals and methods of parties of the European Right. (Contemporaries of his among this intellectual elite included H. F. Verwoerd, Nico Diederichs, and Piet Meyer, all of them destined to become powerful forces in the land). Armed with a doctorate from the University of Amsterdam, he was soon elevated to a professorship in sociology at the University of Pretoria; he remained in academic life until his retirement.

Politically active from early in his life, Cronjé joined the pro-Nazi Dietse Studentebond (Pan-Dutch Student League) and helped found the Afrikaanse Nasionale Studentebond (National Student League). Later he was recruited into the Afrikaner Broederbond (League of Brothers), the secret organization created to advance Afrikaner interests, and became a leading figure in its policy-forming deliberations. During the 1930s the Broederbond had given its energies to cultural politics and the plight of landless poor whites. But with the wartime economic boom generating large-scale black migration to the cities, it began intensive internal discussion of plans for radical racial segregation and self-governing African reserves. The ideas embodied in Cronjé's 'n Tuiste vir die nageslag were seminal in these discussions.[1]

Between 1945 and 1948 Cronjé wrote or made substantial contributions to four influential books: 'n Tuiste vir die nageslag (A Home for Posterity) (1945), Afrika sonder die Asiaat (Africa without the Asiatic) (1946), Regverdige rasse-apartheid (Just Race-Apartheid) (1947) and Voogdyskap en apartheid (Guardianship and Apartheid) (1948).[2] Though he continued to publish steadily thereafter, his reputation rests on these works, on which the National Party drew heavily in constructing a platform for the election that brought it to power in 1948.[3]

After 1948, Cronjé faded, or was allowed to fade, from a vanguard role. In his research and writing he began to focus upon more narrowly conceived social work among poor Afrikaners, and later upon his hobby of classical literature. An evaluation of his life's work, written during the heyday of apartheid by N. J. Rhoodie, gives an idea of how he was seen at that time by the establishment social-science community. During the "years of ferment" after the World War, writes Rhoodie, Cronjé "attempted to bring about a sociologically responsible evaluation and diagnosis" of "the South African race-problematic."[4] The scientific rigor of his policy proposals is to be commended. His books of this period, taken together, constitute "the first comprehensively argued *principled* exposition of [the] system of ethnic relations" that after 1948 would crystallize as apartheid (p. 42). "Numerous policy directions that Cronjé suggested today already form part of statutory apartheid. Others are subscribed to in principle by the Government" (p. 76). With a blend of academic formality and crudeness reminiscent of Cronjé himself, Rhoodie identifies as "arguably Cronjé's greatest contribution" the insight that the key to "the Bantu problematic" is the "physical presence" of blacks in white South Africa, and that the best solution would therefore be the "physical draining away *(wegdreinering)*" of blacks (pp. 67–68). (The term *wegdreinering* belongs to soil conservation but also to sanitary engineering).

In retrospect we can see that, in elaborating the doctrine of a unique *Afrikanervolk* charged with the historical duty of maintaining its own uniqueness, Cronjé and his fellows behaved much like nationalist intellectuals world wide: it was not their nationalistic fervor but the steps they were prepared to take to realise their dreams that set them apart. Born in more than one sense on the periphery of empire, young, educated, ambitious Afrikaans-speaking men like Cronjé, in the decades after the Anglo-Boer War of 1899 to 1902, had found only a few avenues of advancement open to them: the law, the church, teaching, the lower levels of the bureaucracy. Their aspirations thwarted, they turned to ethnicism. Their solution to the crisis of the overproduction and exclusion of intellectuals like themselves was to work for a separate state in which their energies would find employment. They set about forming, in Tom Nairn's words, a "militant, inter-class community rendered strongly (if mythically) aware of its own separate identity vis-à-vis the outside forces of domination." They worked with the only materials at hand: "the people and peculiarities of the region: its inherited *ethnos,* speech, folklore, skin-colour, and so on. Nationalism works through *differentiae* like those because it has to."[5] Taking as their constituency the rural poor and impoverished urban Afrikaners, they built out of them the *Afrikanervolk*.

CRONJÉ: WRITINGS, 1945–48

Cronjé's first book, *'n Tuiste vir die nageslag* (1945), is dedicated to the author's wife and other *"Afrikanermoeders"* as "protectors of the blood-purity of the *Boerenasie.*" This dedication is worth pausing over. The compaction of the noun *moeder*, "mother," with the epithet *Afrikaner*, though not grammatically irregular in Afrikaans, here carries a heavy ideological freight, conscious and unconscious. Consciously, it is an expression of the synthetic character of Afrikaans as a Germanic language, and stands in opposition to the alternative analytic *Afrikaanse moeder*. In its linguistic politics it aligns itself with the nativist movement in Germany for ridding the German language of non-Germanic elements. Unconsciously, it is a morphological figure of introversion, exclusion, enclosure, embrace. It looks forward to a lexicon in which there will be hundreds of entries for emotionally charged nouns starting with *Afrikaner-: Afrikanermoeder, Afrikanergesin, Afrikanerbloed, Afrikanerplaas* . . . (Afrikaner-mother, Afrikaner-family, Afrikaner-blood, Afrikaner-farm . . .). *Afrikanermoeder* is thus a morphological metaphor and lexical metonym for *Afrikanereie*, the uniqueness of Afrikanerness.

There is a second feature of the dedication that deserves note. Cronjé implicitly does *not* cast the Afrikaner father in an equal role as protector of the blood-purity of the people. Translated into biological terms, the dedication implies that by confining herself to men of pure Afrikaner blood, the Afrikaner woman keeps the blood-strain pure; or, to put it in another way, that what keeps the blood-strain pure is women confining themselves to men of pure blood. The question poses itself: why is the blood-strain not equally kept pure by men confining themselves to women of pure blood?

The answer, though simple, is central to Cronjé's genealogical imagination: bastardy. The issue of the intercourse of the Afrikaner man with a woman not of pure blood is defined in Cronjé's scheme of things as a bastard, one who is by custom cast out into the population of bastards *(bastervolk)*. The issue of the intercourse of the Afrikaner woman with a man not of pure blood, on the other hand, may remain as a viper nurtured in the bosom of the *Afrikanervolk*. The child takes on the racial classification of the mother. Bastard women by definition give birth to children who fall into the bastard category. Pure-blooded Afrikaner women, however, give birth to children of the *volk*. If one of these children is in fact a biological bastard, it will grow up a secret bastard, an insidious, weakening force within the nation.

But if the way for the *volk* to remain pure-blooded is for its women to have intercourse only with pure-blooded men, how are its women to know they are not having intercourse with one of these secret bastards? If we expect Cronjé to answer that women have intuitive ways of telling, we will be disappointed: no such power is attributed to them. Thus feminine chastity is in itself no guarantee of continuing blood-purity, and the *Afrikanermoeder* will be the protector of the race only as long as she, too, is protected. Behind Cronjé's dedication therefore lurks a patriarchal threat or promise. As husband, the Afrikaner will guard the chastity of his wife; as father, he will protect the purity of the race by approving the men with whom his daughters will mate.[6]

'n Tuiste vir die nageslag confronts two *problems,* as defined in Cronjé's problematics: the problem of the native *(naturel)* and the problem of the Coloured *(Kleurling).*[7] But before he sets out his solution to these two problems, Cronjé addresses, in one of the most extraordinary paragraphs in the book, a covert word to his readers.

Whenever an Afrikaner expresses himself on South Africa's racial problems, says Cronjé, there are those who "read [him] with a magnifying glass," searching for evidence to present to the "natives and Coloureds" that the Afrikaner is their greatest enemy. Such readers—Cronjé clearly has liberals and their running dogs in mind—are "dangerous," and account must be taken of them (*TN*, p. 7). What his countrymen are about to read, they are warned, will therefore be self-censored. But the warning is double-edged: reminding readers of the need for censorship, it also alerts them to read between the lines, to put back into the text what has been censored out, and thus invites them to constitute themselves as, in Leo Strauss's term, an esoteric reading community.[8] As for the nature of what has been censored, that is clearly signaled though not spelled out: formulations that will make the Afrikaner sound like the enemy of the natives and the Coloureds; that is to say, expressions of hostility toward them. To read Cronjé fully, then, to join those of his readers who are *in the know*, the aspirant reader must put back into the text the hostility whose overt expression has been euphemized or elided.[9]

In defining his problematics in terms of natives, Coloured, and Asians ("Asiatics") as against whites ("representatives of the West European race"), Cronjé sketches a fourfold racial typology (elsewhere he adds a fifth race, the Jews). What scientific basis has this typology? Little, he acknowledges. "The Afrikaner's historical and traditional viewpoint [on race] . . . is based above all else on his experience of racial differences. . . . The race-differences are simply *there*" (*TN*, pp. 8–9). In other words, the categories of folk-ethnology—or *volk*-ethnology—are consciously accepted as the given categories within which the history of ethnic contact and conflict in South Africa will be played out. Races are seen as self-constituting groups, or groups constituted by overpowering definitions exercised by (usually hostile) others. Sociologically speaking, this is a not unsophisticated notion of what race has been in South African political history, though not one that Cronjé consistently holds to: for much of the time he falls back on a conception more in tune with European racial science of the first half of the century.[10]

There are also times when he falls back on the notion of race as preordained, part of the Creation. The "racial diversity" of the planet, he says, must be protected from "bastardization" (*uitbastering*, which implies in addition an irreversible elimination of difference). "A mishmash *(mengelmoes)* of races [is] something unnatural." Each race has its appointed task in God's larger scheme. For instance, the evidence of "monotonous" African music suggests that Africans have a predisposition for "repetitive labour [with] a 'monotonous' rhythm" (*TN*, pp. 10, 19, 18).

But if bastardization—mixing the races—is a sin against Creation, has white-led South Africa, with a "bastard" Coloured population numbering millions, not been implicated in sin from its beginnings? In responding to this charge Cronjé relies on his colleague, G. Eloff's, cavalier rewriting of the history of white colonization. In the early years of Dutch settlement, Eloff (and Cronjé) concede, there may have been a certain amount of sexual mixing with indigenous people. But within a generation or two the "apartheid concept" had taken root. In fact, most Coloured people are likely to be descendants, not of the original colonists, but of British soldiers discharged at the Cape in the nineteenth century (*TN,* p. 21).[11]

"With regard to blood-mixing, the Coloured presents the utmost danger for the European race in South Africa" (*TN,* p. 39). The second chapter of *'n Tuiste,* the heart of the book, deals directly with "bloedvermenging," for which "miscegenation" is a less than adequate translation. The etymology of miscegenation is *miscere,* "to mix," plus *genera,* "kinds" or "stocks"; but because *mis-* is a productive prefix in English with a general negative meaning, there is every reason to think that most people read the word as *mis* plus *cegenation* (where *cegenation* rings no Latin bells), thus losing the kernel notion of mixing. Accordingly I prefer "blood-mixing," which translates *meng,* "mix," directly, though even so it does not capture the perfective force of *vermeng,* mix so that no unmixing will be possible.

In 1939, Cronjé recalls, the South African government appointed a Commission on Mixed [i.e., interracial] Marriages. This commission, whose mandate did not extend to investigating interracial sexual relations in general, recommended that mixed marriages should be banned by law, inter alia because they produced "persons who would pass as European" and thus lead, in Cronjé's words, to a "seeping of non-white blood into the European population" (*TN,* pp. 44–45).

"Seep in" (Afr. *insypel, insyfer*) is another key term for Cronjé's imagination: variable in form in Afrikaans as in Dutch *(sijpelen, zijpelen, siepelen, sieperen),* he uses it in contexts where it easily changes places with its rhyme-word *insluip,* steal in: the secret bastard who tries to find a place in the white community, and the bed of a white woman, is "die sluwe insluiper," the sly stealer-in (*TN,* p. 77). The semantic nexus evoked is one of dark and treacherous fluidity.

Neither the commission nor Cronjé—who of course supports its recommendation—confronts the question of why a person should fly in the face of public opinion to make a mixed marriage; confronts, that is, the question of desire. But Cronjé does approach it indirectly:

There are whites, born in this country, who have degenerated to such an extent in respect of morality, self-respect and racial pride that they feel no objection against blood-mixing. . . . Whites must protect themselves against these conscienceless and criminal bloodmixers by . . . making all blood-mixing (illegal intercourse) punishable. *The individual is responsible to his community for all his activities.* The nation-community [*volksgemeenskap*] is entitled to call to the dock everyone who acts in conflict with its highest interest . . . For the interest of the nation [*volksbelang*] always outweighs personal interest [*eiebelang*]. (*TN*, p. 47; Cronjé's emphasis)

Here, as he moves into full flight, Cronjé leaves behind his more prudent academic/bureaucratic prose: the passage echoes not only the Nazis' notorious Nuremberg statutes but, for a moment, the characteristically denunciatory, minatory tone of Hitlerian oratory itself.

The conditions of social disorder following the Great Depression, says Cronjé, have forced many poor whites to live in mixed residential areas. Concomitantly, a steady pressing-in *(indringing)* of nonwhites *(nie-blankes)* into white areas has taken place, creating "living-higgledy-piggledy" (*deurmekaarwonery: deurmekaar* also means confused, as in mental confusion). Mixed living is one of the prime social causes of blood-mixing. Whites in mixed areas lose their ties with the *volk*. "Unconsciously a gradual process of feeling equal *(gelykvoeling)* [with nonwhites] begins to take place in them." The distance between white and nonwhite diminishes. (Here and elsewhere Cronjé undergoes striking lapses, seeming to be unconscious that his words can be read in another light as an argument that interracial tensions will be reduced by social mixing.) "Mixed areas become the dying-places *(sterfplekke)* of the white race in South Africa and the most fruitful soil [for] bastardization." Social disorder and blood-mixing threaten to create "a single South African mishmash-society" (*TN*, pp. 59, 55).

Mengelmoes-samelewing, "mishmash-society," is another term worth pausing over. *Mengel* contains the *meng* of *rassevermenging,* but in addition implies mixing *up:* it is a cognate of English *mangle. Moes,* cognate with English *mush,* is a term from cuisine. In everyday usage *mengelmoes* is always derogatory, implying a mixture in which not only individual character but all original structure have been lost; what is left behind is shapeless, undifferentiated, and pulpy—much like feces, in fact.

Who, among whites, are the treacherous "blood-mixers"? Cronjé identifies four types. One is the Jew, another the visiting soldier or sailor, a third the mentally retarded poor white. This leaves us with those whites born in South Africa, "low-grade people" (the phrase echoes Alfred Rosenberg) who have "degenerated" in "morality, self-respect, and racial pride" to the extent that they feel no revulsion against blood-mixing. A few marry across the bar, but most "mix blood" *(vermeng die bloed)* extramaritally. "At night, under cover of darkness, they steal *(sluip)* into the [black and Coloured] locations, where they commit treason against the white race." Yet "by day we see them again amongst us in their shops, [in] their occupations, etc., where they usually keep up a respectable front" (*TN*, p. 62). These degenerate *insluipers* have to be distinguished from secret bastards within the white community, the *insypelaars* (infiltrators) of the white blood-pool (see *RRA*, pp. 84–85).

Having in his own eyes demonstrated the threat that blood-mixing holds for the white race, Cronjé proceeds in the second half of *'n Tuiste* to list an arsenal of countermeasures, beginning with residential segregation and segregation in the workplace and culminating in "total racial segregation." If there must be immigration, immigrants should be screened for "blood-purity" (*TN*, p. 83–84). These apartheid measures are not intended solely for South Africa, he concludes. A day will come when a racial policy for the whole of Africa will be needed to ensure the survival of the white race and prevent what he will later call "the return of confusion and heathendom and chaos" (*RRA*, p. 107).

The three chapters that Cronjé contributed to the collaborative book *Regverdige Rasse-Apartheid* (1947) repeat many of the arguments of *'n Tuiste*. He does, however, brood further on the enigma of desire, natural and unnatural.

It is natural, he says, to desire to mix blood with the blood of one's own kind. Is it natural or unnatural to desire to mix blood with the blood of another race? Is the natural kind the species or the race? If the former, then we may expect desire continually to cross race-boundaries, and the struggle to contain it within race-boundaries will be never-ending. If, on the other hand, desire operates naturally only within the race, then desire across racial lines is as unnatural as bestiality, and can in theory be bred out (for instance, by eugenics).

The question is restated in another form: is aversion to sexual contact with other races determined genetically (i.e., racially) or culturally (i.e., by custom)? Cronjé's preference—his own desire—is clearly for the former. His inclination is to treat "blood-mixers" as degenerates, and to identify the blunting *(afstomping)* of aversion as a form of progressive degenerativity.

But the existence of a mixed-blood population in South Africa looms up as a fact of such brute magnitude that it cannot be ignored. To the extent that Coloured people are descended from early white colonists, including his own forebears (and no Afrikaner, not even Cronjé, can deny that some of them may be), the forefathers of the Afrikaner people must have pursued "degenerate" practices. Cronjé is therefore compelled to produce an account of aversion situated within history. Thus he must revise and extend his account of early colonial history.

For a generation or two in the seventeenth century, he concedes, there may have been no prejudice against blood-mixing. However, as the eyes of the colonists became opened to the extent of differences between the races, an aversion grew up in them that became "an integrating part of the everyday attitude toward life"—in fact, was assumed to be "an instinct." *But it was not a true instinct.* Just as it was brought into being by specific circumstances, so changing circumstances could lead to its loss. Such circumstances may already have arrived with the socioeconomic decline of whites and the rise of nonwhites (hence the immediate need for residential segregation) *(RRA,* pp. 76–83).[12]

Clearly Cronjé is in a tight corner. If aversion is not instinctual but socially conditioned, then the decision to maintain the social environment that engenders aversion cannot be justified as a transcendent duty to the future of the biological race. The decision to maintain or recreate—or, if the truth be told, *create for the first time*—circumstances in which blood-mixing will be impossible will have to appeal to a different mandate. This is why Cronjé shifts his ground from biologism to the idea of the organic *Volk,* as elaborated by Herder. For in Herderian theory the individual is born into the *Volk* and has no natural rights apart from it.[13] The *volkswil* to which each individual member must bow is thus more than a political consensus: as the expression of the being of the organic *volk,* it transcends not only the will of the individual member but the historical circumstances of its expression, even though the *volk* may have come into existence within historical time. Thus the Afrikaner who betrays his *volk*-being by mixing blood acts *contra naturam* as well.

Hence the complex status enjoyed by acts of blood-mixing. If blood-mixing were a crime against nature of the same order as bestiality, then people who committed it would be outlaws, and the appropriate (eugenic) measure against them would be of the order of extermination or sterilization. But blood-mixing does not run counter to biological instinct. It runs counter to a commandment in which we can distinguish three strands of force: the force of the *volkswil;* the force of God's will that mankind be divided into nations (Cronjé is not averse to reading the surfacing among whites of recessive "African" traits as God's punishment for "the sins of the fathers" operating through the laws of genetics [*RRA,* p. 85]); and the force of criminal law (for of course Cronjé's plea is above all that blood-mixing be prohibited by statute).

In his third book, *Voogdyskap en apartheid* (1948), Cronjé denies that apartheid is a *Herrenvolk* doctrine, arguing that it has a moral basis in the duty of the white man to the African. Africans are still at a stage of cultural childhood; the white man must act *in loco parentis* until they reach adulthood.

During this growing-up period, the disintegration of indigenous culture must be prevented at all costs. If blacks become detribalized, they, like the Coloured people, will be "swallowed down" *(verswelg)* by the process of westernization. Unable to absorb Western culture, they will in effect become a "cultureless mass" *(kultuurlose massa)* (*VA,* p. 33). Culture, to Cronjé, is always *volkskultuur,* a structure of differences within which the individual lives and which sustains him; loss of difference is typically figured via metaphors of devouring, digestion, and defecation. Detribalized, "cultureless" Africans constitute an undifferentiated mass in two senses: mere amorphous lumpishness, but also post-tribal, pre-political clotting-together.

The negotiation of the perilous growing-up phase under guardianship will require that black and white live in separate homelands under separate socioeconomic systems. This separation *(apartheid)* will remove the white man from the daily view of the black man and thus ensure that an unattainable white culture and lifestyle do not become the object of his envious desire. It will also remove the black from the view of the white and prevent the black from becoming the object of white sexual desire. What must above all be rejected is the present (1948) "race-mishmash" *(rasse-mengelmoes)*, which will all too soon turn into a "mishmash-race" *(mengelmoes-ras)* (*VA*, p. 27).

THEMATICS

There is a small set of themes around which Cronjé's thinking obsessively circles. The chief of these is *mixing*.

The semantic poles of Cronjé's racial vision are marked by, on the one hand, the words *anders* (different), *eie* (own/unique), *apart* (apart), and, on the other, the words *meng* (mix), *moes* (mush), *massa* (mass). This polarity marks not only his thinking but the very texture of his discourse. At one moment he will be marking off boundaries, tracing differences, erecting systems, and in general acting the part of founder-patriarch over his new territory. At the next moment he will descend into hectoring, rumormongering, salacious imaginings, obsessive and uncreative wordplay. *Difference* is the world Cronjé wants to belong to; *mixmushmass* is the world he repudiates with the utmost vehemence but is again and again returned to by his imagination.

There is something Cronjé is haunted by. Let me call it simply C. C is the sign of the undifferentiated but also of indifference: indifference to the law, indifference to everything but the urgings of a devouring appetite. Whatever C devours comes out at the other end undifferentiated, that is, as more C. In the algebra of mixing, C + W = C, C + B = C, C + C = C, even B + W = C. Unless there is apartness (apartheid), asks Cronjé—whether direly or desperately, one is not sure—what can lie ahead but more and more mixing, more and more C? The Coloured is never satisfied with what white blood he has in his veins: he is forever greedy for more ("more white blood . . . is welcomed"). The blood-fantasy grows heady, confused, undifferentiated. In the act of mixing (the act of darkness), Coloured blood drinks down white blood and turns it into Coloured blood. Yet at the same time it infiltrates and contaminates the white blood-pool (*VA*, p. 34).

C, the *sluwe baster-insluiper* who drinks and contaminates, represents to Cronjé the insidious sliding into indifference of a system of order based on keeping things apart, a system that is itself precarious, fragile: in Cronjé's substantial imagination it is (one gropes for the likeness) a kind of integument holding together and holding apart a fluid content ever ready to interflow and flow out. It is like a skin holding together a body whose physical substance is 90 percent fluid, at the same time that it keeps this fluid body, this assemblage of fluids, apart. The *baster* C stands as the figure-in-chief of mixed fluids. Mixed fluids run in his veins; his nature is to trigger the mixing of all fluids, fluids which by their fluid nature are all too ready to mix. What the *baster* threatens is the end of things kept apart at every level: sexual, social, conceptual. The breakdown of the system, the breakdown of repression, threatens the self.

C, the undifferentiated, is never sated: like fire, the more he devours the more he is ready to devour.[14] Therefore apartheid, the law of difference, must be strict, without compromise, perhaps even without pity. Liberals think that "mutual consent" will be enough to prevent mixing. No, says Cronjé: the closer black and white approach each other in developmental level, the more the aversion to race-mixing will be blunted on both sides. "*This*"—this insidious growth of indifference—"is why separation of the races is necessary" (*VA*, p. 156). In other words, the principle of difference transcends in importance human accommodations, even peaceful accommodations, such as take place within history. However it may seem from the outside, the world is a stage for a Manichaean conflict between the principle of difference and the principle of indifference. One cannot compromise between difference and indifference, for (the asymmetrical algebra returns) difference plus indifference equals indifference. Apartheid belongs to the realm not of politics but of eschatology.

A second focus in Cronjé, a continual turbulence beneath the surface of his prose, is the riddle of desire.

A typical Boer, writes Cronjé's colleague Eloff in a singular passage, "simply cannot imagine how it is possible for a white man to be guilty of such a ghastly crime *(gruwelike misdaad)*" as intercourse with a black woman. The deeply engraved Boer tradition is that "a young [white] man does not speak to native or coloured women" except about essential matters like wages. "A more eloquent proof of the disapproval of the Boer for bastardization cannot be given, for this [disapproval] is the actual driving force behind the attitude of a young man toward a *meid.*"[15]

The driving force behind the silence of the young man, behind the repression of his address, is, Eloff insists, his disapproval of—his aversion to—what that address might lead to. To the contrary, one might ask, could a more eloquent clue be given to the true and actual driving force within the young man—his desire—than the ban imposed on his speech? Furthermore, as to the misinterpretation of the young man's silence, as well as the vehemence with which that misinterpretation is presented, does this not point to an actual driving force within Eloff himself, namely, the denial of the desire of white men for black women? And what is the "deeply engraved tradition" to which Eloff points but the ban of the patriarch, on whose behalf Eloff here writes?

It is because Cronjé's apartheid—and, to the extent that Cronjé's apartheid was realized in legislation, real apartheid—develops as a counterattack upon desire that I place his tirades against blood-mixing, rather than his prescriptions for segregated suburbs and native reserves, at the center of my account. Apartheid (and the policies loosely known as segregation that preceded it) certainly had their origins not only in desire and the denial of desire but also in fear and greed. But the text of apartheid deserves to have restored to it the chapter that has been all too smoothly glossed over, censored out, removed, namely, a denial and displacement and re-projection of desire reenacted in further huge displaced projects of displacement: the redrawing of the maps of cities, the redivision of the countryside, the removal and resettling of populations.

CONTAGION

Apartheid served certain economic interests. Therefore, as long as devotion to economic self-interest stands as the measure of rationality, apartheid was not irrational. Furthermore, the continuity of apartheid with the policies of segregation that preceded it, and in general with the so-called South African way of life that had evolved since 1652, is plain for all to see. If there is any madness in the picture of apartheid, then, where does it belong?

If only from having lived in South Africa, I would be reluctant to confine the madness of apartheid to a compartment of Cronjé's mind. And I am strengthened in this reluctance when I observe that not only hostile commentators but Cronjé's ideological heirs have difficulty in integrating his madness into the accounts they give of his reason. His heirs are either silent about it or euphemize it; as clearly as decency permits, they signal that it is extraneous, unnecessary, even an embarrassment.[16]

Why, then, were Cronjé's writings welcomed in the 1940s, treated as a serious account of reality, and acted upon?

Part of the answer is that Cronjé met with a response because he was in crucial respects representative of his class and time. In effect he was one of the instruments used by his class to give voice to its desires and obsessions. In this sense, it was not he who infected his society with craziness about race but his society that infected him. (However, we must be cautious not to fall into circularity here. Cronjé often complains that his fellow-Afrikaners are lax about race-mixing. His own sociological case studies of the 1930s reveal pointedly that his obsessions were not shared by all Afrikaners.)[17]

Another part of the answer is that Cronjé was a participant in a wider enterprise of mobilization from above, constituting Afrikaans speakers as an ethnic group and raising them to national— or nationalist—self-awareness. Yoking together the ethnic and religious varieties of fervor, elaborating what amounted to a civil religion, Cronjé and his ideological confrères, in Bloomberg's words, "captured the imagination of the Afrikaner masses by giving them meaning, community, status, hope and self-respect."[18]

Nevertheless, the rallying-cry of this project of mobilization remained racist exclusivism, and its political model a discredited and defeated European right-wing nationalism. Why should the racist strain of Cronjé's project have spread so successfully too?

The easy answer is simply that he successfully appealed to the underlying racism of the Afrikaner community. The metaphoric model behind such an answer is perhaps of sympathetic vibration: when the right note is struck, the listener vibrates in response. Let me, however, explore a different metaphor: the metaphor of contagion.

Contagion as an explanatory model for the communication of passions among masses of people has been used often in the past. Gustave le Bon, for instance, in a pioneering study for which Freud had great admiration, named susceptibility to contagion, along with heightened suggestibility and the lowering of inhibitions against aggression, as the three main features of the psychology of the crowd.[19]

In itself, the metaphor of contagion explains as little as the metaphor of sympathetic vibration. However, in the context of South African racial custom it does pick up a suggestive cultural and historical coloring. Let me recall one of Cronjé's arguments for total— as opposed to mere residential—segregation. Whites employ blacks as domestic servants, he says, ignoring their "low standards of hygiene" and thereby exposing themselves to "infection" *(besmetting)*. In this way, he claims, venereal diseases are passed on to white babies by their black nurses. Furthermore, when whites send out their washing to be done by blacks, it sojourns in unhygienic black surroundings and comes back contaminated (*TN*, p. 172).

Cronjé is here reiterating a commonplace of South African prejudice. In a justly well-known essay, Maynard Swanson has exposed the outlines of what he calls the "sanitation syndrome." Overcrowded and unhygienic slums are pinpointed, often by public officials with a political axe to grind, as the source of infective disease to the wider community. Soon, by a process of metonymic association, the source is shifted from the slum itself to the (black) slum-dweller. As a public health measure, a double action is then performed: the slum is cleared, and the slum-dwellers are packed off to a site (a "location") outside the town's *cordon sanitaire*. The epidemic that gave rise to the sanitation scare may pass; but the black man, now conceived as *in himself* the carrier of infection, remains segregated, ordered to live indefinitely outside the town.

In this essay and others, Swanson thus argues that public health administration helped to mold the racial ecology of colonial societies. Urban race relations were widely conceptualized in terms of imagery of infection and epidemic disease. In South Africa in particular, the sanitation syndrome was "a major strand in the creation of urban apartheid." The link between blackness and infectiousness was never a real one. Epidemiology was simply used as a rationalization to justify actions whose real ends were economic. Nevertheless, says Swanson, this should not lessen our interest in "the power of a metaphor to shape perceptions and influence or justify behavior."[20]

I would go further, however, and ask: Strictly speaking, is the infection feared by Swanson's whites—and by Cronjé too—a metaphor, *something else* in the disguise of sickness? As we examine the sanitation syndrome closely, it is not metaphor we find at work (a shift from one term to another because the two are in some sense equivalent) but metonymy (a sliding of meaning from one thing to the next because the two are adjacent). In a first sequence of metonymic displacements we see the germ of infection suspected of being harbored by the black carrier being displaced on to his breath, his sputum, his mucus, and then on to the black *as black* who houses that breath, that spittle, that mucus. From being a carrier who is a black, the suspect becomes the black who is a carrier; from being vehicle of infection, blackness itself becomes the infection, therefore subject to public health measures like isolation/segregation.

In the next step, the germ of infection is rapidly displaced, in a kind of fluid motion whose model is the circulation of the blood, throughout the black body. The black body becomes a generator of black essence (as we speak of "essence of rose"). Though *black blood* is the name conventionally applied to this essence, it is understood in the first place that black blood stands for black semen (a kind of semen possessed by both sexes, however, as Cronjé's story of the black woman giving venereal disease to the white baby reveals), but in the second place that this "standing-for" is not stable—is not an equivalence, a metaphor. The circulation of "black blood" through the black body is nothing more or less than the circulating power of metonymy itself, one site unendingly displaced on to another. Thus *the black body is the place of metonymy;* and if this seems a slippery concept, a concept hard to grasp, hard to get a hold on, hard to pin down, that is because the place of metonymy is a nonplace, because its essential "place" is the place where it has just been or is just about to be.

Third, what we may call the idea of infection, but might equally well call the germ of the idea, is itself carried by a process of rapid displacement over the agitated community. Swanson's essay deals, after all, with the behavior of communities in a state of panic (panic which, in his account, is exploited by political interests); and panic is merely the obverse side of the contagious suggestibility that to Le Bon (and to Freud) was a prime trait of the crowd mind. But in contagious suggestibility it is not the contagion that is suggestible but suggestibility itself: being open to suggestion is what is suggestible. Thus we have another vision of unending displacement, another slippery thought: from contagion to suggestibility of contagion to openness to suggestibility of contagion to openness to openness. . .

And finally, as Swanson observes, it is only the already-infected (the already-agitated) who can be infected. The medical officials who ordered the segregation of blacks in turn-of-the-century Cape Town "were [already] imbued with the imagery of infectious disease as a societal metaphor." The idea of being infected is inherited by a process of endless backward displacement, as the myth of the Fall tells us.[21]

If this analysis has any power as an account of the spread of aversion, we may then want to abandon a quest for the origin of the responsiveness of Cronjé's readership, and of the responsiveness of white South Africans in general to racist agitation, in favor of a different kind of analytical movement: a tracking, a following in the footsteps, of the movement by which ideas are displaced—a *reading,* that is to say, rather than an *explanation.*

MADNESS

In the reading I have given to his writings of the period 1945 to 1948, Geoffrey Cronjé, or the "Geoffrey Cronjé" who matters, was crazy. The electorate that bought the package offered by Cronjé and his friends, besides being deceived or self-deceived, was also for a time crazy, or at least crazed—though, since it bequeathed us no text, I cannot back this assertion with a reading.

Was there anyone in the transaction, then, who was neither deceived, nor self-deceived, nor crazy in any sense of the word, but sane throughout, knowing exactly what was what? The recent historiography of apartheid, though it tends to imply that such people existed, more generally and more subtly tends to finesse the question on the grounds that self-knowledge is not necessary for an ideological system to exist and function. Key metaphors like the metaphor of blood-contagion are then not necessarily the invention of grand rhetoricians but are rather *in the air*, waiting for a confluence of material circumstances that will be conducive to their spread. Identifying such circumstances becomes a major part of the historian's task.

It is obvious, of course, that in the notion of ideas floating in the air ready to catch hold and spread through the social body when circumstances are right I have reinvoked the metaphor—the meta-metaphor—of infection. There are finally only two viable positions one can take up with regard to the notion that ideas ("ideological" ideas) are not self-aware constructions used as means to ends, but instead float in the air, ready either to infect whole societies (model 1) or to infect intellectuals, selected or self-selected for their particular kinds of obsessiveness, who as rhetorician-propagandists (carriers) receive, intensify, dramatize, and retail them to whole societies (model 2, Gramsci's). One position is that the whole description is a convenient professional metaphor for a process about whose workings we are more or less ignorant. The other position is that it is philosophically naive to believe that metaphors stand for things that are more real than the metaphors themselves, to believe that if we trace the equivalences far enough back we ultimately come to solid meanings. On the contrary, there is ultimately no "ultimately" in language; metaphors slide into (or interpret) other metaphors which slide into yet others, and so on. If we follow the latter course we may be in a better position to read racism, but we are in no position to eradicate it, not only because it has no root (no "ultimate" root), but because a reading position is not a position at all: it is what I can only call a *following*.

CHAPTER TEN

The Work of the Censor: Censorship in South Africa

The Publications Act (1975) of the Republic of South Africa, as amended in 1978, allowed for a publication to be declared "undesirable" if it was found to answer to any of the following criteria:

(a) it was "indecent or obscene or offensive or harmful to public morals"

(b) it was "blasphemous or offensive to the religious convictions or feelings" of any "section" of the population

(c) it "[brought] any section . . . into ridicule or contempt"

(d) it was harmful to inter-section relations

(e) it prejudiced security, welfare, peace and good order

(f) it disclosed part of a judicial proceeding in which offensive material was quoted.[1]

In 1980, J. C. W. van Rooyen, professor of criminal law at the University of Pretoria, was appointed to the chairmanship of the Publications Appeal Board, the ultimate tribunal in the system of censorship created by the act, succeeding Judge J. H. Snyman. Van Rooyen was by that time the author of a book on the system, *Publikasiebeheer in Suid-Afrika* (Publications Control in South Africa) (1978), which he later followed with *Censorship in South Africa* (1987). These are authoritative works, the second somewhat more liberal in its outlook than the first, written not by a Christian Nationalist ideologue or unbudging defender of the status quo but by one of a new generation of professionally trained people and technocrats who in the 1970s were beginning to move into positions of power in the Afrikaner establishment. Cautious by training and temperament, Van Rooyen was in principle in favor of censorship, but was concerned that the law should be rationally and consistently interpreted and equitably applied. If we wish to understand South African censorship in its systematic phase, from the coming into force of the Publications and Entertainments Act of 1963 to the negotiation of a democratic constitution and Van Rooyen's retirement in 1990—by which time the apparatus had withdrawn into inertia—there is no better place to start than with Van Rooyen's account of its workings.

OBJECTIVITY, IMPERSONALITY, IMPARTIALITY

"The need arose for a comprehensive book to be written on the application of the Publications Act, and someone had to do the work," writes Van Rooyen in his 1987 preface. "So I set about writing this book . . . despite my misgivings" (*CSA*, p. vii). These words set the tone for what follows. *Censorship in South Africa* presents itself as a book written not out of desire but out of duty. The marks of the censor's desire on its pages are few and far between (though not wholly absent). In fact, Van Rooyen's vision of the Publications Appeal Board (hereafter the PAB) is of a committee of technocrats in the field of morality and intergroup relations, their personalities wholly submerged in their work. "The ideal is that the [PAB] should be seen to be an objective and independent arbiter." Its attitude should be "not that of a persecutor but that of an arbiter who weighs all the relevant interests against each other." Even in the sensitive area of state security, "the publications committees and the PAB are arbiters whose function is not to restore order or to defend the country, but to strike a balance between the opposing interests" (*CSA*, pp. 16, 51, 106).

The notion of the censor as an arbiter between contending social forces is close to the heart of Van Rooyen's philosophy as this had developed by the mid-1980s. "A balancing of interests has become the hallmark of control [of publications] in the Republic: general or sectional interests are continually weighed against minority interests." Even the lowly committees that performed the initial scutiny of publications should be set up, in his view, in such a way that "each committee represents diverse interests." After summarizing (rather briefly) the conservative and liberal positions in the philosophical debate about censorship, Van Rooyen even goes to the extent of taking up the position of arbiter between these positions: since "legal philosophy is divided on [the subject of] the basis of control," he opts for a "moderate" approach, which he defines as a middle course between the two (CSA, pp. 3, 16, 8–9).

Nevertheless, reading Van Rooyen's two books attentively, one can recover a submerged history of clashes of personality and compromises over standards within the corridors of the censorship bureaucracy. In the earlier book, written while the dust of the battle provoked by cabinet minister Connie Mulder over Etienne Leroux's novel Magersfontein, O Magersfontein! still hung in the air, Van Rooyen defends Mulder's intervention and represents the PAB as adjudicator between spokesmen of the (white, Afrikaans) community and a minority of intellectuals out of touch with community standards.[2] In the second book, there is no such forthright defense of the handling of the Magersfontein affair, which could by now be recognized as a watershed in the history of censorship in South Africa, marking a split between the conservatives still dominating Afrikaner political organizations and middle-of-the-road academics represented by the Akademie vir Wetenskap en Kuns (Academy for Science and Art). Instead, the reader is given a discreet account of an evolution away from Judge Snyman's legal fiction of the "man of balance," the "reasonable reader/viewer who is not hyper-critical or over-sensitive," whose sensibilities needed to be catered to and whose tolerance should not be "transgressed," toward the "likely reader-viewer" of the particular work under scrutiny. This new touchstone, together with an increased role for advisory committees of experts and (not least) the retirement of Judge Snyman in favor of Van Rooyen himself, mark 1980, in Van Rooyen's account, as the beginning of a new, more rational, less confrontational dispensation (CSA, pp. 56–57, 9–10).

If there is one feature of the publications control system Van Rooyen commanded that emerges from his writings as a source of personal pride, it is the standard of impersonality the system attained. This impersonality is not to be confused with objectivity. Van Rooyen knows all too well how vain it is to aspire to objectivity in the arena of morals. "It cannot be argued that the concepts of indecency, obscenity, offensiveness or harmfulness are objective concepts which exist apart from any consideration of the likely readers/viewers." Hence the importance to him of the likely-reader test. By interrogating this hypothetical reader's response to a publication, the censor can reach an answer independent of his own, subjective response to the question of whether the publication offends against the putative standards of the specific sector(s) of society (demarcated perhaps by age and social class) likely to read it. This response cannot, of course, serve as the sole criterion of whether the publication should be declared "undesirable" and suppressed. But it will constitute one of the more significant opposing opinions between which the censor, in his role as social mediator, may then proceed to adjudicate. "Academically," writes Van Rooyen, the problem is thereby reduced from one of identifying a "reasonable man" to finding "a solution which is reasonable in the light of all competing interests" (*CSA*, pp. 60, 13).

Between Snyman and Van Rooyen the theoretical difference can thus be captured in the opposition between the ideological construct *the reasonable reader* and the sociological construct *the likely reader*. Rejecting the troublesome ideological burden of the former, Van Rooyen presses for the latter as a value-free, probabilistic concept. The shift of ground marked here is certainly not insignificant. But rather than pursue further the differences between the two regimes, I prefer to ask what is involved in the kind of reading that both Snyman and Van Rooyen propose, a reading via an interposed fictional figure, whether "reasonable" or "likely" (for we should remember that the PAB's procedures have never included identifying real-life reasonable or likely readers and polling their opinions). If someone is or is not to be offended, why should it not be the censor himself? What did it mean—in the South Africa of 1963 to 1990 in particular—to be offended?

THE OFFENSIVE

Offensiveness and its closer semantic cousins are at the core of the Publications Act. Clause (a) proscribes publications that are "indecent or obscene or offensive or harmful to public morals." Clause (b) proscribes, inter alia, publications "offensive to . . . religious convictions or feelings," clause (c) those that "bring any section . . . into ridicule or contempt." Van Rooyen calls the language of the act "vague" and holds it to be the first task of the PAB to give it specific meaning.[3] Although in discussing offensiveness he concedes that "we are working with subjective feelings," there is also a "judicial offensiveness" with a limited meaning; similarly with the terms ridicule, contempt.[4] Again: "Each of the terms (e.g., 'indecent,' 'obscene') employed by the Act has . . . a juridical meaning. . . . The jurisdictional postulates of obscenity, offensiveness, harmfulness and blasphemy are the basic issues which must ultimately be addressed" (*CSA*, p. 11).

What else does Van Rooyen have to say about these notoriously difficult terms? Of the following observations, some are based on legal precedent, while some reflect his own best judgment.

1. "It cannot be argued that the concepts of indecency, obscenity, offensiveness or harmfulness are objective concepts which exist apart from any consideration of the likely readers/viewers" (*CSA*, p. 60). This is Van Rooyen's clearest statement on the subject, and marks his most forthright divergence from the touchstone of the "reasonable reader." His reasoning, though not spelled out, is plain: there is no way of defining the reasonable reader, in a context of censorship, except as the reader who either does or does not pass the test of finding publication X or Y indecent/obscene/offensive/harmful. Thus the definition of the indecent/obscene/offensive/harmful remains circular. The likely reader, on the other hand, to the extent that he has an objective or at least a statistically definable existence outside the censor's mind, allows the *possibility* of noncircular definition.

2. "No word is undesirable in itself. . . . The criterion is . . . whether [the word] is used in a manner that . . . is in fact 'offensive' as defined in [legal precedent]" (*CSA*, p. 79). Since the precedent to which Van Rooyen proceeds to refer cites the potential of words to cause repugnance, mortification, pain, or other unwelcome feelings, the test is again one of how words affect a reader/listener, and specifically of whether they "transgress" his "tolerance." However, before legal action can be taken, a fairly gross transgression of tolerance will need to have taken place. With regard to religion, the

offensive does not "mean merely something that displeases, but . . . something that is repugnant, that mortifies or pains" (*CSA*, pp. 79, 56–57, 54).

3. Everything obscene is indecent, but not vice versa. Nevertheless, "a common characteristic of the [two] terms seems to be the blatantly shameless intrusion upon that which is private (usually sexually) by whatever is horrifying, disgusting, lascivious, lewd, depraving or corrupting." Again, "obscene material is material which . . . *blatantly* violates privacy" (*CSA*, pp. 53, 11). Leaving aside the typically legalistic scatter-gun multiplication of defining terms, we may note that the key notion of intrusion upon or violation of privacy is here introduced.

4. "The meanings of the terms 'ridiculing' or 'bringing into contempt' [in clause (c)] are circumscribed. Ordinary scorn or political criticism is not sufficient for a finding of undesirability. The material must be degrading, humiliating or ignominious" (*CSA*, p. 100). Here we move away from the hypothetical likely reader to what is better termed the target reader, the reader whose pain rather than whose pleasure is the writer's desire. But even if such target readers testify to feeling degraded, humiliated, or brought into ignominy by a publication, such testimony does not in itself justify a ban. Again a validating displaced reading has to be performed by the censor in the person of the target reader. Thus this case entails no departure from the paradigmatic test for offensiveness.

It is clear by now that, to Van Rooyen, "Is X offensive?" translates as "Does the likely reader of X find X offensive?" The censor's task, as he sees it, is to identify the likely reader, read X *as if* it were being read by its likely reader, and then introduce the result of this inquiry as one among several considerations to be weighed up and adjudicated among before a decision is reached.

Nevertheless, Van Rooyen does not regard the likely reader and his responses without curiosity. (How could he?—the only reader in the real world is, after all, the censor himself.) As we see under item 3 above, both the indecent and the obscene involve, in Van Rooyen's view, blatant intrusion on the reader's privacy. Van Rooyen, to say nothing of the PAB itself, comments extensively on the relation between privacy, particularly sexual privacy, and obscenity. In its judgment on *Magersfontein*, the PAB had denounced the "excessively filthy language" of the book, citing reference to "masturbation, loss of virginity, contraception. . . , orgasms, periods, sex organs and ailments of the prostate" as "an intrusion into the respect [of the individual] for sexual privacy" (*CSA*, p. 18). "At the basis for the protection accorded [by the law] to sexual relationships lies the respect for privacy and dignity," writes Van Rooyen in his own person. "At the basis of control of the arts" lie, inter alia, "respect for the privacy of the sexual act [and] for the privacy of the nude human body" (*CSA*, pp. 65, 3).

It is clear that "privacy" here is being used in a metaphorical sense. A right to privacy means a right to a physical space where one shall be secluded, undisturbed (in a range of senses of this word), and unobserved. To assert that one's privacy has been disturbed by words or images in a book requires that the notion of private space be extended to cover the space of the language, images, and general view of the world within which one is used to living: it is this essentially conceptual space that is claimed to be violated. Even when an obscene spectacle or act is forced upon an unwilling or surprised individual—for instance, by a prominently displayed image—the privacy claimed to be invaded is metaphorical. Unless it is conceded that the extension of privacy from the physical to the conceptual is metaphorical, defining obscenity or indecency as a form of violation of privacy makes no sense.[5] The "respect [of the individual] for sexual privacy" identified by Van Rooyen as that which needs to be protected is a clear example of a conceptual space—a space defined here with notable vagueness. What it is that the South African censor had in mind when he acted to protect the privacy of the reader has therefore yet to be identified.

Let us return to the case of *Magersfontein*. Is it an accident that, in its verdict, the PAB defines the outrage of the reader at Leroux's book as a *man's* outrage ("The broad public . . . personified in the average man [*gemiddelde man*]") and elsewhere as a *man's* feeling for woman's honor? "The average man puts a high premium on the sexual privacy of woman," avers the PAB, objecting to "the dishonor of the female body" caused by the book (*CSA*, pp. 18, 59). I by no means suggest that Van Rooyen and the PAB defend only the right of the female body to be shielded from representation (its right to "privacy"); but as the censor, in Van Rooyen's account, is required to read on behalf of the average man (here) or the likely reader (elsewhere) to protect, not that person's privacy, but that person's *respect* for privacy from being offended, so he must also protect from outrage a man's feeling that a woman's body should be private. The censor acts for the man, who feels for others and/or for the woman; and who may, indeed, himself be displaced so far from his own better self that his better self needs to be represented by another.[6] A double or triple or quadruple displacement has therefore taken place in the name of privacy.

Just as the kind of reading Van Rooyen describes is a displaced reading, the kind of argument he conducts is an argument by displacement. All definition is, of course, a displacement: in a dictionary each word is defined by being displaced onto a subset of the other words in the dictionary. Nevertheless, displacement runs through Van Rooyen's text (and indeed through the censor's text in general) like wildfire. What is being displaced?

PROTECTING OTHERS

Van Rooyen situates censorship (or "publications control") in the South Africa of the 1980s in the context of a debate in the area of morals about the rights of the individual vis-à-vis the demands of society, as that debate was being conducted in Britain and the United States during the 1960s and 1970s. He sees the poles in the debate as occupied by, on the one hand, Patrick Devlin, arguing for the community's right to preserve its standards, and, on the other, Herbert Hart and Ronald Dworkin, following John Stuart Mill in arguing for the priority of individual rights.[7] Van Rooyen himself claims to follow "a moderate approach" between these poles (*CSA*, pp. 8–9). Nevertheless, as he expands upon his approach, it becomes clear that he is closer to Devlin than to Hart.

Van Rooyen concedes that the state cannot and should not legislate morality ("morality finds its source in man himself"). But he proceeds to define morality as "the sum total of rules which society has developed to regulate man's behavior towards others" (*CSA*, p. 2), that is, to give it the kind of definition that Dworkin distinguishes as merely "anthropological," without any distinct moral foundation (*TRS*, p. 254). Van Rooyen proceeds: "Should the basis of control not . . . be sought in the protection of interests which underlie morality?"—that is, which underlie morality as just defined (*CSA*, pp. 2–3). But this is precisely Devlin's position, namely, that the principle underlying the enforcement of moral standards—a principle which itself is not a moral standard—is the right of a society to take what steps are necessary to protect its organized existence.[8]

Thus, when Van Rooyen claims for himself a "moderate" position, it is not a position mediate between Devlin's functionalism and the liberalism of Hart and Dworkin, but rather moderate in the sense in which Hart uses it, namely, moderate by comparison with the extreme position that the enforcement of morals is a good in itself. To Hart, the "moderate thesis" is that "a shared morality is the cement of society" and a breach of moral principle is therefore "an offense against society as a whole" (*LLM*, pp. 48–49). It is this kind of moderation that Hart attributes to Devlin, and it is this kind of moderation that Van Rooyen follows.

The divergence between Devlin and Van Rooyen on one side and Hart and Dworkin on the other rests on a disagreement about the status of moral systems. To Devlin and Van Rooyen, nothing is lost if we understand morality as a set of habits and beliefs whose basis may be either shared, customary, and unquestioned, or else political, in the sense that they reflect the expressed will of society.[9] (Devlin and Van Rooyen diverge, of course, when it comes to identifying how society expresses its will.) To Hart and Dworkin, this conception of morality is inadequate. True morality, says Hart, must include a yet-to-be-defined element of *value* lacking in mere customary rules (*LLM*, p. 58). Public opinion does not necessarily understand itself, says Dworkin: when the public claims to be condemning something or other in the name of morality it may be doing no more than expressing "passionate . . . disapproval" (*TRS*, p. 24).

Of course, concedes Dworkin, the legislator must take account of what presents itself as a moral consensus among the public. But before such a consensus can claim the status of "a consensus of moral conviction," it must provide proof in the form of "moral reasons or arguments which the average member of society might sincerely and consistently advance," otherwise we are in the realm not of justice but of politics (*TRS*, p. 258). Van Rooyen paraphrases this argument of Dworkin's (the judge/censor's decision should not be based, he says, on "parroting and not relying on a moral conviction of [his] own"), but the gloss he gives to the argument reveals that he has not understood its force, and is in his own way "parroting": "This means that sound objective reasons must be given" (*CSA*, p. 1). On the contrary, it is precisely because "objective reasons" cannot be advanced to prove that one holds a belief with conviction that Dworkin has to add a criterion of sincerity. The question only halfway faced by Dworkin and not faced at all by Van Rooyen is whether people know whether the convictions they hold are sincerely held. Dworkin assigns to his legislator the task of adjudicating between sincere and insincere moral beliefs. It is no wonder that Devlin, a lawyer rather than a philosopher, chooses the more matter-of-fact distinction between moral beliefs that are merely held and moral beliefs that are loudly and persistently expressed.

Clause (a) of the South African Publications Act named four categories of publication that might be found undesirable: the indecent, the obscene, the offensive, and the harmful to public morals. From the preceding discussion it is clear that the fourth category differs in kind from the first three. The concepts of indecency, obscenity, offensiveness, and harmfulness can indeed, as Van Rooyen says, be given a meaning only relative to a specific reader/viewer (*CSA*, p. 60). But harmfulness to public morals cannot be defined in a relative manner. The censor here must either act on his own initiative to protect what he defines as public morals or take his cue from public protest. No displacement of reading is possible; the censor's position is inescapably political.

A frequent criticism of the activities of the Publications Appeal Board under Van Rooyen was that its practice did not accord with its theory. The "rhetoric" of the PAB in defense of freedom of speech, writes Gilbert Marcus, was "both impressive and seductive..., [but] an analysis of [its] decisions reveals that its stated commitment to these guiding principles [was] often fragile." "Decisions...[were] often strikingly inconsistent...with the professed guiding principles. Certain decisions [seemed] to be devoid of principle altogether."[10] The record bears out Marcus's charge. To give one instance: *Having it All* by Helen Gurley Brown was banned "as a result of its advice to women to use extramarital sex in the promotion of a career." This decision—cited by Van Rooyen himself (*CSA*, p. 71)—reveals the PAB behaving not in its claimed role as arbiter between competing interests but in an authoritarian Devlinian role of guardian of public morals.

But it was not in the sphere of morals that the authoritarianism of the South African censorship system emerged most clearly. In respect of state security as much as in respect of morals, Van Rooyen claimed that the PAB was nonpartisan: "The publications committees and the PAB are arbiters whose function is not to restore order or to defend the country, but to strike a balance between the opposing interests" (*CSA*, p. 106). However, another decision cited by Van Rooyen reveals how this principle could be bent. The question before the PAB: Should a writer of fiction be permitted to bring the police into ridicule or contempt? The answer: "Although the police force is not regarded as a section of the population [as required by clause (c) of the Publications Act], it was decided that the rendering of the police ridiculous or contemptible in this book was intended to prejudice state security, the general welfare and good order within the meaning of [clause (e)]" (*Publikasiebeheer*, p. 118).

CENSORS AND WRITERS

The truth is that the censors played a highly partisan role in South African intellectual life in the 1960s and 1970s. As for the 1980s, it can at least be said that their partisanship was not given overt rein. In his own overview of the system, Van Rooyen acknowledges that "tension between authors and a large section of the public reached a crisis point between 1960 and 1978." He implicitly attributes this tension to the conservatism of the (white) South African way of life, and even on a conservative reaction against a current of permissiveness from abroad.[11] "In 1980, however, matters changed. The PAB, under the chairmanship of the acting chairman" (i.e., Van Rooyen himself), passed *Magersfontein*. A new policy allowing "strong protest" was adopted "based on the philosophy that it is often in the interests of state security to permit the expression of pent-up feelings and grievances" (*CSA*, pp. 15–16). In practice this meant that publications "with a sophisticated likely readership [were] found to be not undesirable in spite of . . . material expressing hatred against the authorities. Such publications were regarded as useful safety-valves for pent-up feelings in a milieu where they would be understood not as a call to political violence but as a literary experience" (*CSA*, p. 115).

As a measure of the cooling of tempers between censors and writers that Van Rooyen alludes to, we may contrast with the level-headed crisis management that Van Rooyen advocates the highly confrontational response of the PAB under Snyman to those Afrikaans intellectuals who had testified on behalf of *Magersfontein*:

> The point at issue is whether the position of the literary experts *[letterkundiges]* regarding unsavory language (however revolting *[vieslik]*) can really be justified.
>
> The law protects the morals of the entire community *[gemeenskap]*. The Appeal Board wishes to state expressly that, according to its assessment of the community view *[gemeenskapsopvatting]* of public morals, this approach of the literary experts is at odds with the Publications Act. (*Publikasiebeheer*, p. 14)

The PAB concluded:

> The writer built into [his] novel excessive filthy language, excessive idle use of the Lord's name, vulgar references to excretion, masturbation, [etc.]. . . . [This novel is] highly regarded by literary experts. The broad public, however, as personified by the average man, regards the use [of such language] as an infringement of the dignity of the individual and an invasion of his respect for sexual privacy. (Ibid., p. 18)

Magersfontein was therefore banned.

In a double sense of the term, we see the PAB here *deciding for* the public: first posing the public and the intellectuals as antagonists, and then deciding on behalf of the public. The PAB under Snyman acted as both champion of the public (whose feelings it embodied in a fiction called "the average man" and assessed according to its own methods) and arbiter between the public and the intellectuals in a *cause célèbre* that it did as much as any other party to set up and stage-manage. In the role of champion—a role Van Rooyen later made an attempt to drop—Snyman's PAB at least acted in accord with its conservative views. But even in the role of arbiter, Van Rooyen kept alive the notion that there was a conflict to arbitrate—or, in his terms, that the interests of writers and public were at odds. Van Rooyen is very clear about the matter: the 1978 amendment to the act that created committees of experts gave recognition, he writes, to the "minority rights of literature, art and language." "I have described these as 'minority rights,'" he goes on, "since there is little doubt that, were a referendum to be held as to the value which should be given to these interests, majority opinion would deny them recognition" (*CSA*, p. 9). Thus, if the PAB under Snyman set aside intellectuals as a group marginal to the "broad public," Van Rooyen, in conceding them no more than "minority rights," perpetuated their constitution as a minority.

Nor is the kind of aggressive emotionalism that breathes from the 1977 judgment on *Magersfontein*, rendering the body that gave the judgment so suspect in the role of arbiter, wholly absent from the post-1980 PAB. In his 1978 book Van Rooyen does not hesitate to characterize certain instances of obscenity as the emanations of sick minds.[12] Though there is little of this crudity in the 1987 book, there remain pronouncements in the area of politics that come from a quite specific political viewpoint. Thus, for instance, the PAB claims that Nadine Gordimer's *Burger's Daughter* "contains various anti-white sentiments." Wessel Ebersohn's *Store up the Anger* is said to "deal with alleged atrocities committed by the security police." The television series *Roots* is banned in 1984 because "a substantial number of likely viewers would identify with the cause of the oppressed American slaves" (*CSA*, pp. 100, 103, 104).

With regard to these three pronouncements one need only observe that, while Gordimer's dialogue includes racial insults, most of them directed against Afrikaners, the book "contains" these insults only in the sense that the Board's own records "contain" them;[13] that it is possible for a work of fiction to deal with atrocities or with allegations of atrocities but not with alleged atrocities; and that while the decision on *Roots* may be logically impeccable, Van Rooyen seems to be blind to the implication of its premise.

Such pronouncements serve only to confirm Marcus's view that "the assessment of factors such as 'the security of the State' will inevitably be bound up with the personalities, background and general life experience of the members of the Board. 'State Security' . . . involves an emotional dimension which often precludes rational debate."[14] We might add: an emotional dimension invisible to the participants.

PARANOIA

The further we explore the workings of censorship, the more pivotal the issue of attribution turns out to be, specifically the attribution of blame, and the dynamic of counterblaming that blaming initiates. It is hard not to be sucked into this dynamic, impossible not to be touched by it: those who claim to observe it judiciously or scientifically may be the most deceived. We do not step outside the dynamic simply by acknowledging its existence. It has its own inevitability. Paranoia gives rise to paranoia.

At the close of his major case study of paranoid fantasy, the case of Judge Schreber, Freud confronts the (phantasmal?) suspicion that his brand-new theory of the etiology of paranoia is already detectable in outline in Schreber's autobiographical memoir and therefore is not original.

> Since I neither fear the criticism of others nor shrink from criticizing myself, I have no motive for avoiding the mention of a similarity which may possible damage our libido theory in the estimation of many of my readers. . . . I can nevertheless call a friend and fellow-specialist to witness that I had developed my theory of paranoia before I became acquainted with the contents of Schreber's book.[15]

In both its lack of occasion and its hand-on-heart style, this asseveration betrays a certain paranoia in Freud himself; alternatively, seeing paranoia everywhere, even in Freud, belongs to a perception that has been touched by paranoia.

The principal manifestation of Schreber's paranoia is an end-of-the-world fantasy. Discussing this fantasy and the general question of the paranoiac's relation to the world, Freud gives his support to the explanation that part of paranoia is a general detachment of libido from the world.[16] In the psychohistory of the white South African in the last years of apartheid, detachment of libido from the world took the form of an inability to imagine a future, a relinquishing of an imaginative grasp upon it. At a political level, this loss of hope manifested itself most markedly in an end-of-the-world fantasy of a "total onslaught" of hostile powers against the South African state and against Western Christian civilization in Africa, an onslaught in which no means would go unused, even the most unsuspected. Though the censorship laws antedated the flowering of the full total-onslaught worldview, they became an avenue through which total-onslaught thinking expressed itself, and the construction of a bureaucracy of censorship entrusted with the task of scrutinizing every book, every magazine, every film, every record, every stage performance, every T-shirt to appear in the land, was what one might legitimately call a manifestation of total-onslaught paranoia.

By comparison with other officers of the South African state, particularly with those entrusted with state security, Van Rooyen may seem far from paranoid. Yet precisely because of his heavy emphasis on the maintenance of balance, neutrality, and health, one is led to scrutinize the pages of his books for traces of the contagious paranoid discourse that he, by his office, must mediate.

Reading Van Rooyen closely, we find a range of such traces. At one end of the range, there are fault-finding insults such as the attribution of mental or moral sickness that he either utters in his own person or quotes approvingly. In the middle of the range occur various instances of self-censorship, in the interest of presenting a cooler, more judicious face, from the 1978 volume to the 1987 volume. At the other end, there is the overall enterprise—a legal and philosophical enterprise but finally an exercise of power, to which Van Rooyen gives his professional loyalty—of abstracting judicial authority, including the censorship system, from interrogations of its authority and from the dynamic of blame, eliding it from that discourse in advance, by means of what one can call the meta-rule of contempt: certain acts of blaming, certain questionings of authority, are ruled inadmissible under penal sanction and form no part of the record ("No person shall insult, disparage or belittle any member of the Publications Appeal Board, or do anything in relation to the Publications Appeal Board which if done in relation to a court would constitute contempt of court.")[17] The entire argument of the 1987 book—that the PAB occupies a position of arbiter between contending interests—can be seen as an effort to place censorship outside the paranoid dynamic of blaming.

But the ultimate and most pervasive expression of paranoia lies in the habits of denial, projection, and displacement in Van Rooyen's texts to which I pointed earlier. Offense, taking offense, always belongs to *someone else:* the man in the street, the man in the street taking offense on behalf of someone else, woman or child, and so forth. When Freud draws up a table of the transformations of inadmissible impulses that paranoiacs perform, the projective transformation is at the head.[18] As Jacques Lacan observes, it is characteristic of this transformation—the transformation into "He is persecuting me" ("He is part of the onslaught")—that it takes place immediately, without reflection. The efforts of the paranoiac to explain his attribution as an act of judgment (as Van Rooyen's two books do) or to proclaim it an act of judgment (as the Publications Act itself does) thus founder under the suspicion of being retrospective or prospective rationalization.

The suspicion that the censor acts on the basis of unadmitted impulse itself belongs to the mode of paranoia. It is answered by the suspicion of the censor, also paranoid, that the call for the end of censorship in the name of free speech is part of a plot to destroy order. Polemics around censorship tend all too soon to fall into a paranoid mode in which every argument presented by the other is seen as a mask for a hostile intention. Once paranoid discourse is entered upon and its dynamic takes over, the intentions of the other cannot but be hostile, since they are constituted by one's own projections.

In this sense, the entry into paranoia is an entry into an automatism, of which there can be no clearer illustration than the fact that, of all the pathologies, paranoia has been the most amenable to artificial simulation. A computer program embodying a system of "beliefs" to be protected and a set of defense mechanisms for protecting those beliefs has simulated the discourse of paranoid patient and therapist convincingly enough to pass Turing tests: qualified psychiatrists have been unable to tell whether what is being relayed to them is the verbal behavior of a human being or an automaton.[19]

Paranoia has a paradoxically double character. On the one hand it manifests itself in behavior whose rationale is not apparent to the outsider. On the other it presents a highly intellectual front of rationality or pseudo rationality. It is highly judgmental, though its judgments are aberrant. For this reason classical (pre-Freudian) psychiatry focused on the question of judgment in paranoia, treating paranoia as a syndrome whose essence is that the faculty of judgment becomes perverted.[20]

But what, in a psychoanalytic context, is judgment? In his 1925 paper on negation and denial, Freud discusses the relation of judgment to primary instinctual impulses. "Judging is a continuation, along lines of expediency, of the original process by which the ego took things into itself or expelled them from itself, according to the pleasure principle." This original process has to remain compulsive (and, in the sense in which I have used the word, automatic), governed by the pleasure/unpleasure principle, until "the creation of [a] symbol of negation" is achieved. This "No" marks the liberation of thinking from the primitive alternatives of incorporating and expelling. Thus we can take "No" both as the mark (the birthmark) of language and as the first speech of the Freudian unconscious. "There is no stronger evidence that we have been successful in our effort to uncover the unconscious," says Freud, "than when the patient reacts to [an interpretation] with the words 'I didn't think that,' or 'I didn't (ever) think of that.'"[21]

The therapeutic move Freud describes here ought not to escape suspicion—and is indeed interrogated by Freud himself—as sleight-of-hand on the therapist's part: "If the patient agrees . . . then the interpretation is right; if [not] . . . that is only a sign of resistance."[22] But let us turn our attention for the present to Freud's claim that when we hear "No," we know for sure the unconscious speaks (or else that we know for sure it is the unconscious that is speaking).

By linking the faculty of judgment to instinctual impulses, Freud allows us to suggest that the essential gesture of censorship, the judgment to admit or refuse entry, continues to bear a primitive incorporative or expulsive character. What does it mean, to admit and consider this suggestion? It has required only the slightest shift of logical angle on my part as reader (a shift characteristic of the paranoid mode, which shares a world of signs with the "healthy" or "normal" subject but reads them at a peculiar angle) for the censorship laws themselves to come into focus as a set of conditions and tests which have to pass the judge's primitive Yes/No response. From this point of view, laws and judgment are on the same level: under suspicion, on the defensive. The (paranoid) wisdom of the law is that society must guard itself on all sides, against its own defenses too. The defense of the ego (which, at least in his earlier account of the psychological apparatus, he describes as "the dominant mass of ideas," whose analogue at a social level is ideology) is assigned by Freud to a function that—like a border official charged with preventing the entry of subversive materials—he calls censorship. The defenses that guard the ego "are not just unconscious in the sense that the subject is ignorant of their motive and mechanism, but more profoundly so in that they present a compulsive, repetitive and unrealistic aspect which makes them comparable with the very repressed against which they are struggling."[23]

In the discourse I am conducting, a discourse of criticism (from the verb *krino*, 'to accuse,' 'to bring to trial'), I have placed censorship under suspicion. But just as I place censorship under suspicion of hiding its true nature, of being secretly governed by paranoia, my criticism too cannot escape from the paranoid dynamic of judging, expulsion. The blame always lies elsewhere, it is always displaced.

In the discourse of law and legal philosophy as it confronts the matter of the offensive, we encounter again and again these rationalizing displacements, as though there were a fear of confronting the offensive itself. I have already pointed to the processes of displacement in Van Rooyen's texts. Here is the same process at work in the writing of the most rationalistic of all writers on offense, Jeremy Bentham. The law, says Bentham, should define no act as an offense "which is not liable, in some way or another, to be detrimental to the community." The test of mischievousness is utility. "An action . . . may be said to be conformable to the principle of utility . . . when the tendency it has to augment the happiness of the community is greater than any it has to diminish it." Thus by a process of abstraction the thing itself, or the word onto which it has been displaced, becomes an *offense* which is then abstracted into the class *detriment* and entered as a term in the calculus of *utility*.

Does the chain of displacements stop with utility? Yes, promises Bentham: "The principle of utility neither requires nor admits any other regulator than itself."[24] Similarly, Dworkin promises that his chain of displacements will end in the principle of sincerity.

One hears the protest: But that is how reason works: reason works by displacement. Yes indeed; but the reasoning of paranoia sees that work from another, shifted angle: what presents itself as reason is displacement in disguise. Reason cannot explain paranoia to itself, explain it away. In paranoia, reason meets its match.

CHAPTER ELEVEN

The Politics of Dissent: André Brink

The 1960s and 1970s saw the deployment of a comprehensive censorship apparatus in South Africa. In the forefront of opposition to censorship stood the novelist André P. Brink. While Brink cannot be said to have stood alone, his position was in two senses exemplary: he exemplified the dissident Afrikaans intellectual rejecting the tutelage of a government that claimed to be protecting the interests of the Afrikaner people; and he took a stand that was consistent, principled, and uncompromising in an exemplary way.

Brink's writings on censorship fall into two groups. The first group belongs to what he calls the *strydperk*, the phase of more or less naked confrontation between dissident writers and official censors. The second group belongs to the 1980s, when the grip of the censors on books and newspapers, if not on films and television, began to relax as part of a gradual liberalization in which—as we can now see in retrospect—not only South Africa but most of Eastern Europe was participating.[1]

WRITER AND STATE

When Brink reflects on the relationship between the writer and the state, it is not only the South African state he has in mind. In his writings of the 1970s he is clearly making an effort to align himself as a dissident writer with dissident writers elsewhere, particularly in Eastern Europe, and to see censorship, and in general the repression of dissent, as inherent in the nature of state power. The South

African state is, in his view, typical of all authoritarian states in the pressure it exerts toward conformity.

Acknowledging the power of the state, Brink quotes from the Afrikaans poet N. P. van Wyk Louw a parable on the countervailing power of the writer. On the eve of his execution, a condemned writer is visited in jail by the head of state. The tyrant promises him a reprieve if he will recant. Convinced that "in the end" he will be the winner, the writer refuses. How can he be so sure he will win, asks the tyrant? Because the tyrant has found it necessary to visit him, he replies (*M*, p. 56).

In Brink's earlier model, as the parable indicates, writer and state are locked in irreconcilable antagonism. The writer may lack material power, but this lack is balanced by his power to annex the kudos of a lone hero resisting persecution. This powerless power is enough to put him on an equal footing with the state. In the long run, indeed, he triumphs, if only because his version of the truth will outlast his foe's. "Let this be a warning to *our* authorities," Brink writes in 1974 (in an essay whose thesis it is that "all great art is offensive"): "in the struggle between authority and artist it is always the artist, in the end, who wins. Because his voice continues to speak long after the members of the relevant government . . . have been laid to rest" (*LS*, p. 64, 67).

In this model, the antagonism between writer and state is straightforward. The writer tries to tell his truth and the state tries to stifle him; or the state offers seductions to which the writer either succumbs or replies with a truth-affirming No. His exemplary, guiding figure is Antigone, "the first rebel of Western tradition." "Antigone's key word is: NO! But it is a paradoxical thing, for she really means: YES!" (*M*, p. 62).

In the second model, which begins to develop in the late 1970s, the relationship between writer and state becomes more complex and more dialectical. Brink returns to the example of Antigone. Like Antigone, the writer obeys the higher authority of his own conscience, wherever it may lead him. A tension inevitably ensues between himself and the state. This tension may for a while be "healthy," to the extent that "reasonable opposition" may lead him to examine his conscience and refine his insights. However, interference from outside may reach a point where it begins to affect his ability to work. This is a point of crisis, but also of paradox. The state appears to have gained the upper hand; yet in fact, in stifling the writer, it is unwittingly putting its own health in danger.

How should the writer respond when such a point of crisis is reached? Brink rejects the option of

> a direct answer on the same level . . . on which the authorities or the people *(volk)* issue their threats and ultimatums. The writer simply does not function, as writer, within the same dimension. . . . He should not even try to think in terms of immediate, practical consequences. A book cannot begin to fight against a sword on a battlefield. If the book does indeed in the end win, it is precisely because [the writer] refuses to take up the same weapons as his opponent. . . . The writer's answer lies in the first place in the quality of his work. He must not allow anything to affect this. . . . Even anger must be distilled into something lasting. (*LS*, pp. 115–17)

Thus in the later model the writer and the state, although necessarily asserting different mandates and starting from different positions, are not, in a wider view, doomed to be antagonists: a level of healthy reciprocal criticism is possible, a level that benefits society in general. It is only when criticism turns into repression that the two become enemies and the earlier, simpler model is in effect reentered.

The later model is elaborated most fully in an essay entitled "Censorship and Literature" (1982). Trying to imagine a dynamic able to accommodate both a writer whose claims to unbounded freedom of expression may threaten anarchy, and a state whose conception of the general good may lead it to trample on individual interests, Brink—clearly gesturing toward the the advanced democracies—suggests that "an intricate [enough] system of checks and balances" would allow their co-existence.

What happens all too often in reality, however, is either that power seeks greedily to extend itself, compelling the writer of conscience to protest; or that, feeling threatened by the writer, the state reacts by mobilizing atavistic forces against him. "This is when taboo, which fulfills a creative and possibly indispensable function in primitive society, expresses itself in the form of censorship: what used to be constructive and wholesome now becomes destructive and a symptom of sickness."

In taking this step, the state fails to recognize that the intellectual, and in particular the writer, is in fact an organ developed by society to respond to the need of the whole for self-understanding. "His domain is that of meaning, not of healing. But unless he performs his function and performs it well, and unless his diagnosis is heeded, healing will not be possible." A healthy society is capable of facing the writer's diagnosis, "but if it is sick it may dread the vision of itself offered by [him]. In this case a mortal sickness would remain undiagnosed." "The creative mind . . . guarantees growth and development and health in a community," while censorship "represents the protective mechanisms and processes of the social organism in a state of excessive, cancerous development" (M, pp. 233–36, 248).

The contrast Brink sees between a state of tension that is in essence constructive and a destructive mutation of tension into repression is further underlined in an essay published in 1984.

> The totalitarian order depends for its very existence on a precarious equilibrium. Without the heretic, the rebel, the writer, the state crumbles: yet by tolerating him, the ruler equally well seals his fate. At least by implication, [in George Orwell's *1984*] Big Brother's mighty system disappears because he wanted to eradicate the dissident—but could not do without him. (*LS*, p. 165)

Whereas the metaphor underlying Brink's earlier and simpler model is one of battle, the metaphorics underlying the later model are of disease. Society is a body that has developed a special organ whose function is diagnostic of the health of the whole. When the body is in reasonable health, it tolerates and benefits from the functioning of this organ. But in a condition of hypertrophic repression it will, through agencies of state, reject those of its own organs that cause it most unease, trying to kill off the messenger who brings the bad tidings. Yet once this is achieved, collapse from unchecked disease is a foregone conclusion.

THE CONTEST

Thus far I have represented Brink's writings on censorship as an analytical account in which he, as theorist of the conflict between writer and state, occupies a position above the contending parties. But in fact his position is more complex. As critic-essayist, and therefore in some sense as judge, he is outside the fray; as writer making a polemical intervention he is one of the parties to the fray. In occupying positions both of judicious distance and of commitment, he mirrors the doubled identity of the censor. For the censor is charged with embodying the standards sketched out by the state (and therefore with occupying the position of a hypothetical ideal citizen) while at the same time acting as judge.

What is the polemical content of Brink's respective models?

In the earlier model we can distinguish seven elements which, together, constitute a myth of the writer as hero of resistance.

1. The couples through whom Brink dramatizes the opposition between writer and state—condemned prisoner and tyrant, Antigone and Creon, Winston Smith and Big Brother—represent, on the one side, overwhelming power and deadly intent, on the other, indomitable steadfastness despite powerlessness and isolation.

2. The contest itself is unequal and in fact anomalous in nature. "A book cannot enter the field of battle against a sword." "The writer simply does not function, as writer, within the same dimension [as the state]" (*LS*, p. 116).

3. The contest is morally clearcut. The state upholds "the great Conspiracy of the Lie," while the writer accepts no compromise with the lie. "Unless [the authorities] are prepared to change, . . . we shall go all the way . . . in making sure that their lies are exposed, . . . that truth will prevail." For, like Antigone, the writer "affirm[s] a higher Order" (*LS*, pp. 67, 93; *M*, pp. 194, 62).

4. The stakes are high. "Where the writer is allowed only the freedom to pronounce the letters from A to M, his word immediately acquires a peculiar weight if he risks not only his comfort but his personal security in choosing to say N, or V, or Z. Because of the risk involved, his word acquires a new resonance: it ceases, in fact, to be 'merely' a word and enters the world as an act in its own right" (*M*, p. 164–65).

5. Victory for the writer is inevitable (this is the paradoxical other side of the anomalousness of the contest).

6. Confrontation is inescapable. This is so not only because the writer's vocation drives him to follow his conscience but because,

being coupled to him as a kind of shadow, the state will not permit him to ignore it.[2]

7. Finally, the writer never initiates confrontation: he enters the fray only in response to outrages on the part of the state, or to efforts by the state to silence him.

In the later model, where the underlying metaphoric opposition is between sickness and health, the myth is not so much of the hero armored in truth as of the physician who moves unharmed in the midst of contagion, contagion which may at one moment manifest itself as a malignant cancer, at another as "fatal folly" or madness (*M*, p. 194).

Why does the state find it so hard to coexist with its own best members? Again Brink quotes Orwell: "The object of power is power" (*LS*, p. 158). He proceeds: "Power . . . is narcissist by nature, striving constantly to perpetuate itself through cloning, approaching more and more a state of utter homogeneity by casting out whatever seems foreign or deviant" (*M*, p. 173). Pointing to the closed character that language took on in Stalin's Russia, Brink proposes that it is one of the most compelling duties of the writer to destroy simplistic polarities and open up complexities (*M*, p. 202–3). Complexity inevitably angers the modern heirs and perverters of rationalism, who "fear the harm it can do to their devastatingly logical systems and tyrannies" (*M*, p. 217). It is in the nature of the state to gravitate toward homogeneity and impose homogeneous conformity on its citizens; the presence of a skeptical, diagnostic intelligence in the social body awakes its antagonism at an almost instinctive level.

CONSCIENCE AND TRUTH

Brink refers repeatedly to Antigone as an exemplar of what the writer should be. She is the citizen who, prescribed to only by her own conscience, rebels against the state in the name of "the truth," of "a higher Order" (*M*, p. 62; *LS*, pp. 98, 115–17). But how does the writer gain access to this "truth"? Brink describes the process as follows:

> Deep inside him [the writer] apprehends a welter and a whorl of truth, a great confounding darkness which he shapes into a word;

surrounding him is the light of freedom into which his word is sent like a dove from the ark. In this way, through the act of writing, truth and liberty communicate. (*M,* p. 163–64)

The writer is, then, the bearer of the divine *logos*. To ignore his moments of illumination, to conceal the truth, is a betrayal of the divine within him. The truth that he bears demands to be told: "When the conspiracy of lies surrounding me demands of me to silence the one word of truth given to me, *that word becomes the one word I wish to utter above all others*" (*M,* p. 165).

Is the writer always an adequate vehicle for the truth entrusted to him? Brink does not dwell on this question. But he hints at two ways in which the writer can betray his mission: first, by subordinating his own aesthetic standards to lust for battle ("Even anger must be distilled to something lasting," *LS,* p. 117); second, by succumbing to the lure of uttering the forbidden simply because it is forbidden.

The prophetic role of the writer belongs more to Brink's first model than to the second. In the second, the writer's monopoly of truth is no longer absolute:

Once the exploration has been undertaken, once the statement has been encoded in writing, it has to be published, 'made public,' in order to test its relevance within the context of communal life. . . . [Truth] *has* to be private and individual to start with; but to become valid it must transcend the life of the individual. (*M,* p. 210)

Truth is now not just a matter of the writer's inspiration: it has to enter into a social dialectic to be tested for wider validity. A necessary condition for such a test, however, is the freedom of the writer to bring his truth before the public, publish it. In the first model, censorship bans the truth from reaching the people; in the second the censor merely bars the road to the attainment of truth.

But why does the state abhor the truth? Brink, writing with white-ruled South Africa and comparably authoritarian states in mind, does not have to answer the question in its general form. Founded on the lie, it is simply in the nature of tyranny to hate the truth.

In the truth embedded in the writer's word lies that ineffable power feared so much by tyrants and tyrannies and other agents of death that they are prepared to stake everything they have against it. For they know only too well that no strategy or system can ever, finally, resist the word of truth. (*M*, p. 195)

Hating the artist's truth, the tyrannous state tries to obliterate it. Nevertheless, one way or another, "truth will out." As an instance of this dictum Brink recalls Osip Mandelstam, martyr to the truth of the Stalinist state, whose words had to be preserved in memory by his wife for thirty years before they could be published (*M*, p. 167). *Ars longa:* let the South African state be warned. "It is always the artist, in the end, who wins."

MADNESS AND LIES

"*Whom the gods wish to destroy. . .* : this must have been a spontaneous reflection in the minds of many as they saw the eruption of violence in Soweto in June, 1976," wrote Brink in 1976 (*M*, p. 128). *Mad* is a word Brink often applies to South Africa of the apartheid years; *sick* is another. The writer stands on the side of health and sanity, the state on the side of sickness and madness.

Though Brink has claimed for the writer the role of diagnostician of society's sickness/madness, he does not—at least in his writings on censorship—produce a diagnosis of what, at the most fundamental level, ails apartheid South Africa. Instead we get a catalog of quick, yet verbally excessive characterizations, marked less by clinical coolness than by shudders of horror. South Africa is "a demented world. . . , [a] swamp of violence and hysteria" (*M*, p. 152) with "an insane structure" (*M*, p. 201), beset by "a sickness of the mind. . . , a psychosis of fear" (*M*, p. 205), "a psychosis about a 'state of emergency'" (*LS*, p. 91). It is a nation of "Gadarene swine" (*LS*, p. 150); the Afrikaner is "a political and cultural schizophrenic" (*M*, p. 95), while the censorship apparatus is "[a] social organism in a state of excessive cancerous development," "the nucleus of a cancerous cell which divides and subdivides and multiplies rapidly to endanger the whole body" (*M*, pp. 236, 249). It is as though the author has been infected by the violence of the state, and infected at the very level of his language. If the state is diseased, its disease has begun to communicate itself.

Accusations of madness seek to infirm the antagonist's response in advance by situating the response outside rational discourse. To the extent that they close off the entry of the antagonist into dialogue, they predict and indeed invite retaliatory violence, which in turn acts as a confirmation of their diagnostic truth. Much the same can be said about accusations of lying when lying is treated not as a trick or scheme or strategy of disputation but as the manifestation of an evil essence, the essence of power itself ("We live in an age of the Lie," *LS*, p. 90).

THE 1980s

The polemical battle waged by Brink against the South African censors, the men and women dubbed by Breyten Breytenbach "the gray ones," lost its urgency as the 1980s wore on and the censorship of works of literature in particular began to relax. Brink's first comment on the thaw was cautious: "[The] puff-adder may only be *playing* dead." In the unfolding situation he sensed an unfamiliar dilemma. The new freedom being allowed to writers was clearly part of a public relations act. "But is that a reason to fall silent, and thereby play even more neatly into the hands of the powers-that-be?" (*M*, p. 256). The game seemed to be moving into a new and subtler phase, whose rules Brink was not as yet sure he knew.

In the meantime, Brink ruminated, could it be concluded that writers had won the first and more naked round of the struggle? Perhaps. But might it not also be that the authorities had decided that naked antagonism toward intellectuals was counterproductive? Might it not be that the energies of the security organs were being diverted toward more pressing matters? Might it even be that, in an age of television, the government had decided it had overestimated the importance of writers? Whatever the explanation, the initiative had clearly been lost. This is the sobering note on which Brink concludes the 1985 preface to his book on the *strydperk*, the period of struggle (*LS*, p. 11–12).

THE CENSORS

How did the censors themselves see the developing situation? In 1980, J. C. W. van Rooyen, an academic lawyer, had been appointed to chair the Publications Appeal Board, the highest tribunal of the censorship system. Though Van Rooyen did not initiate a sharp change of course, his tenure was undoubtedly marked by a more conciliatory attitude toward writers and academics. In a book he later published on the workings of the system, he disclosed, in so many words, that after the banning of the respected novelist Etienne Leroux's *Magersfontein, O Magersfontein!* in 1978—a rancorous affair that had left many moderate Afrikaners with a bitter taste in their mouths—it had been recognized by the more prudent men in the government that the censorship apparatus needed an overhaul.[3]

In the *Magersfontein* case, the board had adopted a highly confrontational posture toward those Afrikaans intellectuals who had come forward to testify on behalf of Leroux's novel. The banning of the book, with the clear proof it gave that the censors were determined to continue to apply the most conservative standards, threatened to alienate even middle-of-the-road Afrikaans academics and intellectuals. The prospect of the defection of this crucial element of its support almost certainly influenced the government in its appointment of Van Rooyen.

In his book, Van Rooyen discreetly admitted that the censors had played too partisan a role in South African intellectual life of the 1960s and 1970s. "Tension between authors and a large section of the public reached a crisis point between 1960 and 1978," he wrote. The new, corrective policies of his own tenure would permit "strong protest," being "based on the philosophy that it is often in the interests of state security to permit the expression of pent-up feelings and grievances" (*CSA*, p. 14–16). In practice this would mean that publications with "a sophisticated likely readership" would be passed "in spite of . . . material expressing hatred against the authorities," such works being treated as "useful safety-valves for pent-up feelings" (*CSA*, p. 115).

It was the policy decision hinted at here—the decision that the stringency of the censorship could be relaxed because novels and poems had been reassessed and found to pose no threat to the existing order after all, and might indeed constitute a "useful safety-valve" where disaffected intellectuals could let off steam within the ambit of an educated and predominantly white middle class—that in the mid-1980s gave Brink cause to ponder. His oppositional writings and those of other disaffected Afrikaners were, it seemed, in the process of being relegated to the category of what in the Soviet Union was called permitted dissent.

The calculations that led to a change of policy on censorship were strategic and political in nature: they had little to do with morality or with community standards, and nothing to do with respect for what Brink calls "the truth." In these calculations, the issue for the authorities was no longer whether the existence of certain offensive or otherwise undesirable writings should be tolerated within the borders of South Africa, but whether (white) South Africa could afford recurrent polarizing crises over symbolic but otherwise insignificant issues—in other words, whether a people holding on to power only tenuously could afford the political consequences of internecine violence between writers and censors.

In the event, as white rule passed through its waning years, mechanisms for control over expression lost both credibility and power. A new constitution was negotiated, including a bill of rights guaranteeing freedom of expression. Books whose very possession had been a criminal offense emerged in the bookstores in gaudy display. The censorship *apparatchiks*, while continuing discreetly to draw their salaries, adopted the lowest of profiles. Brink, it would seem, had been right: the artist, if he is patient enough and persistent enough, always wins, or at least emerges on the winning side. The way was open for a hundred flowers to bloom. If they failed to bloom, there would be no more gray ones at whose door to lay the blame.

CHAPTER TWELVE

Breyten Breytenbach and the Reader in the Mirror

ADDRESSING THE STATE

One of the major poems in Breyten Breytenbach's collection *Skryt*[1] is entitled "Letter from Foreign Parts to Butcher" ("Brief uit die vreemde aan slagter"), subtitled "For Balthazar." *Skryt* did not appear in South Africa. Published in the Netherlands in 1972, the book was banned for distribution in South Africa. In banning it, the responsible committee of the Publications Control Board singled out "Letter from Foreign Parts" and the appended list of names of persons who had died in police detention, reading the poem as having "very strict reference" to then Prime Minister Balthazar John Vorster and interpreting its ending as an accusation against the white man and particularly the Afrikaner.[2]

Breytenbach incorporated several poems from *Skryt* into the 1977 collection *Blomskryf* (Flower-write), which was passed for distribution in South Africa. However, "Letter from Foreign Parts" was not among them. It is this poem for which, during his trial on charges of entering South Africa illegally with the purpose of recruiting saboteurs to a militant underground organization, he apologized in 1975: "I would specifically like to apologize to the Prime Minister for a crass and insulting poem addressed to him. There was no justification for it. I am sorry."[3]

Since the first half of the poem is obscure to the point of being cryptic, it is likely that the committee of censors came to its decision on the basis of the second half of the poem alone, where the torture and killing of detainees by the security police is referred to in unambiguous terms, and B. J. Vorster is directly addressed as the butcher/obstetrician presiding over their deaths. But this is no reason for ignoring the first half of the poem, which is one of Breytenbach's most intensely worked-out treatments of death and resurrection and belongs intimately with the accusations of the second half.

Lazarus, the man who came back from the dead, has been a central figure in Breytenbach's poetic mythology.[4] The first half of the Butcher poem, without naming Lazarus, is spoken in the voice of a man resurrected from the grave/cell, acquainted with death under torture, and thus entitled to accuse Vorster in the name of "the rearisen prisoners of Africa." By its own power, but also by gathering about itself Breytenbach's earlier figurations of the Lazarus-poet, it attempts to establish poetic authority to speak in the name of the *gemarteldes* (the tortured and martyred) of John Vorster Square (security police headquarters), whose names (some fifteen of them) are given in an appendix to the poem. In its I-address, the poem therefore implies two different readers: a reader directly addressed, "jy" (you), butcher Balthazar, but also an invisible third person, a reader over the shoulder, a "prisoner" ready to question Breytenbach's authority to speak as I for him.

The language of the poem progresses from being difficult in a typically modernist manner to being quite plain. This is not only because the poem is designed to grow more and more naked as it builds up to its denunciation (the poet in the person of a history yet to be written, pointing a finger at the oppressor) but because it takes over the language of the security police at their most shameless and cynical, presenting lies as lies in the arrogant certainty that, while no one will believe them, no one will dare repudiate them (I refer to official accounts of detainees jumping out of windows in fits of remorse, slipping on bars of soap and killing themselves, hanging themselves by their own clothing, and so forth).

> I stand on bricks before my fellow-man
> I am the statue of liberation
> who with electrodes on the balls
> tries to scream light in the dusk
> I write slogans in a crimson urine
> over my skin and over the floor

I stay awake
suffocating on the ropes of my entrails
slip on soap and break my skeleton
murder myself with the evening newspaper
tumble out of the tenth floor of heaven
to salvation on a street among people

When Vorster's security police explained a prisoner's death by saying that he had slipped on a bar of soap, the unstated continuation was: And we defy any court in the land to reject that explanation. It has been one of the linguistic practices of totalitarianism to send out coded messages whose meaning is known to all parties, and then to use the censors to enforce a literal interpretation of them, at least in the public arena. Thus "slipped on a bar of soap" was known by all parties to mean "died under torture," but its public interpretation was nevertheless forced to remain "slipped on a bar of soap." When, as here, Breytenbach parodies the codes, his unstated continuation is: Here I create an arena in which the codes are unmasked and denounced. His challenge therefore takes place on the grounds of power itself: against police power, protected from denunciation and reprisal, he sets the power of rhetoric (a skill with words) employed for the purpose of mockery on a public stage. It goes without saying that the motive for banning the poem was, by denying it a public stage, by reasserting control over public staging, to deny it the power of its superior rhetoric to unmask the codes.

But this is where the position of a speaker speaking "uit die vreemde" (from strange parts, from abroad) raises difficulties of a moral as well as of a practical order. Both speaker and poem (published abroad) are operating outside the jurisdiction of the rival power (the police, the censors), as they are operating outside the speech community and political community they address. Is the challenge therefore not morally empty? It is not farfetched to interpret Breytenbach's return to South Africa in 1975 as an existential response to this question, an act by which the poet placed himself on the same footing as the enemy, ready to play out the myth of humiliation, incarceration, and rebirth into the authority of the reborn—a myth not solely Christian in its currency—on which the poem draws.

The attack on Vorster in the poem is twofold. First, he is denounced as the boss of the torturers and killers and therefore as the one who will have to answer to history for their actions:

> say it to me now, butcher
> before the thing becomes a curse
> before it is left to you to plead only by mouth
> of graves
> before the rearisen prisoners of Africa

Insofar as the Lazarus-poet writes his prophetic history of the future here, he is prophesying the reversal of jurisdiction, the inevitability of the judge-executioner becoming the accused. But insofar as the poem itself, as an utterance, an act, and a challenge, places Vorster in the dock, it attempts to bring that future about. In effect Breytenbach claims a power that Vorster, even as self-proclaimed steersman of the state, lacked—the power to make the future come about.

The second prong of Breytenbach's attack is more radical. Picturing the scream of pain issuing from the dying prisoner as a bloody birth in the hands of the butcher-obstetrician, he asks:

> does your heart also tighten in the throat
> when you grasp the extinguished limbs
> with the same hands that will stroke your wife's secrets?

Secrets: Breytenbach might as well have written *secret parts.* The exposure to public gaze is not just of the forbidden secrets of the torture chamber, not just of the (putative) private revulsions of B. J. Vorster himself (the irony is complex here: Breytenbach asserts that Vorster has a conscience and dares him to deny it), but of the mysteries (forbidden to the public gaze by decency itself) of the Vorster marriage bed. The poem is a low blow, a dig at the private parts, not of the man, but of his defenseless wife; an insult to male honor, more rather than less offensive when one considers the age of its targets (Balthazar and Tini were in their mid-fifties in 1972). The excess of the poem is an excess of intimacy.

BREYTENBACH AND THE FORBIDDEN, 1964–1975

Without implying that "Letter from Foreign Parts" by itself gave rise to the animosity against Breytenbach that led to a nine-year (rather than the expected seven- or five-year) sentence, one can assert that, as an insult—that is, as intentionally aggressive and transgressive speech—aimed at Vorster, the security police, and the community whose interests they protected, the poem had its real-world consequences. But it was not Breytenbach's first transgression. In writings dating back to 1964 he had made one attempt after another, with gathering audacity, to turn transgressive speech into transgressive act.

In Breytenbach's first collection (1964), the poem "Breyten Prays for Himself" (*YMS,* pp. 14–15) comes closest to naming the forbidden of what goes on at the hands of the police. In the person of a white bourgeois who wants no more than to slide through life without trouble, he distances himself from those "others" who

> May be arrested, Shattered
>> Stoned
>> Hanged
>> Scourged
>> Used
>> Tortured
>> Crucified
>> Interrogated
>> Placed under house arrest. . .
> Banned to dim islands to the end of their days
> Languish in dank holes. . .
> But not *Me*
> But us never give Pain or lament

In *Kouevuur* (Cold-fire) (1969) the targeted figure of authority is the emperor Tiberius, casting an eye (an "imprisoned" eye) over the seas where his ships sail "an ordered world"

> so that in the evenings—when the red god
> behind the headland leaves a red toga in the breakers—
> in company and pretension of fat-arse senators
> he [can] blessedly wade
> the volumes of his white body
> in the torpid fresh water of his marble swimming pool[5]

The whiteness of Tiberius alerts us that we are reading an allegory of white rule in South Africa. But—except perhaps for the demotic "vetgat" (fat-arse)—the poem lacks a barb: it settles for a mixture of fascination with and revulsion at the stillness of imperial power.

In the allegory of the surrealistic prose piece *Om te vlieg* (To Fly) (1971), white South Africa is a huge institution for the mentally ill, its gardens patrolled by a caretaker wearing a butcher's jacket who shoots patients for misbehaving.[6] A murderous regime presides over a landscape of mass extinction in the name of law and order.

This apocalyptic vision is presented through the eyes of a patient confined inside his blind "white" vision. "God is on the side of prison guards, butchers, and male nurses," he tells himself piously. His greatest pleasure is a private one, defecating. But even that has dangers: using old papers to wipe his backside, he has to be careful not to read them, for they may be "forbidden fruit, . . . subversive propaganda, . . . books of poetry and other declarations of superfluous freedoms." As trouble mounts in the world outside him, he cuts off his penis, cuts out his tongue, puts out his eyes, retires into his mind (*OV,* pp. 33, 19).

Thus Breytenbach achieves a kind of repudiation of the South African order by splitting and casting off a self-confessing, storytelling self who belongs in spirit to it. But then, as if to ensure that the extent of his self-denunciation is not overestimated, he brings back an authorial self to explain his intent:

> Although this essay does not wish to be symbolic, it is to me a representation of our specific cancer and leprosy, our highly civilized refinement and putrefaction that can motivate and explain away murder and mass murder, imprisonment and torture procedures. Daily we passed Auschwitz by train but we did not see the smoke, we looked across the bay at Robben Island but thought it was a leper colony. (*OV,* p. 92)

This anxious authorial intervention does much to subvert the transgressive force of the text—not inconsiderable, given the limitations on public discourse in South Africa of the early 1970s—by in effect repudiating its authority, an authority won by its own fictional power.[7]

Besides "Letter from Foreign Parts," *Skryt* contains several poems of straightforward denunciatory content, for instance, "The Promised Land" (*S,* p. 20). The problem such poems raise for their author—particularly in view of their publication abroad—is that, while they are transgressive, all they can be said to transgress in the end is a certain decorum of address. They cannot be said to become acts, in the sense of completing themselves in the world as the poem on Vorster does. Relying on a rhetoric of abjuration, they remain within the rhetorical realm and so are always vulnerable to being trumped by yet more violent rhetoric.

The strategy Breytenbach sometimes follows as an alternative to frontal rhetorical assault is irony (in such poems as "Life in the Earth," *S*, pp. 22–23). But irony—speaking the enemy's language and seeming to identify with the enemy—particularly when it is sensitively done, raises an unsettling question: is the ironic poem merely a second-best substitute for the private diaries of the tyrant, or does the tyrant truly not know his mind as intimately as the poet does? If the latter, what is the source of the secret sympathy of poet for tyrant? In particular, to repudiate white South Africa, does one first have to be, in one's marrow, a white South African?

The implications of such questions as these are lived out by Breytenbach in the act of writing in the "bastard language" Afrikaans,[8] the language of a split, doubled self. "Letter from Foreign Parts" has to be written in the language of the tyrant, spoken only in the land of the tyrant, yet at the same time the mother-tongue: "I write poetry in afrikaans language of bodyspasms: brew-smell / of my first milk, grain of my father's fingertips" (*YMS*, pp. 20–21). The attack on the Afrikaner has to be an attack on himself, and has to entail a movement back to origins that holds terrible regressive perils. In his poetry Breytenbach has lived out in the most intense way the paradox of being and not being of the Afrikaner tribe.

Before *'n Seisoen in die paradys* (A Season in Paradise), the memoir of a visit to South Africa with his wife in 1973, could appear in Afrikaans, the author had to accept the excision of passages that alarmed or offended his South African publisher.[9] In bowing to that veto, he in effect returned to native ground, reentered the arena of the enemy's discourse and power. But whatever the crippling effect of the veto, Breytenbach was now at least able to implicate himself in his denunciation as both subject and object:

> We South Africans, we will go on haunting the world forever. We are, all of us, slightly nuts, there is a bleeding crack running through

each of us. . . . We are mad, all of us. . . . We are maimed, we are only half human, but we know it, we are mad and realize that we are mad. (*SP,* p. 203)

It is of course "Breytenbach" speaking, but also the Cretan liar. And even if his self-denunciation here is intended as mad speech, the words with which the address ends are clearly intended to cast aside the cloak of madness: "By taking cognizance of the nature of the struggle we are involved in and share . . . we expand our humanity and our language" (*SP,* p. 160). The madness, he seems to say, is not really his own: to the extent that it is real madness, it belongs to other people. Breytenbach may be branded by the scar-like birthmark of a mad formation, and by a second scar (like a whiplash) left by the mad behavior around him ("I too . . . have . . . been placed in the humiliating position of being subjected to the discriminating system I despise," *SP,* p. 166), but not by madness itself. Whatever the nature of his own implication, it continues to elude him.

Hence his recourse, in the same book, to a *deus ex machina*, a savior who will end the reign of madness and institute a new era. To this messiah he plays the role of visionary John the Baptist:

> I say unto you, from the heart of the country
> he will come to you, one of you . . .
> and where he goes a way will be paved
> and women will drop their stitches
> and fire will emerge barking from the barrels of
>   guns
> houses will grow black
> fig trees will wither
> he will command armies
> he will avenge injustice
> and settle old scores . . .
>
> some of you will of course—it's in a man's nature—
> lie down on your stomachs like bloated worms . . .
> offering . . .
> anything, "anything, master Kaffir, no
> matter what, anything but death, oh, my own
> mashter Kaffir"
> he will be wearing a gorgeous smile
> and a halo and a Sten [gun] and he will
> not harm the sparrows of the veld[10]

I have pointed to a shuttling or lurching movement in Breyten-bach between poems of rhetorical denunciation with a certain emp-tiness at their heart, and poems of ironic identification with the enemy. The poem quoted, loose and occasional though it is, corre-sponds to the unsettled position of a poet to whom both speaking from outside and speaking from inside are sources of unease. In essence it is about reversal and about settling scores: the slave be-comes master, while the arrogant master embraces the self-abasing, sickening baby-speech of the powerless, a language beneath lan-guage. The poem invokes a magical, comic-book violence to bring about a millennium in which there will be an end to restlessness and division.

THE PRISON WRITINGS

"Imagine a dialogue of two persons," writes Mikhail Bakhtin,

> in which the statements of the second speaker are omitted, but in such a way that the general sense is not at all violated. The second speaker is present invisibly, his words are not there, but deep traces left by these words have a determining influence on all the present and visible words of the first speaker. . . . Each present, uttered word responds and reacts with its every fibre to the invisible speaker, points to something outside itself, . . . to the unspoken words of an-other person. . . . The other's discourse . . . is merely implied, but the entire structure of speech would be completely different if there were not this reaction to another person's implied words.

Such *hidden polemic* and *hidden dialogue* Bakhtin identifies in all of Dostoevsky's mature novels. He goes on:

> By no means all historical situations permit the ultimate semantic authority of the creator to be expressed without mediation in direct, unrefracted, unconditional authorial discourse. When there is no ac-cess to one's own personal "ultimate" word, then every thought, feeling, experience must be refracted through the medium of some-one else's discourse, someone else's style, someone else's manner.[11]

It would be as naive in Dostoevsky's case as in Breytenbach's to imagine that a change in "historical situation," specifically the removal of external censorship, would have resulted in "direct, un-refracted, unconditional authorial discourse" from which hidden dialogue would have been absent. Censorship, or at least the office of the censor, is not the sole "semantic authority" at which Bakhtin hints. Nevertheless, the work Breytenbach did in the period 1975 to 1982 was carried out under extraordinarily restricted circumstances, and, even though there was opportunity for subsequent revision, bears traces, not always in the most obvious way, of a censored origin. As Bakhtin's concept of hidden contestatory dialogue has opened up hidden areas of Dostoevskian discourse, it also alerts us to the possibility of hidden contestation in Breytenbach. In approaching Breytenbach's prison writings, I will concentrate my attention on the hidden voices *against* which Breytenbach speaks.[12]

Even in detention before his trial, Breytenbach was allowed to write. The poems that emerged were published as *Voetskrif* (Footscript), dedicated to his principal interrogator at the latter's insistence: "You dedicate this to me and I allow you to have it published," as Breytenbach reports (*TC*, p. 156).

In prison, writing was permitted on four conditions: (1) what Breytenbach wrote was to be shown to no other prisoner or warder, (2) it would not be smuggled out, (3) each piece would be handed in for safekeeping when completed, and (4) all notes would be destroyed (*TC*, pp. 156–57, 159). Four volumes of poetry from the prison period, making up Parts 1–4 of *Die ongedanste dans* (The Undanced Dance), were eventually published.[13]

In *True Confessions* Breytenbach recalls his position as a prisoner vis-à-vis his censor: "A bizarre situation ... when you write knowing that the enemy is reading over your shoulder..., knowing also that you are laying bare the most intimate and the most personal nerves and pulsebeats in yourself to the barbarians, to the cynical ones who will gloat over this" (p. 159). Besides this testimony, there is textual evidence that at least some of the poems of *Die ongedanste dans*, as originally published, are, in the most obvious sense, censored.[14]

Not all the poems of the prison period are built around dialogue, whether open or hidden, with the oppressive censor-figure. Nevertheless, even poems that seem monological express less a determination to manage the discourse monologically than a repudiation of dialogue with a detested other.[15] Other poems exhibit a complex and even ambivalent attitude toward dialogue. "(Language Struggle)," for instance, addresses rebellious black children in the lifeless monotone of *baasskap:*

> You will learn to be obedient,
> obedient and subservient.
> And you will learn to use the Language [Afrikaans],
> you will use it subserviently[16]

In Bakhtin's terms, the poem is "double-voiced" but not dialogical: Breytenbach the writer takes possession of the enemy's discourse for a purpose of his own, in this case a grimly satiric one. I have already pointed out how double-edged this procedure can be (something Breytenbach is well aware of): the one taking possession can also be the one taken possession of. Side by side with this poem we may set "The Conquerors":

> because we would not acknowledge them as human
>   beings
> everything human in us dried up
> and we cannot grieve over our dying
>   because we wanted nothing more than fear and
>   hatred
> we did not recognize the human uprising of
>   humanity
> and tried to find rough solutions but too late
> the flowers in the fire
> no one is interested in our solutions—
>
> we are past understanding
> we are of another kind
> we are the children of Cain[17]

The monotone of the last four lines, spoken from from a kind of death in life, pronounces a prospective epitaph on the Afrikaner. But in the earlier lines there is a rudimentary dialogue as the words of the other ("human," "humanity") creep in. These two poems thus speak for two moments in the history of white domination: a moment of somnambulistic blindness and a first moment of fatalistic self-knowledge.

But why does Breytenbach the exile, the prisoner, the rejected son, say "we" in both poems when he means "you"? Why disguise accusation as self-accusation, or take on the voice of someone he repudiates? Can his grim opponents not speak for themselves in their own voices, issue their own ukases, their own despairing epitaphs? Why must he speak for both sides? Why surrogate monologue, but also, why hidden dialogue, why even a hidden polemic with an enemy who at heart belongs among the dead?

The answer is a practical one. The speech of the real-life enemy against whom Breytenbach directs himself is never as naked as Breytenbach would wish it to be. On the contrary, it is evasive, circuitous, self-censored. What Breytenbach performs in these poems is, in effect, ventriloquism, preemption of the enemy's speech, presentation of the enemy's case in heightened, parodic, and self-damaging form in a medium—the discourse of the intelligentsia—to which the enemy had no access.

Because the confrontations they play out are so one-sided, it is hard to detect in poems like these any real creative engagement on Breytenbach's part. In contrast, consider "—'n Spieëlvars—":[18]

> you! you! you!
> it's you I want to talk to cunt
> you ride around without saddle or driver's licence
> in the gutters and yards of my verses
> my death
>
> you dig around with your lance in the white
>   acres
> where I wanted to multiply
> for nation and fatherland
> (but soon there will be nothing left of either)
> my death. . .
>
> you with your yellow eyes you with the left
>   hand
> you with the missing beard you with the sand
> over the tongue
> with your nine-year sentence like a pregnancy
> I'll make you a widower chop-chop
> for you make me shiver
> you make plaints
> of pleasure
> you lay the cold caress of your lips
> here upon my life
> and *here* and *here*
> come kiss me in my mouth
> you hand-picked dog

come and draw lines through my young
   thoughts
and pack stones over my slack wings

must I wait still longer?
o my snow-white shadow Death
o my own secret police
I will be yours forever
and you are
mine mine mine

The imprint of Sylvia Plath lies heavily on this poem, not least
in its jagged rhythms and wild swings of mood. But from Plath
Breytenbach has learned something deeper too: that I and You need
not stand for fixed positions. The I here is the vindictive, death-
ridden jailer and killer, but he is also the self that longs for liberation, despite seeing no other form of liberation looming but death.
You is clearly Breytenbach the prisoner in derided form; but he is
also the persecuting figure of the oppressed slave, as well as the
lover death whose perverse embrace (*"here* and *here"*) he craves,
the ever-watchful other in the mirror, and, finally, a figure with
wings that answer to his own useless wings. In fact, many of the
avatars of the I—censor, secret policeman, winged guardian-
persecutor—are shared by the You. What we have is a true mirror-
poem, *spieëlvers,* in which it is not clear what is self, what image.
It is a poem of accelerating dialogical frenzy in which it is no longer
possible to say what *position* the self holds: the interchange between self and other is, in effect, continuous.

THE MIRROR PHASE

The figure of a man looking into a mirror dominates Breytenbach's
prose works of the prison and immediate post-prison period, *Mouroir* and *True Confessions of an Albino Terrorist.*[19] The surface of the
mirror and the surface of the blank page touched by the pen become
indistinguishable: moving the pen, the self both creates and calls
up on that surface a sardonic counter-self mocking his effort to see
himself transparently, telling him to try again. The figure in the
mirror behaves, in fact, just like the security policemen who, at the
time of Breytenbach's first interrogation, put two blank pages in

front of him and told him to write down the story of his life; then, when he was finished, read them, tore them up, and told him to try again (*TC*, pp. 28–29).

Breytenbach drafted *True Confessions* by talking into a tape recorder, a process he calls "this jumbletalk, this trial." What truth will emerge from the trial? Whatever it is, it cannot be foretold: only in the process of dialogue between self and mirror/page will it reveal itself. If there were to be a new interrogation, a new trial, the truth would come out differently: "I'd be somebody else—as sincere, as keen to help, as obsessed by the necessity to confess," he confesses. Thus the posture of the writer before the mirror/page is assimilated with the attitude of the cooperative prisoner under interrogation. And who is the interrogator? In a sense, the reader who wants to read what Breytenbach has to say; but also the self that writes itself. "Mr. Investigator[:] *you* know that we're always inventing our lives. . . . You and I entwined and related, parasite and prey[,] image and image-mirror."[20]

Thus far we have only another ingenious poststructuralist figure of textual self-production. But the African connection has not been elided. Coming to the end of his long confession, Breytenbach writes:

> Mr. Investigator . . . I see you now as my dark mirror-brother. We need to talk, brother I. I must tell you what it was like to be an albino in a white land. We are forever united by the intimate knowledge of the depravity man will stoop to. (*TC*, p. 260)

Who is the interrogator here? Not (or not only) the white twin who polices the psyche but a black mirror-brother, just as haunting and persecutory, an accomplice in a historical crime in which there have been two parties, not one. Simone Weil is a good guide here. In every destructive act, she writes, the self leaves behind its traces. "A hurtful act is the transference to others of the degradation which we bear in ourselves."[21] Since in the process of suffering the victim takes into himself the degradation of the oppressor, the I becomes double, multiply double: interrogator and revolutionary, criminal and victim, colonizer and colonized, even censor and writer. The black in the mirror is not Other but other/self, "brother I."

The long talking in the empty room with which *True Confessions* began thus culminates, not in dialogue with the dark brother, but in the discovery that, before true knowledge can come about, dialogue must take place with the mirror. So when Breytenbach writes, in retrospect, that he does not regret having gone through the "underground" experience, the word is rich in significance, referring not only to his history as a secret agent and a prisoner, but to a history of blind burrowing that has led not into the light of liberation but instead to the illumination, the insight that light-seeking is a process of blind burrowing. "What one has gone through becomes a new corridor outlining the innards of the labyrinth; it is a continuation of the looking for the Minotaur, that dark centre which is the I (eye), that Mister I [mystery]" (*TC*, p. 87).

The white policeman, the black revolutionary: enemies brought together in the mirror. Is the mirror the place, then, where history is transcended? Does the dialogue with the mirror-self extend to dialogue between the selves in the mirror? Can dialogue with the mirror be trusted to proceed peaceably, or will it degenerate into hysterical confrontation such as we see in "Place of Refuge" and again in the 1986 "Pretext" to *End Papers*, where control of dialogue is allowed to break down in a controlled experiment, and an exhibition is given of hysterical self-accusation, a spiraling descent into "the bottomless pit of deprecation and disgust"?[22]

These questions are beyond the scope of *True Confessions*. It is in *Mouroir*[23] that Breytenbach tries to put into practice—the practice of writing—the theory outlined in *True Confessions*. *Mouroir* is an assemblage of stories, parables, meditations and fragments linked by the coupled symbolisms of mirror and labyrinth. The text itself is the Ariadne's thread that Breytenbach spins behind himself as he advances through the labyrinth of his fictionalizing toward a meeting with something that is both the Self beckoning from the mirror—Mister I—and the monstrous Other who will never be recuperated into amity: Death.

Of course the merging of self with mirror-self is not achieved, the surface of the mirror/page does not melt away, the heart of the labyrinth is not attained. Instead, a new surface recurs at every turn, leading into yet another corridor of the labyrinth. The text moves forward by a process of metamorphosis of images, as in dreams. Text becomes coextensive with life: text will not end till writing ends; writing will not end till breath ends.

Despite its very private nature, *Mouroir* marks a step forward in Breytenbach's thinking and writing. By seeing or claiming to see *through* the hostile identity in the mirror, by making the surface of the mirror something that one goes *through*, an opening to an infinite progress, he has deferred the confrontation with his enemy twin, and further has turned this deferring into a model of textual production. On the basis of the moment of genesis he describes in *True Confessions*—the moment when the police interrogator returned his life-story to him with the comment "Try again"—he has constructed a program of writing indistinguishable from the theoretical justification for that program.

But the moment of "Try again" is not the only crux that his post-prison writing again and again rehearses. Out of the repertoire of memory, it repeats even more gallingly the moment of Breytenbach's confession to the court when pride had to be swallowed and humiliating apologies uttered, *and* when this self-humbling was nevertheless refused as not sincere enough to deflect a punitive sentence.

In his overt or public account of how he came to make this confession, Breytenbach says: "Without being political, it was an attempt to explain how I got to be standing where I was, without rejecting my convictions. Read it—you will also hear the insidious voice of the [security police] controller in it. It was in [his] hands a week before the trial commenced, and Vorster himself had it on his desk before it was read in court" (*TC*, p. 63).

Nowhere in his account does Breytenbach accuse the police, or B. J. Vorster, of trying to influence the trial magistrate. Nevertheless, the implication seems to be there that a deal was made (apologies, self-abasement, public acceptance of the authority of the patriarch in return for a lighter sentence) and that the deal was reneged on. Cryptically, Breytenbach writes: "It [is] not my intention [in *True Confessions*] to take revenge on a system or on certain people—at least, I don't think it [is]." And he goes on: "We are too closely linked for that."[24]

We are too closely linked? Have family ties ever been a barrier to revenge? The motive forces behind *True Confessions* and *Mouroir*—the main texts of Breytenbach's mirror-phase—are extraordinarily complex. Despite what he says, they do include a primitive desire to get back at the people who shut him up, as the torrents of name-calling—in which people's names are turned into, precisely, caco-phony (B. J. Vorster into Chief Sitting Bull, for instance, *TC*, p. 18)—attest. They also include a more cautious project—instigated, perhaps, by a realization of how infantile it is to throw excrement at those figures of power who reject his stories of himself—to incorporate the censor-figure into himself (calling it the figure in the mirror, calling it the I) and thus manage it. The success of this stratagem is doubtful: the test is *Mouroir*, and *Mouroir* finally dwindles into a doodling with Ariadne's thread, the Minotaur forgotten. Breytenbach is not without moments of clarity about how essentially magical his plan is for mastering the voice that says No. Writing is a way of survival, he writes. "But . . . at the same time it becomes the exteriorization of my imprisonment, . . . the walls of my confinement" (*TC*, p. 155).

One of the fates of confession since Rousseau—of secular confession at least—has been to spin itself out endlessly in an effort to reach beyond self-reflection to truth. In Breytenbach the task of taking charge of the process of self-reflection at first seems to the narrating self no more than a preliminary task to be performed (a sentry to be passed) before the real work, the real storytelling, can begin: in this case, the story of life underground. Only later does the realization dawn that getting to the real self (finding the Mystery I) is a life's task, like cleaning the Augean stables.

THE CENSOR

In his public, political persona, Breytenbach expresses attitudes towards censorship typical of the cosmopolitan, progressive intellectual. "Censorship is an act of shame . . . It has to do with manipulation, with power, with . . . repression." For the writer to consent to being censored is fatal. "It takes root inside you as a kind of interiorized paternalism. . . . You become your own castrator." "Once you submit to the thought restrictions of the power managers, enter their game, . . . they have already won the day."[25]

There is no hint in these post-prison utterances that, for a time at least, the policeman/censor of the imagination had been installed in Breytenbach as his mirror-self, and that writing had been, if not playing at the censor's game, at least playing a game with the censor. For public occasions this part of the story was censored out. What we have from Breytenbach is therefore a split account of censorship, split between what Leo Strauss calls the exoteric and the esoteric.[26] The exoteric account is constituted by public utterances of the kind I have quoted. In this account there is an unambiguous contest between a voice struggling to utter itself and a gag that stifles it; the censor is demonized. The esoteric account, the doctrine to be teased out of his more imtimate writings, is that the writer writes *against* and cannot write *without* a manifold of internalized resistances that are in essence no different from an internalized censor-twin, both cherished and hated.

In intense moments, writing can throw up evidences of bloody or asphyxiating struggles against blockages and resistances: gagged words gagged out. The voice struggles to breathe in, to breathe out, against intimate persecutory figures. Breytenbach's poetry, and particularly his poetry of the prison and immediate post-prison period, is writing of this kind. It may during this period have been necessary to him, for the sake of his life's enterprise, to denounce publicly his heritage and call himself a bastard, neither European nor African, afflicted with the schizophrenic consciousness of the bastard. But the very gesture of blaming, so widespread in his writing, mirroring the blaming of him by censor and judge, belongs to an ultimately futile strategy of demonization and expulsion. The poems that emerged with him from prison into the fresh air point to a much harder task: that of living with his daimon and his demons.

Notes

CHAPTER ONE

1. Kimberly W. Benston points to the importance of this "unnaming" process in mythology, where as part of a strategy of power a god may deliberately retreat from being named: "The refusal to be named invokes the power of the Sublime, a transcendent impulse to undo all categories . . . and thrust the self beyond received patterns and relationships into a stance of unchallenged authority." Benston finds this strategy of self-empowerment being used today by those African Americans, descendants of slaves, who unname or rename themselves. "I Yam What I Am: The Topos of (Un)naming in Afro-American Literature," *Black Literature and Literary Theory*, ed. Henry Louis Gates (New York: Methuen, 1984), p. 153.

2. Andrew Altman proposes an alternative framework of analysis for what in contemporary American parlance is called "hate speech" and in South Africa includes terms like *settler*. He suggests that such speech performs the illocutionary act of treating its object as a moral subordinate, someone whose interests are of less intrinsic importance and whose life is inherently less valuable than that of the speaker. "Liberalism and Campus Hate Speech: A Philosophical Examination," *Ethics* 103 (1993): 310.

3. "Toleration and Intellectual Responsibility," in Susan Mendus and David Edwards, eds., *On Toleration* (Oxford: Clarendon Press, 1987), p. 18.

4. "To respect others is not to think well or badly of them, but it is *at least* to abstain from injuring or destroying them, whether physically or morally" (my emphasis). Gabriele Taylor, *Pride, Shame, and Guilt* (Oxford: Clarendon Press, 1985), p. 81.

5. José Ortega y Gasset, *Meditations on Quixote*, trans. Evelyn Rugg and Diego Marin (New York: Norton, 1961), pp. 146–47.

6. See Etienne van Heerden, "Seur en kleur: Oor neo-sensuur, kwets-woorde en lesers," *Tydskrif vir Letterkunde* 24/4 (1986): 58-65. Van Heerden uses the term *suiwering* (purification) for the process.

7. David Saunders, "Copyright, Obscenity and Literary History," *ELH* 57 (1990): 431.

8. See David Edwards, "Toleration and English Blasphemy Law," in John Horton and Susan Mendus, eds., *Aspects of Toleration* (London: Methuen, 1985), p. 94.

9. The latter point is made by Richard Webster, *A Brief History of Blasphemy* (London: Orwell Press, 1990), p. 95.

10. John Milton, *Areopagitica*, ed. J. C. Suffolk (London: University Tutorial Press, 1968), p. 88.

11. Danilo Kis, "Censorship/Self-Censorship," *Index on Censorship* 15/1 (January 1986), 44.

12. This perverse case is made in respect of certain Russian writers by Lev Loseff, *On the Beneficence of Censorship* (Munich: Otto Sagner, 1984). Eugene Goodheart argues that in the case of D. H. Lawrence censorship may have been an enemy but was nevertheless "a necessary and empowering enemy." "Censorship and self-censorship in the fiction of D. H. Lawrence," in George Bornstein, ed., *Representing Modernist Texts* (Ann Arbor: University of Michigan Press, 1991), p. 230.

13. This argument relies in part on Freud's proposal that intellectual curiosity ("epistemophilia") has its origin in sexual curiosity, so that frustration of the child's sexual explorations may result in a stifling of the drive for knowledge. Freud's thinking on sexual curiosity seems to have moved toward this conclusion in the years 1905 to 1910, from the *Three Essays on Sexuality* to the essay on Leonardo. See Toril Moi, "Patriarchal Thought and the Drive for Knowledge," in *Between Feminism and Psychoanalysis*, ed. Teresa Brennan (London: Routledge, 1989), pp. 201–2.

14. Max Scheler, *Person and Self-Value*, ed. and trans. M. S. Frings (Dordrecht: Martinus Nijhoff, 1987), pp. 23–24.

15. *The City of God*, book 14, chap. 16. Translated by John Healey (2 vols.; London: Dent, 1945), vol. 2, p. 47.

16. In distinguishing between "extreme" and "moderate" conservative positions, I follow H. L. A. Hart, *Law, Liberty and Morality*, rev. ed. (Oxford: Oxford University Press, 1981), pp. 48–49, vii, 19. "Intolerance, indignation, and disgust" is Patrick Devlin's phrase: "[these] are the forces behind the moral law." *The Enforcement of Morals* (London: Oxford University Press, 1965), p. 17.

17. Hart, *Law, Liberty and Morality*, p. 12.

18. James Mill, quoted in John C. Rees, *John Stuart Mill's On Liberty* (Oxford: Clarendon Press, 1985), p. 32.

19. Ronald Dworkin, *Taking Rights Seriously* (Cambridge, Mass.: Harvard University Press, 1977), pp. 242–43, 245.

20. Ibid., pp. 253–54.

21. Ibid., pp. 255, 258.

22. John Stuart Mill, *On Liberty*, ed. Gertrude Himmelfarb (Harmondsworth: Penguin, 1974), pp. 68, 63.

23. Jeremy Bentham, *Principles of Morals,* chap. 16, sec. 1; chap. 1, secs. 3–4; chap. 2, sec. 19; quoted in Rees, *John Stuart Mill's "On Liberty,"* pp. 30, 44.

24. Cf. John Gray, *Mill on Liberty: A Defence* (London: Routledge, 1983), p. 29; Susan Mendus, *Toleration and the Limits of Liberalism* (London: Macmillan, 1989), p. 121.

25. See David Edwards, "Toleration and English Blasphemy Law," p. 86. See also Albert Weale, "Toleration, Individual Differences and Respect for Persons," in Horton and Mendus, eds., *Aspects of Toleration,* p. 22.

26. *Collected Works,* X:179, quoted in Rees, *John Stuart Mill's "On Liberty,"* p. 45.

27. Jeremy Waldron, "Mill and the Value of Moral Distress," *Political Studies* 35 (1987): 413, 414, 417.

28. When censure is not only expressed but acted upon by bodies that hold an effective monopoly on particular media of expression (via, for instance, distribution or retail networks), freedom of expression may be stifled as effectively as under outright legal ban. This is a significant problem for anyone who tries to distinguish sharply between censorship and censure, or what Frederick Schauer calls public and private censorship. On the other hand, monopoly holders can argue that in exercising censure they are simply asserting their own freedom of expression rather than stifling anyone else's. The issue is discussed at length in Schauer, *Free Speech: A Philosophical Enquiry* (New York: Cambridge University Press, 1982), pp. 119–25.

29. Bernard Williams, ed., *Obscenity and Film Censorship* (Cambridge: Cambridge University Press, 1981), p. 55.

30. Dworkin, *A Matter of Principle* (Cambridge, Mass.: Harvard University Press, 1985), pp. 336–37.

31. Herbert Marcuse, "Repressive Tolerance," in Robert P. Wolff, Barrington Moore, and Herbert Marcuse, *A Critique of Pure Tolerance* (Boston: Beacon Press, 1969), pp. 90–91.

32. Dworkin, *A Matter of Principle,* p. 352.

33. John Ellis, "On Pornography," in Mandy Merck, ed., *The Sexual Subject* (London: Routledge, 1992), p. 146.

34. See Joel Feinberg: "There is no more unfortunate mistake in the discussion of obscenity than to identify [obscenity] either in meaning or in the scope of designation, with pornography." *The Moral Limits of the Criminal Law,* vol 2: *Offense to Others* (New York: Oxford University Press, 1985), p. 127.

35. Ibid., p. 1.

36. Ibid., p. 123.

37. Max Scheler, *Person and Self-Value,* p. 32. Cf. Howard Poole, "Obscenity and Censorship," *Ethics* 93 (1982): 40; Feinberg, *Offense to Others,* p. 2.

38. At first sight, this categorical distinction between offenses and

harms may seem to go contrary to the taxonomy of harms in U.S. law, where obscenity—along with "insults to human dignity, such as racist or sexist speech"—figures among "injuries to communal sensibilities," which are in turn listed under the third of the categories of harms, "Reactive Harms." The difference is, however, only terminological: as Rodney A. Smolla points out, reactive harms may not, under the U.S. Constitution, be used as a basis for restricting freedom of speech. In this respect a reactive harm is thus like "extreme offense." "Academic freedom, Hate Speech, and the Idea of a University," *Law and Contemporary Problems* 53 (1990): 204–5.

David Edwards finds "any absolute distinction between offense and harm impossible to sustain." However, Edwards includes shame, guilt, anger, and mortification under the category of offense, as "shocks which can cause long-lasting or permanent disorientations or impairments" (even though, he concedes, they may equally well be beneficial in the long run). "Toleration and English Blasphemy Law," p. 86.

39. See Jacqueline MacGregor Davies, "Pornographic Harms," in Lorraine Code, Sheila Mullett and Christine Overall, eds., *Feminist Perspectives* (Toronto: University of Toronto Press, 1988), pp. 127–28; Carole Pateman, "Sex and Power" *Ethics* 100 (1990): 405; Steven Alan Childress, "Reel 'Rape Speech': Violent Pornography and the Politics of Harm," *Law and Society Review* 25 (1991): 209; Richard B. Miller, "Violent Pornography: Mimetic Nihilism and the Eclipse of Differences," *Soundings* 69 (1986): 345; Andrew Altman, "Liberalism and Campus Hate Speech," 302–17. A comparable argument is made on the grounds that, as an aid to masturbation rather than an act of communication, pornography is less speech-like than thing-like. Frederick Schauer, *Free Speech*, pp. 182–85.

40. The private sphere, says Jacqueline Davies, is "historically . . . a sphere of oppression for women": for reasons of strategy feminists should therefore eschew the legal argument that pornography invades their privacy ("Pornographic Harms," p. 132). This contrasts with the classically liberal argument advanced by D. N. MacCormick, that persons who commit indecent acts are "waiving their own privacy" rather than intruding on the privacy of others. "Privacy and Obscenity," in Rajeev Dhavan and Christie Davies, eds., *Censorship and Obscenity* (London: Martin Robertson, 1978), p. 87.

41. Margaret Intons-Peterson and Beverly Roskos-Ewoldsen claim that "research conducted with male subjects has consistently shown that exposure to the assaultive sexuality of violent pornography is associated with lowered opinions of women, increased tolerance of violence toward women, and increased likelihood of actual aggression against women in laboratory settings." "Mitigating the Effects of Violent Pornography," in Susan Gubar and Joan Hoff, eds., *For Adult Users Only* (Bloomington: Indiana University Press, 1989), p. 218. This claim is supported with references to numerous empirical studies. On the other hand, noting an equally

long list of case studies, Marcia Pally claims that "no reputable research today finds a causal link between sexual imagery and violence. . . . None of the wealth of scientific literature on the subject supports the claim . . . that sexual imagery triggers aggression." "Out of Sight and Out of Harm's Way," *Index on Censorship* 22/1, no. 146 (January 1993): 5. These two positions are not absolutely incompatible; but to reconcile them requires extraordinary logical scrupulosity, more perhaps than an essentially political debate can cope with. The question of whether pornography indeed causes sexual violence is further complicated by suspicion on the part of some feminists about the rules and procedures of empirical demonstration itself.

42. "Society as a whole is harmed in its moral fiber when the moral status of all its members is not considered of equal worth by all the members of the society." Eva Feder Kittay, "Pornography and the Erotics of Domination," in Carol Gould, ed., *Beyond Domination* (Totowa, N.J.: Roman and Allanheld, 1984), p. 161. Similarly, John Horton points to a failure among liberals (specifically, members of the Williams Committee) to understand the argument made by conservatives, but also by some feminists, that pornography may in itself *be* a harm—that "the harm of pornography lies in its nature and not its effects." "Toleration, Morality and Harm," in Horton and Mendus, eds., *Aspects of Toleration*, p. 131.

43. "Because women, in particular, have internalized male versions of their sexuality for so long, it is difficult for them even to begin to articulate the nature of their suffering from pornography, let alone how their perceptions of their own sexuality differ from male proscriptions about it." Joan Hoff, "Why Is There No History of Pornography?" in Gubar and Hoff, eds., *For Adult Users Only*, p. 33. Carol Smart labels this position "standpoint feminism." Standpoint feminism privileges the views of women "who have collectivized and reinterpreted their experiences through processes of consciousness-raising or similar political activity." "Unquestionably a Moral Issue: Rhetorical Devices and Regulatory Imperatives," in Lynne Segal and Mary McIntosh, eds., *Sex Exposed* (London: Virago, 1992), p. 197.

A novel version of the false-consciousness argument is given by David Dyzenhaus. Dyzenhaus uses J. S. Mill's *The Subjection of Women* as the "authoritative text," the one "with which *On Liberty* should cohere." In *The Subjection of Women* Mill asserts that men demand more from women than they demand of slaves: they demand a willingness, a complicity in their own subjection—in effect, false consciousness. A person who is not fully autonomous, argues Dyzenhaus, cannot be expected to testify one way or the other about harms done to her. David Dyzenhaus, "John Stuart Mill and the Harm of Pornography," *Ethics* 102 (1992): 540–43. Cf. J. S. Mill: "All men, except the most brutish, desire to have, in the woman most nearly connected with them, not a forced slave but a willing one, not a slave merely, but a favourite. They have therefore put everything in practice to enslave their minds"; "No other class of dependents have had their character so entirely distorted [as women] from its natural proportions by their relation with their masters." *The Subjection of Women* (Cambridge, Mass.: MIT Press, 1970), pp. 16, 22.

44. Jacqueline Davies, "Pornographic Harms," pp. 137, 135.

45. See, for instance, Feinberg, *Offense to Others*, pp. 69, 159–63.

46. Alasdair MacIntyre, *After Virtue* (London: Duckworth, 1981), p. 8. See also Jeffrey Stout, *Ethics after Babel* (Boston: Beacon Press, 1988), p. 205.

47. Susan Mendus, "Harm, Offence and Censorship," in Horton and Mendus, eds., *Aspects of Toleration*, p. 110.

48. Quoted in Mendus, *Toleration and the Limits of Liberalism*, p. 125.

49. Catharine MacKinnon, *Feminism Unmodified* (Cambridge, Mass.: Harvard University Press, 1987), p. 149.

50. John Horton, "Toleration, Morality and Harm," p. 132.

51. Mendus, *Toleration and the Limits of Liberalism*, p. 128.

52. Susan Sontag, *Styles of Radical Will* (London: Secker and Warburg, 1969), pp. 71–72.

53. For instance, Kathleen Mahoney proposes that the law should have no compunction about "prioritizing the needs of the impoverished, disempowered, and disadvantaged over those who are more privileged." "The Canadian Constitutional Approach to Freedom of Expression in Hate Propaganda and Pornography," *Law and Contemporary Problems* 55 (1992): 103.

54. Carol Smart, *Feminism and the Power of Law* (London: Routledge, 1989), pp. 12, 161.

55. See Carole Pateman, "Sex and Power," *Ethics* 100 (1990): 404; Smart, *Feminism and the Power of Law*, pp. 81, 130.

56. Pateman, "Sex and Power," 407.

57. Surveying U.S. Supreme Court judgments on pornography up to the early 1980s, Joel Feinberg finds that the court has "moved back and forth among our various legitimizing principles, applying now a liberal offense principle mediated by balancing tests and later a thinly disguised moralism, here flirting with paternalism, there sniffing for subtle public harms, and never quite distinguishing with clarity among them." *Offense to Others*, p. 166.

58. *Feminism and the Power of Law*, pp. 114–16, 123–25. It is telling that, in an otherwise well-informed survey of the feminist antipornography movement, Marcia Pally should misidentify MacKinnon as a "right-wing feminist." "Out of Sight and Out of Harm's Way," 4.

59. Luce Irigaray, *This Sex which is not One*, trans. Catherine Porter with Carolyn Burke (Ithaca, N.Y.: Cornell University Press, 1985), pp. 88, 129–30, 162.

60. *This Sex which is not One*, pp. 162–63.

61. Feinberg, *Offense to Others*, pp. 1–2. This is not to say that *in pro-*

pria persona, and not as interpreter of the law, Feinberg cannot give exceedingly fine analyses of inner states: see, for instance, his account of the embarrassment people feel when they watch sexual spectacles in groups (p. 19).

62. Because pornography challenges taboos imposed on us early in psychosexual life, says Richard S. Randall, we must expect a measure of inchoateness in our responses to it. However, if we group these inchoate stirrings under the heading of offense, then "patent offensiveness" is as good a legal criterion as we are likely to find for defining pornography. *Freedom and Taboo* (Berkeley and Los Angeles: University of California Press, 1989), p. 247.

63. Edward Westermarck, *The Origin and Development of the Moral Ideas* (2 vols.; London: Macmillan, 1924), vol. 1, pp. 21, 92–93.

64. Ibid., p. 9.

65. *Feminism and the Power of Law,* p. 118.

66. David Saunders points to a similar move in the 1979 Williams Report. Without invoking the erotic/pornographic distinction to separate the sheep from the goats, the Committee uses the criterion of whether or not a "mediating aesthetic consciousness" has intervened during the manufacture of the material. The test palpably favors written pornography, which is herewith, as Saunders remarks, in effect decriminalized, leaving photographic pornography out in the cold. "Copyright, Obscenity and Literary History," 441.

67. Sontag, *Styles of Radical Will,* pp. 56–58.

68. Georges Bataille, "Sade," in *Literature and Evil,* trans. Alastair Hamilton (London: Calder and Boyars, 1973), pp. 102–3.

69. "Obscenity law helps keep pornography sexy by putting state power . . . behind its purported prohibition on what men can have sexual access to." *Feminism Unmodified,* p. 162. Bataille writes: "Nobody, unless he is totally deaf to it, can finish *Les Cent Vingt Journées de Sodome* without feeling sick." "Sade," p. 99.

70. Linda Williams, "Fetishism and Hard Core," in Gubar and Hoff, eds., *For Adult Users Only,* p. 215.

71. Smart, *Feminism and the Power of Law,* p. 136.

72. Rosalind Coward, *Female Desire* (London: Paladin, 1984), pp. 59, 102, 75.

73. "Is not the most erotic potion of the body *where the garment gapes?" The Pleasure of the Text,* trans. Richard Miller (London: Cape, 1975), p. 9.

CHAPTER TWO

1. Though by no means as extreme, the South African system showed odd parallels with the Soviet system. Andrei Sinyavsky recollects finding no entry for *tsenzura,* "censorship," in a 1955 dictionary of foreign-derived

words in Russian: "The word 'censorship' was itself censored." Quoted in Marianna Tax Choldin and Maurice Friedberg, eds., *The Red Pencil* (Boston: Unwin Hyman, 1989), p. 94.

2. Quoted in Carlos Ripoll, *The Heresy of Words in Cuba* (New York: Freedom House, 1985), p. 36.

3. Leonard W. Levy, *Treason against God* (New York: Schocken, 1981), pp. 25–26.

4. George Mangakis, "Letter to Europeans" (1972), in George Theiner, ed., *They Shoot Writers, Don't They?* (London: Faber, 1984), p. 33.

5. Kis, Danilo. "Censorship/Self-Censorship." *Index on Censorship* 15/1 (January 1986): 45.

6. Lucien Febvre and Henri-Jean Martin, *The Coming of the Book,* trans. David Gerard (London: New Left Books, 1976), pp. 160, 84, 261; Elizabeth L. Eisenstein, *The Printing Press as an Agent of Change* (2 vols.; Cambridge: Cambridge University Press, 1979), vol. 1, p. 230; Alain Viala, *Naissance de l'écrivain* (Paris: Editions de minuit, 1985), p. 85.

7. Michel Foucault, "What Is an Author?" trans. Donald F. Bouchard and Sherry Simon, in Robert Con Davis and Ronald Schleifer, eds., *Contemporary Literary Criticism,* 2d ed. (New York: Longman, 1989), p. 268.

8. As regards this mystique, we may note that even well-educated people misunderstood the etymology of the word *author,* believing that it went back not only to Latin *augere,* to add something to something else— which it does—but also to Greek *autos,* self—which it does not. Thus there grew up around the word a field of connotations: the author was a man of authority, and his authority was backed by a certain parthenogenic power to create out of himself. See Viala, *Naissance de l'écrivain,* p. 276.

9. Tony Tanner, "Licence and Licencing," *Journal of the History of Ideas* 38/1 (1977): 10.

10. Quoted in D. M. Loades, "The Theory and Practice of Censorship in Sixteenth-Century England," *Transactions of the Royal Historical Society,* 5th series, vol. 24 (London: Royal Historical Society, 1974), p. 142.

11. In the sixteenth century, suggests Annabel Patterson, authors began to use "the indeterminacy inveterate in language" to evade censorship. Authors built ambiguity into their texts, while censors concentrated their attention on the ambiguous word or phrase. "Functional ambiguity," in both writing and interpretation, thus became a distinguishing practice of literature. *Censorship and Interpretation* (Madison: University of Wisconsin Press, 1984), p. 18. A succinct account of mechanisms of control used in Europe between the sixteenth and nineteenth centuries—of which institutional censorship is only the most blatant—is give in Robert J. Goldstein, *Political Censorship of the Arts and the Press in Nineteenth-Century Europe* (New York: St. Martin's Press, 1989), pp. 34–54.

12. Patterson outlines the tacit conventions signaled by the authorities in early modern England to allow authors to address contentious issues

without making it necessary for the authorities to take steps against them. *Censorship and Interpretation*, pp. 10–11.

13. Joseph Jacobs, quoted in Annabel Patterson, *Fables of Power* (Durham: Duke University Press, 1991), p. 17.

14. "Sometimes silence expresses more than whole discourses." *The Spirit of the Laws*, quoted in Patterson, *Censorship and Interpretation*, p. 9. Similarly, writing about films made under censorship in Poland, Jeffrey C. Goldfarb points out that silence on a particular live issue could be so complete that it called attention to itself as a political critique. *On Cultural Freedom* (Chicago: University of Chicago Press, 1982), p. 93.

15. Seamus Heaney, *The Government of the Tongue* (London: Faber, 1988), p. 39.

16. Thomas Carlyle, "The Hero as Poet. Dante. Shakspeare," in *On Heroes, Hero-Worship and the Heroic in History* (1841) (London: Chapman and Hall, n.d.), pp. 78–114.

17. Thus Terrence Des Pres suggests that, while many people may still "harbor heroic sentiments about what poetry is or ought to be," they do so nowadays only "quietly, in secret." "Poetry and Politics," *TriQuarterly*, no. 65 (1986): 20, 23.

18. Trilling defines "mature masculinity" as "a direct relationship to the world of external reality, which, by activity, it seeks to understand, or to master, or come to honorable terms with; and it implies fortitude, and responsibility for both one's duty and one's fate, and intention, and an insistence upon one's personal value and honor." "The Poet as Hero: Keats in His Letters," in *The Opposing Self* (London: Secker and Warburg, 1955), pp. 22, 24.

19. Ben Jonson, *Sejanus*, act 4; quoted in Patterson, *Censorship and Interpretation*, p. 52.

20. Mario Vargas Llosa, "The Writer in Latin America" (1978), in George Theiner, ed., *They Shoot Writers, Don't They?* p. 166.

CHAPTER THREE

1. As David Saunders has shown, the "deprave and corrupt" test derives from Victorian medical and administrative science in its mission of supervising the moral health of the populace, particularly that of the literate urban working class. As for the new literary-critical features of the act, Saunders points out that, in addition to the two criteria named, four other essentially literary-critical arguments were used by the defense and admitted by the bench. "Copyright, Obscenity and Literary History," *ELH* 57 (1990): 438–39; "The Trial of *Lady Chatterley's Lover*," *Southern Review* (Adelaide) 15 (1982): 165–70.

2. C. H. Rolph, ed. *The Trial of Lady Chatterley* (London: privately printed, 1961), pp. 70–72, 89–90, 159.

3. *Lady Chatterley's Lover* (New York: Modern Library, 1957), p. 252, hereafter referred to as *LCL*. Unless otherwise stated, all references are to this, the third version of the novel.

4. *A Propos of Lady Chatterley's Lover* (London: Mandrake Press, 1930), pp. 9–10.

5. Tylor, quoted in Mary Douglas, *Purity and Danger,* rev. ed. (London: Routledge and Kegan Paul, 1969), p. 13.

6. Rolph, *The Trial of Lady Chatterley,* p. 98.

7. David Saunders, for instance, writes of "the ridiculousness of [the] confessional antics" of the clergyman and the publisher who, during the 1967 prosecution of *Last Exit to Brooklyn,* testified that the book had tended to corrupt them. "The Trial of *Lady Chatterley's Lover,"* p. 166.

8. Rolph, *The Trial of Lady Chatterley,* pp. 253, 255.

9. The force of "bad language" that the gamekeeper exerts on Connie is clearest in the first version of the story. In one episode, Parkin/Mellors derides Connie's word "lover" and confronts her with himself as her "fucker." "'Fucker!' he said, and his eyes darted a flash at her, as if he shot her." *The First Lady Chatterley* (London: Heinemann, 1972), p. 108. This aggressive verbal act is directed not only by Parkin at Connie: as Evelyn J. Hinz points out, the baring of obscene words is also a baring of the teeth by Lawrence at his (British) readers. "Pornography, Novel, Mythic Narration: The Three Versions of *Lady Chatterley's Lover,"* *Modernist Studies* 3 (1979): 41.

10. For the first three, see Lawrence, *Selected Literary Criticism,* ed. Anthony Beal (New York: Viking, 1966), pp. 26–30, 32–51, 52–67. Hereafter referred to as *SLC.*

11. "The Lady's Dressing Room," "Cassinus and Peter," "A Beautiful Young Nymph Going to Bed," and "Strephon and Chloe." *Complete Poems,* ed. Pat Rogers (New Haven: Yale University Press, 1983), pp. 448–66.

12. For a detailed reading along these lines, see T. B. Gilmore, "The Comedy of Swift's Scatological Poems," *PMLA* 91 (1976): 33–41.

13. Lawrence writes: "There is a poem of Swift's . . . written to Celia, his Celia—and every verse ends with the mad, maddened refrain: 'But— Celia, Celia, Celia shits!'" (*SLC,* p. 29). Huxley published his essay on Swift in 1929. See *On Art and Artists,* ed. Morris Philipson (New York: Harper, 1960), pp. 168–76.

14. Letter to Lady Ottoline Morrell, 28 December 1928, *SLC,* p. 26; Introduction to *Pansies, SLC,* p. 29; *A Propos of Lady Chatterley's Lover,* p. 14.

15. See, for instance, David Burnley, *A Guide to Chaucer's Language* (Norman: University of Oklahoma Press, 1983), chap. 8.

16. At this point Lawrence writes most clearly under the influence of Frazer. To Frazer, what characterizes the savage is a failure to distinguish between *unholiness* and *uncleanness.* As Mary Douglas points out, by rel-

egating uncleanness to the kitchen and bathroom, Christianity makes it a matter of (secular) hygiene, leaving holiness as a purely moral/spiritual category (*Purity and Danger,* pp. 10–11). From this point of view—which Lawrence, with his nonconformist Christian background, seems to share—to revive what ought to be a matter of simple hygiene as a taboo with the force of religion (or superstition) behind it, is precisely a throwback to savagery.

17. See Rolph, *The Trial of Lady Chatterley,* pp. 221–24. At least one observer came away convinced that the jury failed to understand the prosecution's innuendoes. John Sparrow, "Regina vs. Penguin Books, Limited," *Encounter* 18/2 (February 1962): 35–43.

18. Georges Bataille: "Organized transgression together with the taboo make social life what it is. The frequency—and the regularity—of transgressions do not affect the intangible stability of the prohibition since they are its expected complement . . . just as explosion follows upon compression. The compression is not subservient to the explosion, far from it; it gives it increased force." Bataille quotes Sade: "The best way of enlarging and multiplying one's desires is to try to limit them." *Death and Sensuality* (New York: Walker, 1962), pp. 65, 48.

19. Accepting *Lady Chatterley's Lover* as an obscene book, rejecting the notion that obscenity needs to justify itself, Miller concludes: it is "a pity . . . that Lawrence ever wrote anything *about* obscenity, because in doing so he temporarily nullified everything he had created." *The World of D. H. Lawrence* (Santa Barbara: Capra Press, 1980), pp. 175–77. Censorship may have been Lawrence's enemy, writes Eugene Goodheart, but it was "a necessary and empowering enemy," since it preserved the "transgressive force" of sexuality in his books. "Censorship and Self-Censorship in D. H. Lawrence," in George Bornstein, ed., *Representing Modernist Texts* (Ann Arbor: University of Michigan Press, 1991), p. 230.

CHAPTER FOUR

1. I refer to two collections of essays by MacKinnon: *Feminism Unmodified* (Cambridge, Mass.: Harvard University Press, 1987), cited hereafter as *FU;* and *Toward a Feminist Theory of the State* (Cambridge, Mass.: Harvard University Press, 1989), cited hereafter as *FT.* Some of the essays in the second collection are revised versions of essays in the first. Under the normal protocols of scholarship, one would always prefer the revised version to the original. In the present context, however, I cannot ignore revisions that may constitute self-censorship. Where relevant I therefore note differences between earlier and later versions.

2. I call the unmodulated male-female opposition in MacKinnon simplistic; other critics have labeled it essentialist. See the review of *Feminism Unmodified* by Katharine T. Bartlett in *Signs* 13 (1988): 883; the review of *A Feminist Theory of the State* by Carrie Menkel-Meadow in *Signs* 16

(1991): 603; and Carol Smart, *Feminism and the Power of Law* (London: Routledge, 1989), p. 76. MacKinnon concedes at one point that "people do not always know what they want, have hidden desires and inaccessible needs, lack awareness and motivation, have contorted and opaque interactions, and have an interest in obscuring what is really going on" (*FT*, p. 153). But her analysis of pornographic transactions takes no account of this complexity.

3. This is not to say that MacKinnon wholly ignores print pornography: see, for instance, the case history discussed in *FU*, pp. 185–86.

4. Under the latter statute, pornographic materials "are actionable . . . only by women coerced to make [these materials] or assaulted because of them." *FU*, p. 236 n. 35.

5. Women fighting pornography have to contend with the "individuated, atomistic, linear, isolated, tortlike—in a word positivistic—conception of injury" enshrined in obscenity law, a conception unsuited to dealing with the way in which pornography harms women: "not *as* individuals in a one-at-a-time sense, but as members of the group 'women'" (*FU*, p. 156).

6. *Totem and Taboo*, in *Standard Edition*, vol. 13, ed. and trans. James Strachey (London: Hogarth Press, 1955), pp. 18, 311.

7. "To define the pornographic as that which is violent, not sexual, as liberal moral analyses tend to, is to trivialize and evade the essence of this critique, while seeming to express it" (*FU*, p. 160). Rape and pornography "are not the erotization of something else, like power; eroticism itself exists in this form. Nor are they perversions of art and morality. They are art and morality from the male point of view" (*FT*, p. 113).

8. Laura Mulvey, "Visual Pleasure and Narrative Cinema," in Bill Nichols, ed., *Movies and Methods*, vol. 2 (Berkeley and Los Angeles: University of California Press, 1985), p. 307.

9. Seminar of 1953–54, quoted in Betty Cannon, *Sartre and Psychoanalysis* (Lawrence: University Press of Kansas, 1991), pp. 237–38. The puzzling blindness to Sartre in feminist film criticism is remarked by Gertrud Koch in "Ex-changing the *Gaze:* Re-visioning Feminist Film Theory," *New German Critique* 34 (1985): 149.

10. "The essence of relations between consciousnesses is not the *Mitsein* [of Heidegger]; it is conflict." *Being and Nothingness*, trans. Hazel Barnes (New York: Washington Square Press, 1966), p. 555; cited hereafter as *BN*.

11. Martin Heidegger, *Sein und Zeit*, 16th ed. (Tübingen: Niemeyer, 1986), pp. 171–72 (sec. 36). See also Martin Jay, *Downcast Eyes* (Berkeley and Los Angeles: University of California Press, 1993), pp. 274–75.

12. Jay, *Downcast Eyes*, p. 288.

13. Cf. Jay, *Downcast Eyes*, pp. 327–28, 541–42.

14. Cf. MacKinnon's reservations about depictions of "normal dominance and submission . . . , of female-only nudity . . . or even of mutual sex in a social context of gender inequality" (*FU*, p. 157).

15. Declaring the male point of view objective is part of the dizzying strategy of male power. "Objectivity . . . creates the reality it apprehends by defining as knowledge the reality it creates through its way of apprehending it" (*FT*, p. 114). How should feminism respond? "To be realistic about sexuality socially is to see it from the male point of view, and to be feminist is to do so with a critical awareness that that is what one is doing. Because male power creates the reality of the world to which feminist insights . . . refer, feminist theory will simply capture that reality but expose it as specifically male for the first time" (*FT*, pp. 124–25). Feminist theory exposes reality as a male construct, but refuses to fall into the trap of constructing an opposing reality and thereby set itself up as the rival—and mirror—of male power. Here MacKinnon follows Irigaray: "[Woman power] clearly cannot be a matter of substituting feminine power for masculine power. Because this reversal would still be caught up in the economy of the same . . . [as] a phallic 'seizure of power.'" Luce Irigaray, *This Sex which is not One*, trans. Catherine Porter with Carolyn Burke (Ithaca, N.Y.: Cornell University Press, 1985), pp. 129–30.

16. "So long as it's not sex and violence: Andrea Dworkin's *Mercy*," in Lynne Segal and Mary McIntosh, eds., *Sex Exposed* (London: Virago, 1992), pp. 216–30.

17. See, for instance, *FU*, p. 177.

18. *FT*, p. 124. MacKinnon's critique of the foundations of scientific knowledge renders all the more surprising her recourse to the literature of experimental psychology to support her case. "Our critique of the objective standpoint as male is a critique of science as a specifically male approach to knowledge. With it, we reject male criteria for verification," she writes (*FU*, p. 54). Yet elsewhere she quotes "statistical realities" to show that "all women live all the time under the shadow of the threat of sexual abuse" (*FT*, p. 149). "Recent experimental research on pornography," she writes, "shows that materials covered by our definition [of pornography] cause measurable harm to women through increasing men's attitudes and behaviors of discrimination in both violent and nonviolent forms" (*FU*, p. 187). Pages 144–45 of *FT* consist of a review of laboratory findings on violence as a trigger to male sexual arousal.

19. MacKinnon's defense against critics who argue that she should devote some of her energies to the harms of advertising is brief, weak, and evasive: "They want a law to regulate ads maybe?" (*FU*, p. 223).

20. The most notorious of these photographic records is in the film entitled *Snuff*, in which, on camera, a woman hired as a production assistant—not an actress—is stabbed, dismembered, and eviscerated. An account is given in Leo Groarke, "Pornography: From Liberalism to Censorship," *Queen's Quarterly* 90 (1983): 1110–11.

21. Here MacKinnon relies heavily on the autobiography of Linda Marchiano, the principal actress in *Deep Throat* (see *FU*, pp. 127–33), from which it emerges that certain of the acts in the film were performed under

duress. What is more unsettling—or more real, in MacKinnon's sense—is that filming these acts and exhibiting the film seems to have been part of a project of humiliation aimed personally at Marchiano by the man who made the film. See the fuller account given by Susan Griffin in *Pornography and Silence* (London: Women's Press, 1981), pp. 112–15. Anne McClintock argues that MacKinnon misrepresents Marchiano's story to fit her own case; see "Gonad the Barbarian and the Venus Flytrap: Portraying the Female and Male Orgasm," in Segal and McIntosh, eds., *Sex Exposed*, pp. 128–29.

22. As Marcia Pally observes, "Woman and men working in the sex industries are not stupid: it makes good economic sense to make a sex film at a fee of $3000 for two days' work rather than to clean office lavatories or sling meat patties at McDonald's for minimum wages." "Out of Sight and Out of Harm's Way," *Index on Censorship* 22/1 (January 1993): 6.

23. Leo Bersani: "To be penetrated is to abdicate power." Quoted in Mandy Merck, "From Minneapolis to Westminster," in Segal and McIntosh, eds., *Sex Exposed*, p. 78.

24. Julian Pitt-Rivers, "Honour and Shame," in J. G. Peristiany, ed., *Honour and Shame* (Chicago: University of Chicago Press, 1966), p. 26.

25. In a culture that takes shame seriously, says Gabriele Taylor, loss of honor can mean "total extinction of the individual, . . . total loss of identity." Shame is "a moral emotion," as long as morality is taken to include "personal morality, a person's own view of how he ought to live and what he ought to be." *Pride, Shame, and Guilt* (Oxford: Clarendon Press, 1985), pp. 56, 76–77.

26. "Unquestionably a Moral Issue: Rhetorical Devices and Regulatory Imperatives," in Segal and McIntosh, eds., *Sex Exposed*, pp. 189, 196.

27. Conversely, according to Lynne Segal, Japan has plenty of violent pornography yet very little sex crime. Introduction to Segal and McIntosh, eds., *Sex Exposed*, p. 7. On the basis of data from a range of societies, Peggy Reeves Sanday concludes that rape is common only where interpersonal violence is a way of life; where interpersonal violence is rare, rape is rare. "The Social Context of Rape," *New Society* 61, no. 1037 (30 September 1982): 542. The argument that pornography promotes sexual violence is not supported by statistics from countries like Ireland and South Africa, where violence against women has been rife despite stringent laws against pornography; see the researches of Aryeh Neier, cited in Joel Feinberg, *The Moral Limits of the Criminal Law*, vol 2: *Offense to Others* (New York: Oxford University Press, 1985), p. 149. The most extensive bibliography of research into the contentious question of the relation between pornography and sexual violence is given in Ronald E. Berger, Patricia Searles, and Charles E. Cottle, *Feminism and Pornography* (New York: Praeger, 1991), pp. 143–68.

CHAPTER FIVE

1. The quotations from Erasmus and Luther are taken, respectively, from Roland H. Bainton, *Erasmus of Christendom* (London: Collins, 1972), p. 217; Richard L. DeMolen, *Erasmus* (London: Edwin Arnold, 1973), p. 131; and Bainton, p. 261. Duhamel is quoted in Walter Kaiser, *Praisers of Folly* (London: Gollancz, 1964), p. 39.

In letters of 1519, Erasmus decries the attacks on him by the theologians of Louvain as "insane" and the gathering strife as "a deadly pestilence." "I would never have believed theologians could be such maniacs. One would think it was some disastrous infection. And yet this poisonous virus, starting in a small circle, spread to a larger number, so that a great part of this university was carried away by the spreading contagion of this epidemic paranoia." Quoted in James McConica, "The Fate of Erasmian Humanism," in Nicholas Phillipson, ed., *Universities, Society, and the Future* (Edinburgh: Edinburgh University Press, 1983), p. 45.

2. Michel Foucault, *Madness and Civilization*, trans. Richard Howard (New York: Random House, 1967), p. x.

3. Jacques Derrida, "Cogito and the History of Madness," in *Writing and Difference*, trans. Alan Bass (Chicago: University of Chicago Press, 1978), p. 34. Cited hereafter as *WD*.

4. Quoted in Shoshana Felman, *Writing and Madness*, trans. Martha N. Evans and Shoshana Felman (Ithaca, N.Y.: Cornell University Press, 1985), p. 43. Cited hereafter as *WM*.

5. Ibid., pp. 48–49.

6. Ibid., p. 122, quoting Lacan, "La méprise du sujet supposé savoir."

7. The Greek is, *o gar logos emas erei*, 'logos demands it' (*Republic*, s.607). *Erei* is from the verb *aireo*. *Logos airei* is the idiom for 'reason shows,' but in a legal context *aireo* means 'convict.' *Republic*, ed. James Adam, 2d ed. (Cambridge: Cambridge University Press, 1963), vol. 2, pp. 418–19; *The Republic*, trans. H. D. P. Lee (Harmondsworth: Penguin, 1955), pp. 384–85.

8. *Things Hidden since the Foundation of the World*, trans. Stephen Bann and Michael Metteer (Stanford: Stanford University Press, 1987), p. 286, hereafter cited as *TH*. Abbreviations employed for other works by Girard are: *DDN* for *Deceit, Desire, and the Novel*, trans. Yvonne Freccero (Baltimore: Johns Hopkins University Press, 1965); *VS* for *Violence and the Sacred*, trans. Patrick Gregory (Baltimore: Johns Hopkins University Press, 1977); *DBB* for *To Double Business Bound*, trans. Paisley N. Livingston and Tobin Siebers (Baltimore: Johns Hopkins University Press, 1978).

9. The double character of paranoia has always struck observers as paradoxical. On the one hand, it manifests itself in behavior whose rationale is unclear to the outsider. On the other, it presents a highly intellectual front, a front of rationality or pseudo rationality. It is highly judgmental, though its judgments seem to be without basis. For this reason, Lacan sug-

gests in his 1932 study of paranoia, pre-Freudian psychiatry focussed on the question of judgment in paranoia, treating paranoia as a syndrome whose distinguishing characteristic is that "[the faculty of] judgment [becomes] perverted." Jacques Lacan, *De la psychose paranoïaque dans ses rapports avec la personnalité* (Paris: Seuil, 1975), p. 293.

10. See *DDN*, pp. 110–12; Homer O. Brown, "Oedipus with the Sphinx," *MLN* 92 (1977), 1103.

11. *TH*, p. 299; Cesareo Bandera, "The Doubles Reconciled," *MLN* 93 (1978), 1010.

12. *VS*, pp. 64, 56. In the present context, a critique of the eschatalogical thrust of Girard's anthropology is superfluous. The most obvious criticism is that Girard's grand theory lacks an empirical basis and may even be unfalsifiable. As Homer O. Brown points out, the universality of the social practices that Girard explains by the hypothesis of mimetic violence, crisis, scapegoating, and sacrifice raises the questions: Was there one single, originary "event" which was then imitated elsewhere? How was this original event diffused? Or did originary events occur spontaneously everywhere? One is ineluctably led to postulate a single human nature and to minimize cultural difference. "Oedipus with the Sphinx," 1102–3.

At another level, Girard's claim to be revealing a single, final truth is precisely the kind of violent act that he describes as occurring in epochs when belief in universal truths is crumbling, and thus provides an example of—indeed represents—the very violence it seeks to transcend.

13. *The Praise of Folly*, trans. Hoyt H. Hudson (Princeton: Princeton University Press, 1941), p. 51. Page references are to this translation; when two page references are given, the second is to Erasmus's Latin, in *Stultitiae laus*, ed. I. B. Kan (The Hague: Nijhoff, 1898).

14. On the basis of 1 Corinthians 1:25, Erasmus makes of Paul—*tu moron tou theou*—a maniac in the Platonic sense. In his reading of Mark 3:21, Christ is suspected of being a madman by his own family. See M. A. Screech, "Good Madness in Christendom," in W. F. Bynum et al., eds., *The Anatomy of Madness* (London: Tavistock, 1985), vol. 1, pp. 26–27, 31, 34. On the links between Erasmus's folly, Christian theolepsy, and the Neoplatonic *furor divinus*, see Kaiser, *Praisers of Folly*, pp. 89–90.

15. Erasmus's phrase is in Greek: *oti ken epi glossa elthoi*, 'whatever comes to the tongue.' I. B. Kan glosses this from the *Adages: quicquid verbi temere in linguam . . . venerit*, whatever word comes at random to the tongue (*The Praise of Folly* 5/9).

16. Of the language of Erasmus's handbook on writing, *De copia*, Terence Cave writes: "His own analytic discourse reveals itself as figurative, caught in the tropical movement; the terminology of rhetoric is . . . subordinated to a sense of the virtually infinite possibilities of displacement inherent in a natural language. . . . The centrifugal movement which constantly asserts and reasserts itself . . . [is a] movement of discourse towards pleasure, towards a place of celebrations which is also a place of fiction."

De copia, completed in its first version in 1512, is more or less contemporary with *The Praise of Folly;* Cave argues convincingly that, particularly as a meditation on the nature of discourse, it deserves a prominent place in the Erasmian oeuvre. *The Cornucopian Text* (Oxford: Clarendon Press, 1979), pp. 24, 33, 9–10.

17. Playing on Horace's dictum that a writer of wit needs a reader with a discriminating nose, Erasmus in his prefatory letter suggests that *The Praise of Folly* will remain a closed book to readers with blocked noses. H. A. Mason takes over Erasmus's metaphor: Erasmus's irony, he suggests, has the evanescence of a subtle odor, and is lost in paraphrase; a fine nose for its nuances is the "key" to the work ("They Haven't Got No Noses!" *Cambridge Quarterly* 18 [1989]: 132–36). Similarly, Gerhard Schweppenhauser sees the goal of the critic to be to "unlock" the paradoxes of Folly ("Narrenschelte und Pathos der Vernunft: Zum Narrenmotiv bei Sebastian Brant und Erasmus von Rotterdam," *Neophilologus* 71 [1987]: 568). In the notion of the key that will unlock Erasmus's irony or paradox I detect an ambition to freeze it in a single, locked position. Here I diverge from both of these critics.

18. Desiderius Erasmus, *Adages,* trans. Margaret M. Phillips (Cambridge: Cambridge University Press, 1964), p. 357.

19. "Folly as Illusion," in Ernesto Grassi and Maristella Lorch, *Folly and Insanity in Renaissance Literature* (Binghampton: Medieval and Renaissance Texts and Studies, 1986), pp. 60–61.

20. "The Allegorical Fable," in Grassi and Lorch, *Folly and Insanity,* pp. 77–78.

21. Huizinga, *Erasmus* (Haarlem: Willink, 1936), pp. 81–82.

22. Elizabeth L. Eisenstein, *The Printing Revolution in Early Modern Europe* (Cambridge: Cambridge University Press, 1983), p. 247. Erasmus was well aware of this mechanism of appropriation. In a letter of 1520 to Pope Leo X, he cautions that the effect of attacks on Luther's writings is only "to provoke the world to read [them]" (DeMolen, *Erasmus,* p. 129).

23. Huizinga's book was commissioned by an American publisher and made its first appearance in English in 1924. Huizinga subsequently revised it twice for publication in the Netherlands. I cite the 1936 edition: *Erasmus,* pp. 204, 165, 164.

24. Stefan Zweig, *Erasmus [and] The Right to Heresy,* trans. Eden and Cedar Paul (London: Souvenir Press, 1979), pp. 9, 7. See also Thomas J. Schlereth, *The Cosmopolitan Idea in Enlightenment Thought* (South Bend: Notre Dame University Press, 1978), pp. xxii, 105; A. Bance, "The Idea of Europe: From Erasmus to ERASMUS," *Journal of European Studies* 22 (1992): 3.

25. Klaus Heydemann, "Das Beispiel des Erasmus: Stefan Zweigs Einstellung zur Politik," *Literatur und Kritik,* no. 169–70 (1982): 27–28, 34–35. Heydemann quotes a 1933 letter from Zweig to Hermann Hesse: "I have chosen as my helper in adversity Erasmus of Rotterdam, the man of

the center, the man of reason, ground between the millstones of Protestantism and Catholicism just as we are between the great counterforces of today" (27).

CHAPTER SIX

1. Osip Mandelstam, *Complete Poetry*, trans. Burton Raffel and Alla Burago (Albany, N.Y.: State University of New York Press, 1973), pp. 98–99. In McDuff's more literal translation, the quoted lines read:

He forges his decrees like horseshoes—
some get it in the groin, some in the forehead, some in the brows,
    some in the eyes.

Whatever the punishment he gives— raspberries,
and the broad chest of an Ossete.

Osip Mandelstam, *Selected Poems*, trans. David McDuff (Cambridge: Rivers Press, 1973), p. 131.

2. In a letter from early 1937, Mandelstam writes: "Everything [has been] taken away from me: my right to life, to work, and to [medical] treatment. I [have been] put in the position of a dog, a cur. . . . I am a shadow. I do not exist. I have only the right to die. My wife and I are being driven to suicide." *The Complete Critical Prose and Letters*, ed. Jane G. Harris, trans. Jane G. Harris and Constance Link (Ann Arbor: Ardis, 1979), p. 562; cited hereafter as *P&L*.

3. Nadezhda Mandelstam, *Hope against Hope*, trans. Max Hayward (New York: Athenaeum, 1970), p. 203; cited hereafter as *HaH*

4. "Mandelstam's 'Ode' to Stalin," *Slavic Review* 34 (1975): 683–691.

5. Bengt Jangfeldt, "Osip Mandel'shtam's 'Ode to Stalin,'" *Scando-Slavica* 22 (1976): 35–41; Gregory Freidin, "Mandel'shtam's *Ode to Stalin:* History and Myth," *The Russian Review* 41 (1982): 401.

6. Nadezhda Mandelstam tells the following anecdote: "In Voronezh we were once visited by an 'adjudant' of the semi-military kind . . . and questioned about the sense of the line 'wave follows wave, breaking the back of the one ahead.' 'Could that be about the Five Year Plans?' he asked. [Mandelstam] . . . replied with a look of astonishment: 'Is that what you think?' When the man had gone, I asked [Mandelstam] what to do when they inquired about the hidden meaning like this. 'Look surprised,' said M[andelstam]. I didn't always see the hidden meaning, and [Mandelstam] never explained it to me, in case I should ever be interrogated in prison" (*HaH*, p. 171n). This is not to say that Mandelstam wrote no Aesopian verse about Stalin. Peter Zeeman quotes numerous instances of poems from the 1930s in which a "powerful and sinister unreal living being"

appears who "is" Stalin, though in a deniable way. *The Later Poetry of Osip Mandelstam* (Amsterdam: Rodopi, 1988), pp. 138–39, 150–51.

7. "Into the Heart of Darkness: Mandelstam's Ode to Stalin," *Slavic Review* 26 (1967): 603.

8. Ibid.

9. Freidin, "Mandel'shtam's *Ode*," 401. The rehabilitation of Mandelstam in the Soviet Union began in 1957 with the appointment by the Writers' Union of a committee to process his archive and arrange for publication. But—in the account given by Ronald Hingley—this required someone to write an introduction giving a reading of Mandelstam acceptable to the official orthodoxy, a task no one could be found prepared to undertake. So it was not until 1973 that a selection appeared, in an edition of 10,000—small by Russian standards—most of which was then exported. Ronald Hingley, *Russian Writers and Soviet Society 1917–78* (London: Methuen, 1979), pp. 222–23; Igor Pomeranzev, "The Right to Read," *Partisan Review* 49 (1982): 61.

10. *Mandelstam: The Later Poetry* (Cambridge: Cambridge University Press, 1976), p. 177.

11. "Mandel'shtam's *Ode*," 403.

12. See particularly section 1 of the "Conversation" (*P&L*, pp. 397–400). On Shklovsky and *ostranenie*, see Viktor Erlich, *Russian Formalism*, 3d ed. (The Hague: Mouton, 1969), pp. 176–78.

13. It has been pointed out that Mandelstam took Pindar as his model: Gregory Freidin, *A Coat of Many Colors* (Berkeley and Los Angeles: University of California Press, 1987), p. 260; cited hereafter as *CMC*. The Pindaric ode certainly starts with an invocation, and this invocation is sometimes an announcement of the poet's own position and ambition (as in, for example, the third Olympian Ode). To that extent the invocation constitutes a denaturalizing or framing of the poem's address. But it should not be forgotten that, if Pindar—an unfamiliar model for a Russian poet—was indeed the model, he was chosen, denaturalizing invocation and all, by Mandelstam himself.

14. I quote throughout from Freidin's translation (*CMC*, pp. 258–60).

15. Katerina Clark demonstrates that from 1935 the propaganda organs deliberately set out to modify the earlier ideal of a nation of equal brothers and sisters in favor of a model of sons and daughters under the guidance of one all-wise father. "Utopian Anthropology as a Context for Stalinist Literature," in Robert C. Tucker, ed., *Stalinism: Essays in Historical Interpretation* (New York: Norton, 1977), pp. 180–91.

16. Freidin, *CMC*, p. 262; *HaH*, p. 203; Brown, "Into the Heart of Darkness," 594.

17. *HaH*, p. 146. To Mandelstam the Russian word *master* had come to mean a poet whose reputation and whose skills were being yoked to the service of the state. He therefore disdained it (Freidin, *CMC*, p. 379 n. 78).

Mikhail Bulgakov attempted to rehabilitate the term in his novel *The Master and Margarita*.

18. *Writers in Russia 1917–78*, ed. Patricia Blake (New York: Harcourt, Brace, Jovanovich, 1983), p. 194. On the other hand, some one thousand less well-known writers died in prisons or camps during the Stalin years. Writers from smaller nationalities were particularly at risk. See the figures collected by Eduard Beltov, summarized in John and Carol Garrard, *Inside the Soviet Writers' Union* (New York: Free Press, 1990), p. 49.

19. D. M. Thomas—no doubt consciously—reasserts the ancient rivalry of poet and tyrant, and proclaims the triumph of the poet, in the introduction to his translations from Anna Akhmatova: "In relation to [Akhmatova], the politicians, the bureaucrats, the State torturers, will suffer the same fate that, in Akhmatova's words, overtook Pushkin's autocratic contemporaries: 'The whole epoch, little by little, . . . began to be called the time of Pushkin.'" Introduction to Anna Akhmatova, *Selected Poems*, ed. and trans. D. M. Thomas (Harmondsworth: Penguin, 1988), p. 8.

20. *P&L*, pp. 321–22; Osip Mandelstam, *The Noise of Time*, ed. and trans. Clarence Brown (San Francisco: North Point, 1986), pp. 185–86.

21. "[Mandelstam] was only seldom overcome by . . . bouts of what is now called 'patriotism,' and once he had come to his senses he himself dismissed them as madness" (*HaH*, p. 126).

22. Nadezhda Mandelstam's memoirs show her to be fully aware of the perils of alienation entailed in bowing to, and using, the father's language. Like millions of other Soviet citizens, she records, she wrote petitions "addressed to the most metallic of names" (i.e., Stalin, from *stal'*, steel). But these petitions, speaking of "all the hurts, humiliations, blows, pitfalls and traps of our existence," could not be written in the language of the self: they had to be couched in "the special style of Soviet polite parlance," a language *handed down*, in which the self cannot find expression (*HaH*, p. 93).

CHAPTER SEVEN

1. See Girard, "The Underground Critic," trans. Paisley N. Livingston and Tobin Siebers, in *To Double Business Bound* (Baltimore: Johns Hopkins University Press, 1978), p. 56.

2. See Girard, "Strategies of Madness—Nietzsche, Wagner, and Dostoevski," in *To Double Business Bound*, pp. 79–81.

3. Sidney Monas, *The Third Section* (Cambridge, Mass.: Harvard University Press, 1961), pp. 22–48, 63. See also Leon I. Twarog, "Literary Censorship in Russia and the Soviet Union," in *Essays on Russian Intellectual History*, ed. Leon B. Blair (Austin: University of Texas Press, 1971), pp. 100–108.

4. *The Diary of a Russian Censor*, ed. and trans. Helen S. Jacobson (Amherst: University of Massachusetts Press, 1975), p. 116.

5. Peter Chaadayev, *Philosophical Letters and Apology of a Madman*,

trans. Mary-Barbara Zeldin (Knoxville: University of Tennessee Press, 1969), pp. 36, 10–13; Monas, *The Third Section,* p. 169; Richard Tempest, "Madman or Criminal: Government Attitudes to Petr Chaadaev in 1836," *Slavic Review* 43 (1984): 281–87. The draconian reaction to Chaadayev's letter was not as surprising as may seem: the portrayal of Russians as non-European barbarians was one of four absolutely proscribed themes. See Marianna Tax Choldin, *A Fence Around the Empire* (Durham: Duke University Press, 1985), p. 7.

6. P. S. Squire discusses the paradox that on the one hand the Third Section was "the most frightful instrument of tyranny," while on the other "its Chiefs and many of its members appear in themselves to have been worthy individuals." *The Third Section* (Cambridge: Cambridge University Press, 1968), p. 230.

7. Monas, *The Third Section,* pp. 290–91.

8. *Censorship in Russia 1865–1905* (Washington, D.C.: University Press of America, 1979), pp. 28–29; Charles A. Ruud, *Fighting Words: Imperial Censorship and the Russian Press, 1804–1906* (Toronto: University of Toronto Press, 1982), p. 228. My account of the system of censorship in Tsarist Russia is taken largely from Balmuth and Ruud.

9. As demonstrated (through a census of the language used about the censors) by I. P. Foote, "'In the Belly of the Whale': Russian Authors and Censorship in the Nineteenth Century," *Slavonic and East European Review* 68 (1990): 294–98.

10. Monas, "Censorship as a Way of Life," in Geoffrey A. Hosking and George F. Cushing, eds., *Perspectives on Literature and Society in Eastern and Western Europe* (New York: St. Martin's, 1989), pp. 8–11.

11. Balmuth, *Censorship in Russia,* pp. 142–43.

12. Monas, "Censorship as a Way of Life," p. 18.

13. Patterson analyzes the strategies of indirection that allowed writers to have their say without provoking or confronting the authorities, as well as the rules, never openly enunciated, on how explicitly certain issues could be addressed and "how [the writer] could code his opinions so that nobody would be *required* to make an example of him." Patterson is able to reconstruct a code of unwritten rules making up "an implicit social contract between authors and authorities." Censorship trials took place only as a sign that "one side or the other had broken the rules." *Censorship and Interpretation* (Madison: University of Wisconsin Press, 1984), pp. 10–11, 17, 44–45.

14. In 1979, at a time when the Writers' Union had some 7,000 members, Glavlit was reputed to have a staff of 70,000. Ronald Hingley, *Russian Writers and Soviet Society 1917–78* (London: Methuen, 1979), pp. 209–10. For an outline of the routine operations of Soviet censorship, see also Maurice Friedberg, "Soviet Books, Censors and Readers," in Max Hayward and Leo Labedz, eds., *Literature and Revolution in Soviet Russia 1917–62* (London: Oxford University Press, 1963), pp. 198–210.

15. Lenin, "Party Organization and Party Literature" (1905), quoted in Harold Swayze, *Political Control of Literature in the USSR, 1946–1959* (Cambridge, Mass.: Harvard University Press, 1962), pp. 8–9. See also John and Carol Garrard, *Inside the Soviet Writers' Union* (New York: Free Press, 1990), pp. 22–23. As Swayze points out, because it seemed to identify the writer's true freedom with adhering to the party line, this slight document became a fertile source of quotation for Soviet ideologists. Max Hayward argues that, in the use he made of it, Zhdanov "was certainly resorting to conscious fraud," since he knew that Lenin had not intended his generalization to apply to creative writers. Introduction to Hayward and Labedz, eds., *Literature and Revolution in Soviet Russia 1917–62*, pp. xiv–xv.

16. See Swayze, *Political Control of Literature*, pp. 15–17.

17. See Garrard and Garrard, *Inside the Soviet Writers' Union*, p. 175; Geoffrey A. Hosking, "The Institutionalization of Soviet Literature," in Hosking and Cushing, eds., *Perspectives on Literature and Society in Eastern and Western Europe*, p. 59.

18. Aksyonov made these remarks in 1982. "Looking for Colour," *Index on Censorship* 11/4 (August 1982), 3.

19. Ernest J. Simmons, "The Organization Writer (1934–46)," in Hayward and Labedz, eds., *Literature and Revolution in Soviet Russia 1917–62*, p. 77. See also: Dina R. Spechler, *Permitted Dissent in the USSR* (New York: Praeger, 1982), pp. 2–3; Michael Nicholson, "Solzhenitsyn and *Samizdat*," in John Dunlop et al., eds., *Aleksandr Solzhenitsyn*, 2d ed. (New York: Macmillan, 1975), pp. 68–69; Max Hayward, *Writers in Russia 1917–78*, ed. Patricia Blake (New York: Harcourt, Brace, Jovanovich, 1983), p. 58.

20. See Efim Etkind, *Notes of a Non-Conspirator*, trans. and with an introduction by Peter France (Oxford: Oxford University Press, 1978), pp. 174–75. On Babel, see Hayward, *Writers in Russia*, p. 136.

21. Gayle Durham, "Political Communication and Dissent in the Soviet Union," in Rudolf L. Tökés, ed., *Dissent in the USSR* (Baltimore: Johns Hopkins University Press, 1975), p. 257.

22. Solzhenitsyn, *The Oak and the Calf*, trans. Harry Willetts (London: Collins, 1980), p. 6.

23. "Sexuality and Solitude," in Marshall Blonsky, ed., *On Signs* (Oxford: Blackwell, 1985), p. 366. On the general aims of *kritika-samokritika*, see Sue Curry Jansen, *Censorship* (New York: Oxford University Press, 1988), pp. 108–12.

24. Quoted in Abraham Rothberg, *The Heirs of Stalin* (Ithaca, N.Y.: Cornell University Press, 1972), p. 21. I have amended Rothberg's translation slightly.

25. Cited in Priscilla Johnson, *Khrushchev and the Arts* (Cambridge, Mass.: MIT Press, 1965), pp. 206–10.

26. See Garrard and Garrard, *Inside the Soviet Writers' Union*, p. 235.

27. Spechler, *Permitted Dissent*. For other estimates of the significance of *Novy Mir* in Soviet intellectual life, see Garrard and Garrard, *Inside the Soviet Writers' Union*, pp. 156–57; Hosking, "The Institutionalization of Soviet literature," pp. 67–71.

28. See Michael Scammell, *Solzhenitsyn: A Biography* (New York: Norton, 1984), pp. 433–36.

29. Spechler, *Permitted Dissent*, pp. 249–53, 258.

30. See Rothberg, *The Heirs of Stalin*, p. 128; Hosking, "The Institutionalization of Soviet literature," p. 65. Brodsky wryly suggests that what offended the authorities about his writing is that it was "private enterprise." Interview in *Points of Departure: International Writers on Writing and Politics*, ed. David Montenegro (Ann Arbor: University of Michigan Press, 1991), p. 142.

31. Frederick C. Barghoorn, "The Post-Khrushchev Campaign to Suppress Dissent," in Tőkés, ed., *Dissent in the USSR*, pp. 67, 73. See also Rothberg, *The Heirs of Stalin*, pp. 214–15.

32. Rothberg, *The Heirs of Stalin*, p. 180.

33. *The Oak and the Calf*, p. 424.

34. After Solzhenitsyn's first visit to the United States, during which he made such sweeping pronouncements as "That which is against communism is for humanity," Aleksandr Schmemann criticized him for having become just another ideologist, a Marxist turned inside out (Scammell, *Solzhenitsyn*, pp. 922–23)—someone more *like* a Marxist than unlike one. But the position of *rival* that Solzhenitsyn made his own before leaving the Soviet Union had already made this identity-despite-opposition foreseeable. Michael Nicholson is quite wrong to label as "breathtakingly apolitical" Solzhenitsyn's rejection of Marxist aesthetics in favour of fidelity to universal values. In a Soviet context, by claiming the authority to assert his own standards, Solzhenitsyn was claiming a status as an originator equal to that of such founders of Soviet aesthetics as Belinsky, Plekhanov, and Lenin—not an apolitical position at all. Nicholson, "Solzhenitsyn and Samizdat," p. 64.

35. Isaac Deutscher, *The Great Purges* (Oxford: Blackwell, 1984), p. 95.

36. George Orwell, *1984*, ed. Bernard Crick (Oxford: Clarendon Press, 1984), p. 201.

37. Yuri Glazov, *The Russian Mind since Stalin's Death* (Dordrecht: Reidel, 1985), p. 145.

38. Valentin Turchin, *The Inertia of Fear*, trans. Guy Daniels (Oxford: Martin Robertson, 1981), pp. 33–34.

39. Gayle Durham even points to functional reasons why the media could not afford to say what they meant: since they were routinely used as "channels for esoteric communications" (e.g., to inform Party members of changes in the Party line and changes among Party personnel), the ev-

eryday public grew accustomed to a, so to speak, *overhearing* relationship to information. "Political communication and dissent in the Soviet Union," p. 258.

40. Nobel Lecture, in Dunlop et al., eds., *Aleksandr Solzhenitsyn,* 2d ed., p. 575.

41. A. Kemp-Welch, "Stalinism and Intellectual Order," in T. H. Rigby, Archie Brown, Peter Reddaway, eds., *Authority, Power and Policy in the USSR* (London: Macmillan, 1980), pp. 126–27.

42. George Feifer, "No Protest: The Case of the Passive Minority," in Tökés, ed., *Dissent in the USSR,* p. 433.

43. Peter France, in Etkind, *Notes of a Non-Conspirator,* p. ix.

44. Rothberg, *The Heirs of Stalin,* p. 73; Marshall S. Shatz, *Soviet Dissent in Historical Perspective* (Cambridge: Cambridge University Press, 1980), p. 124.

45. Rothberg, *The Heirs of Stalin,* pp. 34–35.

46. Johnson, *Khrushchev and the Arts,* pp. 102–5.

47. Rothberg, *The Heirs of Stalin,* pp. 162–64.

48. Etkind, *Notes of a Non-Conspirator,* pp. 208-9.

49. Zhores A. Medvedev and Roy A. Medvedev, *A Question of Madness,* trans. Ellen de Kadt (New York: Knopf, 1971), p. 132.

50. Durham, "Political Communication and Dissent," p. 261.

51. *The Oak and the Calf,* p. 52.

52. See Paul N. Siegel, "The Political Implications of Solzhenitsyn's Novels," *Clio* 12 (1983): pp. 211–13; Scammell, *Solzhenitsyn,* p. 983. Herman Ermolaev traces the complicated history of the revisions of *The First Circle* and finds that for publication in 1968 Solzhenitsyn made "extensive revisions in his portrayal of Stalin": "Solzhenitsyn's Self-Censorship: Two Versions of *V kruge pervom,*" *Russian Language Journal* 38 (1984): 181. Lev Loseff similarly demonstrates numerous "concessions to the censorship" in the 1968 edition. *On the Beneficence of Censorship* (Munich: Otto Sagner, 1984), p. 145.

53. Vladimir Lakshin, *Solzhenitsyn, Tvardovsky, and Novy Mir,* trans. Michael Glenny (Cambridge, Mass.: MIT Press, 1980), pp. 59, 61.

54. Leopold Labedz, ed., *Solzhenitsyn: A Documentary Record* (New York: Harper and Row, 1970), p. 194.

55. Scammell, *Solzhenitsyn,* p. 574.

56. Ibid., p. 836. Scammell refers to the spate of interviews Solzhenitsyn gave to Western reporters, published in the West but not the USSR, and the spate of articles about Solzhenitsyn written by Communist sympathizers from the West, published in the USSR but not in the West. One might more tellingly compare the efforts of Solzhenitsyn to get his novels published in the West in a way that would not infringe Soviet legality with the efforts of the KGB to get his compromising play *The Feast of the Conquerors,* concealed by Solzhenitsyn but stolen from him, published in the West. For details, see Scammell, *Solzhenitsyn,* pp. 692–93.

57. Ibid., p. 825.

58. Ibid., pp. 829–31.

59. Lakshin, *Solzhenitsyn, Tvardovsky, and Novy Mir,* pp. 59–62.

60. Labedz, ed., *Solzhenitsyn,* p. 126.

61. Ibid., p. 177.

62. Rothberg, *The Heirs of Stalin,* pp. 281–82. On the sociology of the Union membership and its hostility to mavericks like Solzhenitsyn, see Hosking, "The Institutionalization of Soviet Literature," pp. 61–66.

63. Scammell, *Solzhenitsyn,* p. 683.

64. Nobel Lecture, in Dunlop et al., eds., *Aleksandr Solzhenitsyn,* p. 575.

65. Scammell, *Solzhenitsyn,* p. 952.

66. The details are drawn from Johnson, *Khrushchev and the Arts,* pp. 110–11.

67. Rothberg, *The Heirs of Stalin,* p. 202; Friedgut, "The Democratic Movement," p. 129. See also Feifer, "No Protest," p. 423.

68. Rothberg, *The Heirs of Stalin,* p. 301; Medvedev and Medvedev, *A Question of Madness,* pp. 28–29, 33, 43; Turchin, *The Inertia of Fear,* p. 101.

69. Scammell, *Solzhenitsyn,* p. 691.

70. Eleanor Rowe, *Hamlet: A Window on Russia* (New York: New York University Press, 1976), p. 148. Rowe's book is devoted to the significance of the Hamlet figure in Russian intellectual life.

71. Deming Brown, *Soviet Russian Literature since Stalin* (Cambridge: Cambridge University Press, 1978), p. 316.

72. Gary Kern, "Solzhenitsyn's Portrait of Stalin," *Slavic Review* 33 (1974): 3.

73. Daniel Rancour-Laferriere, "The Deranged Birthday Boy: Solzhenitsyn's Portrait of Stalin in *The First Circle," Mosaic* 18 (1985): 62.

74. *The Oak and the Calf,* p. 78. See also David M. Halperin, "Solzhenitsyn, Epicurus, and the Ethics of Stalinism," *Critical Inquiry* 7 (1981): 490.

75. Scammell, *Solzhenitsyn,* p. 391.

76. Aleksandr Schmemann, "On Solzhenitsyn," in Dunlop et al., eds., *Aleksandr Solzhenitsyn,* 2d ed., p. 35.

CHAPTER EIGHT

1. Max Hayward, *Writers in Russia 1917–78,* ed. Patricia Blake (New York: Harcourt, Brace, Jovanovich, 1983), p. 136.

2. Stanislaw Baranczak, "The Gag and the Word," *Survey* 25/1 (1980): 58.

3. Miklos Haraszti, *The Velvet Prison: Artists under State Socialism,* trans. Katalin and Stephen Landesmann (New York: Basic Books, 1987), pp. 7, 97.

4. George Schöpflin, "The Black Book of Polish Censorship," in George

Schöpflin, ed., *Censorship and Political Communication in Eastern Europe* (New York: St Martin's, 1983), pp. 52–54; Jane Leftwich Curry, ed. and trans., *The Black Book of Polish Censorship* (New York: Random House, 1984), pp. 8, 382–86. On the history of censorship in Poland between 1949 and the early 1980s, see Stanislaw Baranczak, "Poland: Literature and Censorship," in *The Writer and Human Rights*, ed. Toronto Arts Group for Human Rights (New York: Anchor, 1983), pp. 173–83; Chris Pszenicki, "Polish Publishing 1980–81," *Index on Censorship* 11/1 (February 1982): 8–11; Chris Pszenicki, "Freedom of Expression in Jaruzelski's Poland," *Index on Censorship* 12/6 (December 1983): 19–24.

5. Quoted in Curry, *The Black Book*, p. 8.

6. Stanislaw Baranczak, "My Ten Uncensorable Years," in Schöpflin, ed., *Censorship and Political Communication in Eastern Europe*, pp. 113–14.

7. Stanislaw Baranczak, "Poems and Tanks," *TriQuarterly*, no. 57 (1983): 53.

8. Tadeusz Konwicki, "Interview: The Delights of Writing under Censorship," *Index on Censorship* 15/3 (March 1986), 30.

9. Konwicki, quoted in Jeffrey C. Goldfarb, *On Cultural Freedom* (Chicago: University of Chicago Press, 1982), p. 90.

10. Ibid., p. 90.

11. Quoted in Jacek Trznadel, "An Interview with Zbigniew Herbert," *Partisan Review* 54 (1987): 567. On Herbert's career, see also A. Alvarez, "Noble Poet," in *The Mature Laurel*, ed. Adam Czerniawski (Chester Springs, Pa.: Dufour, 1991), pp. 163–71; Marek Oramus and Maria Szmidt, "A Poet of Exact Meaning," *PN Review* 8/6, no. 26 (1982): 8–12; Donald P. A. Pirie, "Engineering the People's Dreams: An Assessment of Socialist Realist Poetry in Poland 1949–1955," in Czerniawski, ed., *The Mature Laurel*, pp. 135–59.

12. *Selected Poems*, trans. Czeslaw Milosz and Peter Dale Scott (Harmondsworth: Penguin, 1968), p. 22; hereafter cited as Milosz/Scott.

13. Milosz/Scott, pp. 137–38.

14. *Report from the Besieged City and Other Poems*, trans. John and Bogdana Carpenter (Oxford: Oxford University Press, 1987), pp. 10–11; hereafter cited as *Report*. As Stanislaw Baranczak points out, the stoicism adhered to by Herbert in these poems and elsewhere is darker than classical stoicism. The latter identifies virtue with nature and founds its ethics on concord with nature; there is no such faith in Herbert. *A Fugitive from Utopia* (Cambridge, Mass.: Harvard University Press, 1987), p. 118.

15. Haraszti, *The Velvet Prison*, p. 145.

16. In his 1962 book of essays on France and Italy, Herbert emerges from the caves of Lascaux confirmed in his belief that he is "a citizen of the earth, an inheritor not only of the Greeks and Romans but of almost the whole of infinity." Later he quotes T. S. Eliot approvingly: "No poet,

no artist . . . has his complete meaning alone. . . . You must set him, for contrast and comparison, among the dead." *Barbarian in the Garden*, trans. Michael March and Jaroslaw Anders (Manchester: Carcanet, 1985), pp. 16, 78.

17. Milosz/Scott, pp. 46–47.

18. Goldfarb, *On Cultural Freedom*, p. 92.

19. See Milosz/Scott, pp. 68, 74, 75, 133. That so pointed a reading is within the ambit of Herbert's intention is confirmed by his guarded admission that in the poem "Damastes (also known as Procrustes) Speaks" (*Report*, p. 44) there is indeed a certain resemblance between Procrustes and Lenin. See John and Bogdana Carpenter, "Zbigniew Herbert: The Poet as Conscience," *Slavic and East European Journal* 24 (1980): 46–47.

20. Milosz/Scott, pp. 96–97.

21. Trans. Czeslaw Milosz, in Milosz, ed., *Postwar Polish Poetry*, 3d ed. (Berkeley and Los Angeles: University of California Press, 1983), pp. 69–71. For another and, in my view, inferior translation, see *Report*, pp. 39–42.

22. *A Fugitive from Utopia*, p. 119.

23. *Selected Poems*, trans. John and Bogdana Carpenter (Oxford: Oxford University Press, 1977), pp. 79–80.

24. In this vein, in the introduction he wrote in 1973 for a selection of his poems, Herbert quotes Cyprian Norwid: "Let words mean only what they mean, and not whom they were used against" (quoted in Baranczak, *A Fugitive from Utopia*, p. 66). Similarly, one may cite "Mr. Cogito and the Imagination" (*Report*, pp. 17–19): Mr. Cogito

> adored tautologies
> explanations
> *idem per idem*
> that a bird is a
> > bird
> slavery means
> > slavery
> a knife is a knife
> death remains
> > death

25. Milosz/Scott, pp. 58–60.

26. *A Fugitive from Utopia*, pp. 12, 64.

27. Milosz/Scott, p. 93.

28. "The Longobards," in Milosz/Scott, p. 127.

29. Milosz/Scott, pp. 35–37, 82–83.

30. Milosz/Scott, pp. 51–52, 131.

31. *Report*, pp. 29–31.

32. "Gardens of Stone: The Poetry of Zbigniew Herbert and Tadeusz Rozewicz," in Czerniawski, ed., *The Mature Laurel*, p. 178.

CHAPTER NINE

1. André du Toit, "Ideological Change, Afrikaner Nationalism, and Pragmatic Racial Domination," in Leonard Thompson and Jeffrey Butler, eds., *Change in Contemporary South Africa* (Berkeley and Los Angeles: University of California Press, 1975), p. 40. On Cronjé's early career, see also T. Dunbar Moodie, *The Rise of Afrikanerdom* (Berkeley and Los Angeles: University of California Press, 1975), p. 274; Saul Dubow, *Racial Segregation and the Origins of Apartheid in South Africa, 1919–36* (London: Macmillan, 1989), p. 22. A. N. Pelzer claims that as early as 1933 a Broederbond study group had recommended a system of self-governing reserves, but that its report had been passed over. *Die Afrikaner-Broederbond* (Cape Town: Tafelberg, 1979), p. 158.

2. Geoffrey Cronjé, *'n Tuiste vir die nageslag* (Johannesburg: Publicité, 1945), hereafter referred to as *TN*; *Afrika sonder die Asiaat* (Johannesburg: Publicité, 1946); *Voogdyskap en apartheid* (Pretoria: Van Schaik, 1948), referred to as *VA*; Geoffrey Cronjé et al., *Regverdige Rasse-Apartheid* (Stellenbosch: Christen-Studenteverenigingsmaatskappy, 1947), chapters 3–5, referred to as *RRA*.

3. Charles Bloomberg adjudges Cronjé "by far the most articulate" of the theorists of apartheid: *Christian-Nationalism and the Rise of the Afrikaner Broederbond in South Africa, 1918–1948*, ed. Saul Dubow (Bloomington: Indiana University Press, 1989), p. 29. Patrick J. Furlong calls *Regverdige rasseapartheid* "one of the most important books on the ideology of apartheid": *Between Crown and Swastika* (Hanover and London: Wesleyan University Press, 1991), p. 226. In the estimation of Shula Marks and Stanley Trapido, Cronjé's books give "the most comprehensive theoretical statement" of apartheid we have: "The Politics of race, class and nationalism," in Shula Marks and Stanley Trapido, eds., *The Politics of Race, Class and Nationalism in Twentieth-Century South Africa* (London: Longmans, 1987), p. 19.

4. N. J. Rhoodie, "G. Cronje se beskouing van die Suid-Afrikaanse Blank-Bantoe-problematiek, soos weerspieël in sy onmiddellik na-oorlogse geskrifte," in J. E. Pieterse et al., eds., *Mens en gemeenskap* (Pretoria and Cape Town: Academica, 1969), p. 42.

5. Tom Nairn, *The Break-Up of Britain*. 2d ed. (London: Verso, 1981), p. 340. On vanguard nationalist intellectuals, see also Anthony D. Smith, *The Ethnic Revival* (Cambridge: Cambridge University Press, 1981), pp. 124–26; Ernst Gellner, *Nations and Nationalism* (Oxford: Blackwell, 1983), pp. 55–57. On the South African case, see Dan O'Meara, *Volkskapitalisme* (Johannesburg: Ravan, 1983), pp. 59–66; John Sharp, "The Roots and Development of *Volkekunde* in South Africa," *Journal of Southern African Studies* 8/1 (1981): 28; Isabel Hofmeyr, "Building a Nation from Words: Afrikaans Language, Literature and Ethnic Identity, 1902–1924,"

in Marks and Trapido, eds., *The Politics of Race, Class and Nationalism in Twentieth-Century South Africa*, pp. 95–123..

6. G. Eloff, an enthusiast of racial science and eugenics to whom Cronjé owed much, advocated that, to prevent the "infiltration" of "impure blood," Afrikaners should return to the neglected custom of keeping a genealogical register of the family. "Proof of pure descent should be your first qualification for marriage as a white." *Rasse en rassevermenging* (Cape Town: Nasionale Pers, 1942), pp. 93, 100. Leonard Thompson attributes much of Cronjé's racist virulence to his reading of Eloff: *The Political Mythology of Apartheid* (New Haven: Yale University Press, 1985), p. 44. But one should not forget that Cronjé was a "general" in the pro-Nazi Ossewabrandwag organization during World War II and must have been open to other influences besides his reading: see Moodie, *The Rise of Afrikanerdom*, pp. 274–75.

7. The "problem" of people of Asian descent is addressed in *Afrika sonder die Asiaat*. In foreword Cronjé explains that, but for its length, this book would have been incorporated into *'n Tuiste*.

8. Leo Strauss, *Persecution and the Art of Writing* (Glencoe: Free Press, 1952), p. 36.

9. *'n Tuiste* was of course written under conditions of wartime censorship. Though Smuts had allowed pro-German organizations an extraordinary degree of latitude, he did finally, in 1944, order Military Intelligence to investigate the Broederbond, and subsequently proclaimed it a subversive organization. By this time its office-holders had prudently destroyed its more incriminating records (Bloomberg, *Christian-Nationalism*, pp. 52–53, 192). It is ironic that Cronjé is written out of the history commissioned by the Bond, perhaps because his language was too crude by the standards of the ethnic-pluralist Newspeak of the late 1970s: Pelzer, *Die Afrikaner-Broederbond*.

10. Cronjé reiterates the more sophisticated position in *Voogdyskap en apartheid*. Whether or not there is such a thing as a pure race does not matter, he says. "Suffice it to say that differences, and often deep differences, do exist between races, and that [in South Africa] these differences . . . are so important that reckoning has to be taken of them." He calls his scheme of five races "purely practical" (*VA*, p. 31). In singling out the Jews as the fifth actor on the South African stage, he creates an opening for an anti-Semitism that is a recurrent if minor strain in his writings of 1945–48.

11. See Eloff, *Rasse en rassevermenging*, pp. 93–94. Eloff builds in turn on H. T. Colenbrander, *De afkomst der Boeren*, and G. M. Theal, *History of South Africa from 1795*, vol. 1.

12. In *Voogdyskap en apartheid* Cronjé extends this account further. From the end of the seventeenth century, once the colonists' eyes had been opened, no blood-mixing took place. British immigrants, with their liberal-

istic attitudes, at first saw nothing unnatural in miscegenation; but as their descendants became acclimatized, their eyes too were opened (*VA*, pp. 38–39).

13. F. M. Barnard, *Herder's Social and Political Thought* (Oxford: Clarendon Press, 1965), p. 56.

14. Like fire, like fluid: in the material imagination of Cronjé, "black blood" moves like one of these undifferentiated primary substances. When Cronjé thinks of the contact of white blood with white blood, on the other hand, as in the early years of the Cape Colony, metaphors of devouring, contamination, interflow do not occur to him. The new *Boerbloed* (Boer-blood) of the *Boereras* is "saamgesmee" from the blood of various West-European nations. The choice of "saamgesmee," forged, over "saamges-melt," melted together, is a denial of liquidity: *smee* comes from the Dutch verb *smeden*, cognate with English *smite*. Cronje, "Die huisgesin in die Afrikaanse kultuurgemeenskap," in P. de V. Pienaar and C. M. van den Heever, eds., *Kultuurgeskiedenis van die Afrikaner* (3 vols.; Cape Town: Nasionale Pers, 1945), vol. 1, p. 338.

15. Eloff, *Rasse en rassevermenging*, pp. 95–96.

16. Even P. J. Coertze, a close ideological ally of Cronjé's, reviewing *'n Tuiste vir die nageslag* in 1945 in the right-wing journal *Wapenskou*, gives bare mention to the chapters on blood-mixing. There is a comparable silence in Rhoodie.

17. On the laxness of Afrikaners, see Cronjé, "Rassevermenging as maatskaplike vraagstuk" (Race-mixing as a social question), *Rassebakens* 1/1 (1939): "We sleep . . . blissfully while a portion of our race is committing suicide"; "If succeeding generations are as shortsighted and indolent *(lamlendig)* as we are, then the southern reaches [of Africa] will remain no white man's land" (41, 47). For reference to case-studies, see *TN*, pp. 61–62.

18. Bloomberg, *Christian-Nationalism*, pp. 100–101.

19. Gustave le Bon, *The Crowd* (1897) (Dunwoody, Ga.: Norman S. Berg, n.d.), pp. 15–44; Freud, "Group Psychology and the Analysis of the Ego" (1921), in *Standard Edition*, vol. 18, ed. and trans. James Strachey (London: Hogarth Press, 1955), pp. 74–75.

20. Maynard Swanson, "The Sanitation Syndrome: Bubonic Plague and Urban Native Policy in the Cape Colony, 1900–09," *Journal of African History* 18 (1977): 387, 388, 391. Twenty years before Swanson, I. D. Mac-Crone had hinted at the same syndrome. Reporting a survey of white attitudes, he lists "sanitary work" as the kind of work white South Africans most readily identify as "Kaffir work," and proposes that the association of blacks with dirty work comes about via the association of black people with slum conditions. *Race Attitudes in South Africa* (Johannesburg: Witwatersrand University Press, 1957), pp. 269, 293.

21. "The Sanitation Syndrome," 387. See Benedict Anderson: "Racism dreams of eternal contaminations, transmitted from the origins of time

through an endless sequence of loathsome copulations, outside history." *Imagined Communities* (London: Verso, 1983), p. 136.

CHAPTER TEN

1. J. C. W. van Rooyen, *Censorship in South Africa* (Cape Town: Juta, 1987), p. 7; hereafter cited as *CSA*.

2. As Van Rooyen presents the story in his earlier account of the workings of the system, Mulder's intervention had nothing to do with his personal feelings about Leroux's book. As the responsible minister, "he [did] not choose sides, but simply [referred] the book to the Appeal Board when uncertainty [arose] as to whether the decision of the [relevant] committee was right [*juis*]." *Publikasiebeheer in Suid-Afrika* (Cape Town: Juta, 1978), pp. 13–14; hereafter cited as *Publikasiebeheer*.

3. *CSA*, p. 7. In calling its language vague, Van Rooyen by no means intends criticism of the act.

4. Publications Control Board, "Die tweede beslissing oor *Magersfontein, o Magersfontein!*" *Standpunte* 33/4 (no. 148) (1980): 11.

5. Similarly, D. N. MacCormick argues that in general "offensive obscenity" and "offensive intrusions on privacy" are "entirely different categories and types of wrong." "Privacy and obscenity," in Rajeev Dhavan and Christie Davies, eds., *Censorship and Obscenity* (London: Martin Robertson, 1978), pp. 83–93.

6. "Though [the average man] might, in an unguarded moment, laugh at or become interested in the [reading] matter in question, these actions of his very often differ from his ideals of what should be allowed to be published and distributed." *Publikasiebeheer*, p. 64.

7. Patrick Devlin, *The Enforcement of Morals* (Oxford: Oxford University Press, 1965); H. L. A. Hart, *Law, Liberty and Morality*, rev. ed. (Oxford: Oxford University Press, 1981), cited hereafter as *LLM*; Ronald Dworkin, *Taking Rights Seriously* (Cambridge, Mass.: Harvard University Press, 1977), cited hereafter as *TRS*.

8. "The law exists for the protection of society. It does not discharge its function [merely] by protecting the individual. . . ; the law must protect also the institutions and the community of ideas, political and moral, without which people cannot live together." Devlin, *The Enforcement of Morals*, p. 22.

9. "The morals which underly the law must be derived from the sense of right and wrong which resides in the community as a whole, [but] it does not matter whence this community of thought comes, whether from one body of doctrine or another or from the knowledge of good and evil which no man is without." Devlin, *The Enforcement of Morals*, p. 22.

10. Gilbert Marcus, "Reasonable Censorship?" in Hugh Corder, ed.,

Essays on Law and Social Practice in South Africa (Cape Town: Juta, 1988), pp. 353, 356.

11. Van Rooyen writes of a "tide of conservative reaction" against a permissiveness washing upon South Africa's shores from Britain and the United States (*CSA*, pp. 14–15).

12. "A sickly *[sieklike]* treatment of sex." An instance of digital manipulation of a woman's sex organs is "perverse," part of "a sickly and morbid treatment of the sexual." Of a novel in which a murderer castrates his victim and leaves his testicles in his mouth: "Something of this kind belongs in a book about psychiatry. To give these revolting descriptions in fiction amounts to a dehumanization and bestialization of man." Van Rooyen, *Publikasiebeheer*, pp. 17, 18, 81.

13. For Gordimer's own response to these charges, see Nadine Gordimer et al., *What Happened to Burger's Daughter* (Johannesburg: Taurus, 1980), pp. 22–23.

14. Marcus, "Reasonable Censorship?" p. 352.

15. Sigmund Freud, "Psychoanalytic Notes on an Autobiographical Account of a Case of Paranoia" (1911), in *Pelican Freud Library*, vol. 9, ed. James Strachey and Angela Richards (Harmondsworth: Penguin, 1979), p. 218; hereafter cited as "Paranoia."

16. "Paranoia," pp. 213–14.

17. *CSA*, p. 147. As an instance of the extension of this meta-rule to the day-to-day operations of the censorship, I cite an extraordinary judgment dating from 1971, which Van Rooyen quotes in no spirit of criticism. The court prohibited a play in which interracial sex was favorably presented on the grounds not that its performance represented indecent/obscene/offensive/harmful acts but that in representing illegal acts (in this case interracial sexual acts) it tended to bring the law against such acts into contempt. *Publikasiebeheer*, p. 124.

18. "Paranoia," pp. 200–201. Far from taking Freud's little table of transformations lightly, Lacan argues that it constitutes a powerful explanatory account. *De la psychose paranoïaque dans ses rapports avec la personnalité* (1932) (Paris: Seuil, 1975), pp. 261–62.

19. See Kenneth M. Colby, *Artificial Paranoia: A Computer Simulation of Paranoid Processes* (New York: Pergamon, 1975); Margaret A. Boden, "Freudian Mechanisms of Defence: A Programming Perspective," in Richard Wollheim, ed., *Freud: A Collection of Critical Essays* (New York: Anchor Doubleday, 1974), particularly pp. 252–53, 263–64; William S. Faught, *Motivation and Intentionality in a Computer Simulation Model of Paranoia* (Basel: Birkhauser, 1978).

20. Lacan, *De la psychose paranoïaque*, p. 293.

21. Freud, "Negation" (1925), in *Standard Edition*, vol. 19, ed. and trans. James Strachey (London: Hogarth Press, 1961), p. 239.

22. Freud, in a 1937 paper quoted in J. Laplanche and J.-B. Pontalis, *The*

Language of Psycho-Analysis, trans. Donald Nicholson-Smith (New York: Norton, 1973), pp. 262–63.

23. Laplanche and Pontalis, *The Language of Psycho-Analysis,* pp. 133, 139.

24. Jeremy Bentham, *An Introduction to the Principles of Morals and Legislation* (1823) (Oxford: Clarendon Press, 1907), pp. 205, 3, 23.

CHAPTER ELEVEN

1. Brink's essays on censorship have been republished in two collections, *Mapmakers* (London: Faber, 1983) and *Literatuur in die strydperk* (Literature in the Time of Struggle) (Cape Town: Human and Rousseau, 1985). I use the abbreviations *M* and *LS* respectively for these collections. Where relevant, I supply the dates of individual essays.

2. Brink reports that, after he had advised writers to pay no attention to the censorship apparatus, the Security Police began to collect evidence to support a charge that he had thereby encouraged people to break the law (*LS,* pp. 105–6). In this connection, he quotes (with approval) Czeslaw Milosz: the writer may prefer to ignore the state, but a time comes when silence may be taken as "an avowal." At such a time, the writer "is commanded to resort to all ruses to deceive [his] adversary" (*LS,* p. 138).

3. *Censorship in South Africa* (Cape Town: Juta, 1987), cited hereafter as *CSA.*

CHAPTER TWELVE

1. Amsterdam: Meulenhoff, 1972; cited hereafter as *S.* The neologism *Skryt* is a composite of *skryf* (write) and *skyt* (shit). It also recalls *stryd* (struggle). Breytenbach's Afrikaans, which is full of wordplay and neologism, presents sometimes insuperable problems to the translator. In the cases of *True Confessions of an Albino Terrorist, Mouroir, End Papers,* and *Judas Eye,* I use the English-language versions prepared by Breytenbach himself. Other translations (except that of *A Season in Paradise*) are my own.

2. André P. Brink, "Die vreemde bekende," in *Woorde teen die wolk,* ed. A. J. Coetzee (Johannesburg: Taurus, 1980), pp. 1–2.

3. Jack Viviers, *Breytenbach* (Cape Town: Tafelberg, 1978), p. 59.

4. Lazarus first appears in "Death Begins at the Feet," in *Die ysterkoei moet sweet* (The Ironcow Must Sweat) (Johannesburg: Afrikaanse Pers Boekhandel, 1964), pp. 6–7. Cited hereafter as *YMS.*

5. "Tiberius' Cave near Sperlonga in Latium," in *Kouevuur* (Cape Town: Buren, 1969), p. 67.

6. *Om te vlieg* (Cape Town: Buren, 1971), p. 29. Cited hereafter as *OV.*

7. A companion piece, *Die miernes swel op* (The Ant-Nest Swells Up)

(Johannesburg: Taurus, 1980), written in the 1960s, similarly concludes with a casting off of the mask of fiction: "It ought to be crystal clear that I am asking you for Rebellion. The duty of the artist is to overthrow his government. . . . Can't you see that the poem is a curse of protest, . . . that it cannot and may not be an aesthetic cocoon, a watered-down and scented European-derived dribble of piss!" (p. 117).

8. *A Season in Paradise*, trans. Rike Vaughan (New York: Persea, 1980), p. 156. Cited hereafter as *SP.*

9. The English translation, from which I quote, reintroduces "passages omitted, for political or other reasons, from the original [1976] Afrikaans edition" (André P. Brink, introduction to *A Season in Paradise*, p. 16). See also Breytenbach's *True Confessions of an Albino Terrorist* (New York: Farrar, Straus, Giroux, 1985), p. 157, cited hereafter as *TC;* and *Boek: Deel een* (Book: part one) (Johannesburg: Taurus, 1987), where Breytenbach says that *'n Seisoen in die paradys* was "castrated with pruning-shears . . . for the sake of decency and security" (p. 94).

10. "Just Because" (*SP,* pp. 253–55).

11. Mikhail Bakhtin, *Problems of Dostoevsky's Poetics,* ed. and trans. Caryl Emerson (Manchester: Manchester University Press, 1984), pp. 197, 195, 202.

12. The ideal of "direct, unrefracted, unconditional authorial discourse" to which Bakhtin refers seems to lie behind Sheila Roberts's account of how Breytenbach was affected by prison censorship: "His strong impulse to record the complex existential truth of his prison experiences was modified, distorted perhaps, by his desire to confuse this initial police readership and their threatened censorship." "Breyten Breytenbach's Prison Literature," *Centennial Review* 30 (1986): 309.

13. *Eklips* (Eclipse) (1983), *('Yk')* (1983), *Buffalo Bill* (1984) and *Lewendood* (Living-death; Life-and-death) (1985), all published by Taurus of Johannesburg. *Yk:* to give the stamp of approval; there is further play on *ek* (I) and English *ache.* For Breytenbach's account of the coming into being of the volumes, see *Boek: Deel een,* p. 98.

14. For instance, an untitled poem in *Lewendood,* a rather inconsequential two-stanza lullaby, appears in translation in *Judas Eye* in what one must conclude was the originally intended form: with a third stanza in which a litany of South African relocation camps and razed settlements ("night-hooded names / I'm not yet allowed to say") is added to the litanies of sacked cities and death camps in the earlier stanzas. *Lewendood,* p. 42; *Judas Eye* (London: Faber, 1988), p. 72.

15. "Place of Refuge" (*Eklips,* pp. 3–4) is an extreme example: the enemy other is demonized or bestialized, his speech becomes "an idiot babble," and no exchange is possible with him.

16. *Lewendood,* pp. 143–44.

17. *Buffalo Bill,* p. 115.

18. "A Mirror-Verse" (*Buffalo Bill,* pp. 41–42), with play on *vars/vers,*

fresh/verse. A reworking of the poem in English by Breytenbach himself appears as "Mirror-Fresh Reflection" in *Judas Eye,* pp. 40–41.

19. On the genesis of *Mouroir* and *True Confessions,* see Susanna Egan, "Breytenbach's *Mouroir:* The Novel as Autobiography," *Journal of Narrative Technique* 18/2 (1988): 89–90.

20. *TC,* pp. 13–14, 17, 56. See also *Boek: Deel een,* pp. iii–iv.

21. *Gravity and Grace,* ed. G. Thibon (London: Routledge, 1952), p. 65.

22. *End Papers* (London: Faber, 1986), pp. 33–34.

23. *Mouroir* (New York: Farrar, Straus, Giroux, 1985). *Mouroir* was substantially written in prison.

24. *TC,* p. 339. For a hostile account of Breytenbach's behavior during his trial, see Martin Garbus, *Traitors and Heroes* (New York: Athenaeum, 1987). "Breytenbach panicked and pleaded guilty at the first trial to charges of terrorism. . . . He was given permission to make [his] apology by the prosecutor and by Prime Minister Vorster, both of whom approved every word of his statement before it was read in court" (p. 65). Garbus explains the heavy sentence imposed on Breytenbach as an angry response by the judge to the deal he inferred had been worked out between security police, prosecution, and defense. "Years later, when journalists sought to examine the court files to make sense of the case, they found that all the documents relating to it had disappeared" (p. 21). Garbus does not suggest who was responsible for the disappearance of the files. It is worth noting that, in a letter from prison read out at his second (1977) trial, Breytenbach also offered his services to the security police. Why he should have done so is unclear. See Martin Welz, *Breyten en die bewaarder* (Johannesburg: McGraw-Hill, 1977), pp. 196–97.

25. The quotations are from "Berlin" and "Keep Clear of the Mad," in *End Papers,* pp. 111, 133–34, 109.

26. Leo Strauss, *Persecution and the Art of Writing* (Glencoe: Free Press, 1952), p. 36.

Works Cited

Akhmatova, Anna. *Selected Poems*, ed. and trans. D. M. Thomas. Harmondsworth: Penguin, 1988.

Aksyonov, Vasily. "Looking for Colour: A Soviet Writer Compares Tsarist and Soviet Censorship." *Index on Censorship* 11/4 (August 1982): 3–4.

Altman, Andrew. "Liberalism and Campus Hate Speech: A Philosophical Examination." *Ethics* 103 (1993): 302–17.

Alvarez, A. "Noble Poet." Pp. 163–71 in Adam Czerniawski, ed., *The Mature Laurel: Essays on Modern Polish Poetry*. Chester Springs, Pa.: Dufour, 1991.

Anderson, Benedict. *Imagined Communities*. London: Verso, 1983.

Augustine, Saint. *The City of God*, trans. John Healey. 2 vols. London: Dent, 1945.

Baines, Jennifer. *Mandelstam: The Later Poetry*. Cambridge: Cambridge University Press, 1976.

Bainton, Roland H. *Erasmus of Christendom*. London: Collins, 1972.

Bakhtin, Mikhail. *Problems of Dostoevsky's Poetics*, ed. and trans. Caryl Emerson. Manchester: Manchester University Press, 1984.

Balmuth, David. *Censorship in Russia 1865–1905*. Washington, D.C.: University Press of America, 1979.

Bance, A. "The Idea of Europe: From Erasmus to ERASMUS." *Journal of European Studies* 22 (1992): 1–19.

Bandera, Cesareo. "The Doubles Reconciled." *MLN* 93 (1978): 1007–1014.

Baranczak, Stanislaw. *A Fugitive from Utopia*. Cambridge, Mass.: Harvard University Press, 1987.

———. "The Gag and the Word." *Survey* 25, no. 1 (1980): 58–79.

———, ed. "My Ten Uncensorable Years." Pp. 112–19 in George Schöpflin, ed., *Censorship and Political Communication in Eastern Europe: A Collection of Documents*. New York: St Martin's, 1983.

———. "Poems and Tanks." *TriQuarterly*, no. 57 (1983): 53–58.

———. "Poland: Literature and Censorship." Pp. 173–83 in *The Writer and Human Rights,* ed. Toronto Arts Group for Human Rights. New York: Anchor, 1983.

Barghoorn, Frederick C. "The Post-Khrushchev Campaign to Suppress Dissent." Pp. 35–95 in Rudolf L. Tökés, ed., *Dissent in the USSR.* Baltimore: Johns Hopkins University Press, 1975.

Barnard, F. M. *Herder's Social and Political Thought.* Oxford: Clarendon Press, 1965.

Barthes, Roland. *The Pleasure of the Text,* trans. Richard Miller. London: Cape, 1975.

Bartlett, Katharine T. Review of Catharine MacKinnon, *Feminism Unmodified. Signs* 13 (1988): 879–85.

Bataille, Georges. *Death and Sensuality.* New York: Walker, 1962.

———. "Sade." Pp. 85–103 in *Literature and Evil,* trans. Alastair Hamilton. London: Calder and Boyars, 1973.

Benston, Kimberly W. "I Yam What I Am: The Topos of (Un)naming in Afro-American Literature." Pp. 151–72 in Henry Louis Gates, ed., *Black Literature and Literary Theory.* New York: Methuen, 1984.

Bentham, Jeremy. *An Introduction to the Principles of Morals and Legislation.* Oxford: Clarendon Press, 1907.

Berger, Ronald E., Patricia Searles, and Charles E. Cottle. *Feminism and Pornography.* New York: Praeger, 1991.

Bloomberg, Charles. *Christian-Nationalism and the Rise of the Afrikaner Broederbond in South Africa, 1918–1948,* ed. Saul Dubow. Bloomington: Indiana University Press, 1989.

Boden, Margaret A. "Freudian Mechanisms of Defence: A Programming Perspective." In Richard Wollheim, ed., *Freud: A Collection of Critical Essays.* Garden City, N. Y.: Doubleday/Anchor, 1974.

Breytenbach, Breyten. *Boek: Deel een.* Johannesburg: Taurus, 1987

———. *Buffalo Bill.* Johannesburg: Taurus, 1984.

———. *Eklips.* Johannesburg: Taurus, 1983.

———. *End Papers.* London: Faber, 1986.

———. *Judas Eye.* London: Faber 1988.

———. *Lewendood.* Johannesburg: Taurus, 1985.

———. *Die miernes swel op.* Johannesburg: Taurus, 1980.

———. *Mouroir.* New York: Farrar, Straus, Giroux, 1985.

———. *Kouevuur.* Cape Town: Buren, 1969.

———. *Om te vlieg.* Cape Town: Buren, 1971.

———. *A Season in Paradise,* trans. Rike Vaughan, with an introduction by André P. Brink. New York: Persea, 1980.

———. *Skryt.* Amsterdam: Meulenhoff, 1972.

———. *True Confessions of an Albino Terrorist.* New York: Farrar, Straus, Giroux, 1985.

———. *Die ysterkoei moet sweet.* Johannesburg: Afrikaanse Pers Boekhandel, 1964.

Brink, André P. *Literatuur in die strydperk*. Cape Town: Human and Rousseau, 1985.

———. *Mapmakers*. London: Faber, 1983.

———. "Die vreemde bekende." Pp. 1–28 in A. J. Coetzee, ed., *Woorde teen die wolk: Vir Breyten*. Johannesburg: Taurus, 1980.

Brodsky, Joseph. Interview. Pp. 133–48 in David Montenegro, ed., *Points of Departure: International Writers on Writing and Politics*. Ann Arbor: University of Michigan Press, 1991.

Brown, Clarence. "Into the Heart of Darkness: Mandelstam's Ode to Stalin." *Slavic Review* 26 (1967): 584–604.

Brown, Deming. *Soviet Russian Literature since Stalin*. Cambridge: Cambridge University Press, 1978.

Brown, Homer O. "Oedipus with the Sphinx." *MLN* 92 (1977): 1099–106.

Burnley, David. *A Guide to Chaucer's Language*. Norman: University of Oklahoma Press, 1983.

Cannon, Betty. *Sartre and Psychoanalysis: An Existentialist Challenge to Clinical Metatheory*. Lawrence: University Press of Kansas, 1991.

Carlyle, Thomas. "The Hero as Poet. Dante. Shakspeare." In *On Heroes, Hero-Worship and the Heroic in History*. London: Chapman and Hall, n.d.

Carpenter, John, and Bogdana Carpenter. "Zbigniew Herbert: The poet as conscience." *Slavic and East European Journal* 24 (1980): 37–51.

Cave, Terence. *The Cornucopian Text*. Oxford: Clarendon Press, 1979.

Chaadayev, Peter. *Philosophical Letters and Apology of a Madman*, trans. Mary-Barbara Zeldin. Knoxville: University of Tennessee Press, 1969.

Childress, Steven Alan. "Reel "Rape Speech": Violent Pornography and the Politics of Harm." *Law and Society Review* 25 (1991): 177–214.

Choldin, Marianna Tax. *A Fence Around the Empire: Russian Censorship of Western Ideas under the Tsars*. Durham: Duke University Press, 1985.

Choldin, Marianna Tax, and Maurice Friedberg, eds. *The Red Pencil: Artists, Scholars, and Censors in the USSR*. Boston: Unwin Hyman, 1989.

Clark, Katerina. "Utopian Anthropology as a Context for Stalinist Literature." Pp. 180–91 in Robert C. Tucker, ed., *Stalinism: Essays in Historical Interpretation*. New York: Norton, 1977.

Coates, Paul. "Gardens of Stone: The Poetry of Zbigniew Herbert and Tadeusz Rozewicz." Pp. 175–88 in Adam Czerniawski, ed., *The Mature Laurel: Essays on Modern Polish Poetry*. Chester Springs, Pa.: Dufour, 1991.

Coertze, P. J. Review of Geoffrey Cronjé, *'n Tuiste vir die nageslag*. *Wapenskou*, October 1945, pp. 16–18.

Colby, Kenneth M. *Artificial Paranoia: A Computer Simulation of Paranoid Processes*. New York: Pergamon, 1975.

Coward, Rosalind. *Female Desire.* London: Paladin, 1984.

Cronjé, Geoffrey. *Afrika sonder die Asiaat: Die blywende oplossing van Suid-Afrika se Asiatevraagstuk.* Johannesburg: Publicité, 1946.

———. "Die huisgesin in die Afrikaanse kultuurgemeenskap." Pp. 309–60 in vol. 1 of P. de V. Pienaar and C. M. van den Heever, eds., *Kultuurgeskiedenis van die Afrikaner.* 3 vols. Cape Town: Nasionale Pers, 1945.

———. "Rassevermenging as maatskaplike vraagstuk." *Rassebakens* 1, no. 1 (1939): 41–55.

———. *'n Tuiste vir die nageslag.* Johannesburg: Publicité, 1945.

———. *Voogdyskap en apartheid.* Pretoria: Van Schaik, 1948.

Cronjé, Geoffrey, et al. *Regverdige Rasse-Apartheid.* Stellenbosch: Christen-Studenteverenigingsmaatskappy, 1947.

Curry, Jane Leftwich, ed. and trans. *The Black Book of Polish Censorship.* New York: Random House, 1984.

Davies, Jacqueline MacGregor. "Pornographic Harms." Pp. 127–45 in Lorraine Code, Sheila Mullett, and Christine Overall, eds., *Feminist Perspectives: Philosophical Essays on Method and Morals.* Toronto: University of Toronto Press, 1988.

DeMolen, Richard L. *Erasmus.* London: Edwin Arnold, 1973.

Derrida, Jacques. "Cogito and the History of Madness." Pp. 31–63 in *Writing and Difference,* trans. Alan Bass. Chicago: University of Chicago Press, 1978.

Des Pres, Terrence. "Poetry and Politics" *TriQuarterly,* no. 65 (1986): 17–29.

Deutscher, Isaac. *The Great Purges.* Oxford: Blackwell, 1984.

Devlin, Patrick. *The Enforcement of Morals.* Oxford: Oxford University Press, 1965.

Douglas, Mary. *Purity and Danger.* Rev. ed. London: Routledge and Kegan Paul, 1969.

Dubow, Saul. *Racial Segregation and the Origins of Apartheid in South Africa, 1919–36.* London: Macmillan, 1989.

Durham, Gayle. "Political Communication and Dissent in the Soviet Union." Pp. 233–75 in Rudolf L. Tökés, ed., *Dissent in the USSR.* Baltimore: Johns Hopkins University Press, 1975.

Du Toit, André. "Ideological Change, Afrikaner Nationalism, and Pragmatic Racial Domination." Pp. 19–50 in Leonard Thompson and Jeffrey Butler, eds., *Change in Contemporary South Africa.* Berkeley and Los Angeles: University of California Press, 1975.

Dworkin, Ronald. *A Matter of Principle.* Cambridge, Mass.: Harvard University Press, 1985.

———. *Taking Rights Seriously.* Cambridge, Mass.: Harvard University Press, 1977.

Dyzenhaus, David. "John Stuart Mill and the Harm of Pornography." *Ethics* 102 (1992): 534–51.

Edwards, David. "Toleration and English Blasphemy Law." Pp. 75–98 in

John Horton and Susan Mendus, eds., *Aspects of Toleration*. London: Methuen, 1985.

Egan, Susanna. "Breytenbach's *Mouroir*: The Novel as Autobiography." *Journal of Narrative Technique* 18, no. 2 (1988): 89–104.

Eisenstein, Elizabeth L. *The Printing Press as an Agent of Change*, vol. 1. Cambridge: Cambridge University Press, 1979.

———. *The Printing Revolution in Early Modern Europe*. Cambridge: Cambridge University Press, 1983.

Ellis, John. "On Pornography." Pp. 146–70 in Mandy Merck, ed., *The Sexual Subject: A Screen Reader in Sexuality*. London: Routledge, 1992.

Eloff, G. *Rasse en rassevermenging*. Cape Town: Nasionale Pers, 1942.

Erasmus, Desiderius. *Adages*, trans. Margaret M. Phillips. Cambridge: Cambridge University Press, 1964.

———. *The Praise of Folly*, trans. Hoyt H. Hudson. Princeton: Princeton University Press, 1941.

———. *Stultitiae laus*, ed. I. B. Kan. The Hague: Nijhoff, 1898.

Erlich, Viktor. *Russian Formalism*. 3d ed. The Hague: Mouton, 1969.

Ermolaev, Herman. "Solzhenitsyn's Self-Censorship: Two Versions of *V kruge pervom*." *Russian Language Journal* 38 (1984): 177–85.

Etkind, Efim. *Notes of a Non-Conspirator*, trans. Peter France. Oxford: Oxford University Press, 1978.

Faught, William S. *Motivation and Intentionality in a Computer Simulation Model of Paranoia*. Basel: Birkhauser, 1978.

Febvre, Lucien, and Henri-Jean Martin. *The Coming of the Book*, trans. David Gerard. London: New Left Books, 1976.

Feifer, George. "No Protest: The Case of the Passive Minority." Pp. 418–37 in Rudolf L. Tökés, ed., *Dissent in the USSR*. Baltimore: Johns Hopkins University Press, 1975.

Feinberg, Joel. *The Moral Limits of the Criminal Law*, vol. 2: *Offense to Others*. New York: Oxford University Press, 1985.

Felman, Shoshana. *Writing and Madness*, trans. Martha N. Evans and Shoshana Felman. Ithaca, N.Y.: Cornell University Press, 1985.

Foote, I. P. "'In the Belly of the Whale': Russian Authors and Censorship in the Nineteenth Century." *Slavonic and East European Review* 68 (1990): 294–98.

Foucault, Michel. *Madness and Civilization*, trans. Richard Howard. New York: Random House, 1967.

———. "Sexuality and Solitude." Pp. 365–72 in Marshall Blonsky, ed., *On Signs*. Oxford: Blackwell, 1985.

———. "What Is an Author?" trans. Donald F. Bouchard and Sherry Simon. Pp. 262–75 in Robert Con Davis and Ronald Schleifer, eds., *Contemporary Literary Criticism*. 2d ed. New York: Longman, 1989.

Freidin, Gregory. *A Coat of Many Colors*. Berkeley and Los Angeles: University of California Press, 1987.

———. "Mandel'shtam's *Ode to Stalin:* History and Myth." *The Russian Review* 41 (1982): 400–426.

Freud, Sigmund. "Group Psychology and the Analysis of the Ego." Vol. 18, pp. 67–143 in *Standard Edition of the Complete Psychological Works,* ed. and trans. James Strachey. London: Hogarth Press, 1955.

———. "Negation." Vol. 19, pp. 235–39 in *Standard Edition of the Complete Psychological Works,* ed. and trans. James Strachey. London: Hogarth Press, 1961.

———. "Psychoanalytic Notes on an Autobiographical Account of a Case of Paranoia." Vol. 9, pp. 129–223 in *Pelican Freud Library,* ed. James Strachey and Angela Richards. Harmondsworth: Penguin, 1979.

———. *Totem and Taboo.* Vol. 13 in *Standard Edition of the Complete Psychological Works,* ed. and trans. James Strachey. London: Hogarth Press, 1955.

Friedberg, Maurice. "Soviet Books, Censors and Readers." Pp. 198–210 in Max Hayward and Leo Labedz, eds., *Literature and Revolution in Soviet Russia, 1917–62.* London: Oxford University Press, 1963.

Friedgut, Theodore. "The Democratic Movement." Pp. 116–36 in Rudolf L. Tökés, ed., *Dissent in the USSR.* Baltimore: Johns Hopkins University Press, 1975.

Furlong, Patrick J. *Between Crown and Swastika: The Impact of the Radical Right on the Afrikaner Nationalist Movement in the Fascist Era.* Hanover: Wesleyan University Press, 1991.

Garbus, Martin. *Traitors and Heroes: A Lawyer's Memoir.* New York: Athenaeum, 1987.

Garrard, John, and Carol Garrard. *Inside the Soviet Writers' Union.* New York: Free Press, 1990.

Gellner, Ernst. *Nations and Nationalism.* Oxford: Blackwell, 1983.

Gilbert, Harriet. "So Long as It's Not Sex and Violence: Andrea Dworkin's *Mercy.*" Pp. 216–30 in Lynne Segal and Mary McIntosh, eds., *Sex Exposed.* London: Virago, 1992.

Gilmore, T. B. "The Comedy of Swift's Scatological Poems." *Publications of the Modern Language Association* 91 (1976): 33–41.

Girard, René. *Deceit, Desire and the Novel,* trans. Yvonne Freccero. Baltimore: Johns Hopkins University Press, 1965.

———. *Things Hidden since the Foundation of the World,* trans. Stephen Bann and Michael Metteer. Stanford: Stanford University Press, 1987.

———. *To Double Business Bound,* trans. Paisley N. Livingston and Tobin Siebers. Baltimore: Johns Hopkins University Press, 1978.

———. *Violence and the Sacred,* trans. Patrick Gregory. Baltimore: Johns Hopkins University Press, 1977.

Glazov, Yuri. *The Russian Mind since Stalin's Death.* Dordrecht: Reidel, 1985.

Goldfarb, Jeffrey C. *On Cultural Freedom.* Chicago: University of Chicago Press, 1982.

Goldstein, Robert J. *Political Censorship of the Arts and the Press in Nineteenth-Century Europe.* New York: St. Martin's, 1989.

Goodheart, Eugene. "Censorship and Self-Censorship in the Fiction of D. H. Lawrence." Pp. 223–40 in George Bornstein, ed., *Representing Modernist Texts: Editing as Interpretation.* Ann Arbor: University of Michigan Press, 1991.

Gordimer, Nadine, et al. *What Happened to Burger's Daughter.* Johannesburg: Taurus, 1980.

Grassi, Ernesto. "Folly as Illusion" and "The Allegorical Fable." In Ernesto Grassi and Maristella Lorch, *Folly and Insanity in Renaissance Literature.* Binghampton: Medieval and Renaissance Texts and Studies, 1986.

Gray, John. *Mill on Liberty: A Defence.* London: Routledge, 1983.

Griffin, Susan. *Pornography and Silence.* London: Women's Press, 1981.

Groarke, Leo. "Pornography: From Liberalism to Censorship." *Queen's Quarterly* 90 (1983): 1108–20.

Halperin, David M. "Solzhenitsyn, Epicurus, and the Ethics of Stalinism." *Critical Inquiry* 7 (1981): 475–97.

Haraszti, Miklos. *The Velvet Prison: Artists under State Socialism,* trans. Katalin Landesmann and Stephen Landesmann. New York: Basic Books, 1987.

Hart, H. L. A. *Law, Liberty and Morality.* Rev. ed. Oxford: Oxford University Press, 1981.

Hayward, Max. *Writers in Russia, 1917–78,* ed. Patricia Blake. New York: Harcourt, Brace, Jovanovich, 1983.

———. Introduction. Pp. vii–xx in Max Hayward and Leo Labedz, eds., *Literature and Revolution in Soviet Russia, 1917–62.* London: Oxford University Press, 1963.

Heaney, Seamus. *The Government of the Tongue.* London: Faber, 1988.

Heidegger, Martin. *Sein und Zeit.* 16th ed. Tübingen: Niemeyer, 1986.

Herbert, Zbigniew. *Barbarian in the Garden,* trans. Michael March and Jaroslaw Anders. Manchester: Carcanet, 1985.

———. *Report from the Besieged City and Other Poems,* trans. John Carpenter and Bogdana Carpenter. Oxford: Oxford University Press, 1987.

———. *Selected Poems,* trans. Czeslaw Milosz and Peter Dale Scott. Harmondsworth: Penguin, 1968.

———. *Selected Poems,* trans. John Carpenter and Bogdana Carpenter. Oxford: Oxford University Press, 1977.

Heydemann, Klaus. "Das Beispiel des Erasmus: Stefan Zweigs Einstellung zur Politik." *Literatur und Kritik,* no. 169/170 (1982): 24–39.

Hingley, Ronald. *Russian Writers and Soviet Society, 1917–78.* London: Methuen, 1979.

Hinz, Evelyn J. "Pornography, Novel, Mythic Narration: The Three Versions of *Lady Chatterley's Lover.*" *Modernist Studies* 3 (1979): 35–47.

Hoff, Joan. "Why Is There No History of Pornography?" Pp. 17–46 in Susan Gubar and Joan Hoff, eds., *For Adult Users Only: The Di-*

lemma of Violent Pornography. Bloomington: Indiana University Press, 1989.

Hofmeyr, Isabel. "Building a Nation from Words: Afrikaans Language, Literature and Ethnic Identity, 1902–1924." Pp. 95–123 in Shula Marks and Stanley Trapido, eds., *The Politics of Race, Class and Nationalism in Twentieth-Century South Africa.* London: Longmans, 1987.

Horton, John. "Toleration, Morality and Harm." Pp. 113–35 in John Horton and Susan Mendus, eds., *Aspects of Toleration.* London: Methuen, 1985.

Hosking, Geoffrey A. "The Institutionalization of Soviet Literature." Pp. 55–75 in Geoffrey A. Hosking and George F. Cushing, eds., *Perspectives on Literature and Society in Eastern and Western Europe.* New York: St. Martin's, 1989.

Huizinga, Johannes. *Erasmus.* 3d, rev. ed. Haarlem: Willink, 1936.

Huxley, Aldous. *On Art and Artists,* ed. Morris Philipson. New York: Harper, 1960.

Intons-Peterson, Margaret, and Beverly Roskos-Ewoldsen. "Mitigating the Effects of Violent Pornography." Pp. 218–39 in Susan Gubar and Joan Hoff, eds., *For Adult Users Only.* Bloomington: Indiana University Press, 1989.

Irigaray, Luce. *This Sex which is not One,* trans. Catherine Porter with Carolyn Burke. Ithaca, N.Y.: Cornell University Press, 1985.

Jacobs, J. U. "Breyten Breytenbach and the South African Prison Book." *Theoria,* no. 68 (December 1986): 95–105.

Jangfeldt, Bengt. "Osip Mandel'shtam's 'Ode to Stalin.'" *Scando-Slavica* 22 (1976): 35–41.

Jansen, Sue Curry. *Censorship: The Knot that Binds Power and Knowledge.* New York: Oxford University Press, 1988.

Jay, Martin. *Downcast Eyes: The Denigration of Vision in Twentieth-Century French Thought.* Berkeley and Los Angeles: University of California Press, 1993.

Johnson, Priscilla. *Khrushchev and the Arts.* Cambridge, Mass.: MIT Press, 1965.

Kaiser, Walter. *Praisers of Folly: Erasmus, Rabelais, Shakespeare.* London: Gollancz, 1964.

Kemp-Welch, A. "Stalinism and Intellectual Order." Pp. 118–34 in T. H. Rigby, Archie Brown, Peter Reddaway, eds., *Authority, Power and Policy in the USSR.* London: Macmillan, 1980.

Kern, Gary. "Solzhenitsyn's Portrait of Stalin." *Slavic Review* 33 (1974): 1–22.

Kis, Danilo. "Censorship/Self-Censorship." *Index on Censorship* 15/1 (January 1986): 43–45.

Kittay, Eve Feder. "Pornography and the Erotics of Domination." Pp. 145–74 in Carol Gould, ed., *Beyond Domination: New Perspectives on Women and Philosophy.* Totowa, N.J.: Roman and Allanheld, 1984.

Koch, Gertrud. "Ex-changing the *Gaze:* Re-visioning Feminist Film Theory." *New German Critique* 34 (1985): 139–53.

Konwicki, Tadeusz. "Interview: The Delights of Writing under Censorship." *Index on Censorship* 15/3 (March 1986): 30–31.

Labedz, Leopold, ed. *Solzhenitsyn: A Documentary Record.* New York: Harper and Row, 1970.

Lacan, Jacques. *De la psychose paranoïaque dans ses rapports avec la personnalité.* Paris: Seuil, 1975.

Lakshin, Vladimir. *Solzhenitsyn, Tvardovsky, and Novy Mir,* trans. Michael Glenny. Cambridge, Mass.: MIT Press, 1980.

Laplanche, J., and J.-B. Pontalis. *The Language of Psycho-Analysis,* trans. Donald Nicholson-Smith. New York: Norton, 1973.

Lawrence, D. H. *Lady Chatterley's Lover.* New York: Modern Library, 1957.

———. *The First Lady Chatterley.* London: Heinemann, 1972.

———. *A Propos of Lady Chatterley's Lover.* London: Mandrake Press, 1930.

———. *Selected Literary Criticism,* ed. Anthony Beal. New York: Viking, 1966.

Le Bon, Gustave. *The Crowd.* Dunwoody, Ga.: Norman S. Berg, n.d.

Levy, Leonard W. *Treason against God: A History of the Offense of Blasphemy.* New York: Schocken, 1981.

Loades, D. M. "The Theory and Practice of Censorship in Sixteenth-Century England." Pp. 140–57 in *Transactions of the Royal Historical Society.* 5th series, vol. 24. London: Royal Historical Society, 1974.

Loseff, Lev. *On the Beneficence of Censorship: Aesopian Language in Modern Russian Literature.* Munich: Otto Sagner, 1984.

MacCormick, D. N. "Privacy and Obscenity." Pp. 76–97 in Rajeev Dhavan and Christie Davies, eds., *Censorship and Obscenity.* London: Martin Robertson, 1978.

MacCrone, I. D. *Race Attitudes in South Africa.* Johannesburg: Witwatersrand University Press, 1957.

MacIntyre, Alasdair. *After Virtue: A Study in Moral Theory.* London: Duckworth, 1981.

MacKinnon, Catharine. *Feminism Unmodified.* Cambridge, Mass.: Harvard University Press, 1987.

———. *Toward a Feminist Theory of the State.* Cambridge, Mass.: Harvard University Press, 1989.

Mahoney, Kathleen. "The Canadian Constitutional Approach to Freedom of Expression in Hate Propaganda and Pornography." *Law and Contemporary Problems* 55 (1992): 77–105.

Mandelstam, Nadezhda. *Hope against Hope,* trans. Max Hayward. New York: Athenaeum, 1970.

Mandelstam, Osip. *Complete Poetry,* trans. Burton Raffel and Alla Burago. Albany, N.Y.: State University of New York Press, 1973.

————. *The Complete Critical Prose and Letters,* ed. Jane G. Harris, trans. Jane G. Harris and Constance Link. Ann Arbor, Mich.: Ardis, 1979.

————. *The Noise of Time,* ed. and trans. Clarence Brown. San Francisco: North Point, 1986.

————. *Selected Poems,* trans. David McDuff. Cambridge: Rivers Press, 1973.

"Mandelstam's 'Ode' to Stalin." *Slavic Review* 34 (1975): 683–91.

Mangakis, George. "Letter to Europeans." Pp. 32–38 in George Theiner, ed., *They Shoot Writers, Don't They?* London: Faber, 1984.

Marcus, Gilbert. "Reasonable Censorship?" Pp. 349–60 in Hugh Corder, ed., *Essays on Law and Social Practice in South Africa.* Cape Town: Juta, 1988.

Marcuse, Herbert. "Repressive Tolerance." Pp. 81–123 in Robert P. Wolff, Barrington Moore, and Herbert Marcuse, *A Critique of Pure Tolerance.* Boston: Beacon Press, 1969.

Marks, Shula, and Stanley Trapido. "The Politics of Race, Class and Nationalism." Pp. 1–70 in Shula Marks and Stanley Trapido, eds., *The Politics of Race, Class and Nationalism in Twentieth-Century South Africa.* London: Longmans, 1987.

Mason, H. A. "They Haven't Got No Noses!" *Cambridge Quarterly* 18 (1989): 129–59.

McClintock, Anne. "Gonad the Barbarian and the Venus Flytrap: Portraying the Female and Male Orgasm." Pp. 111–30 in Lynne Segal and Mary McIntosh, eds., *Sex Exposed: Sexuality and the Pornography Debate.* London: Virago, 1992.

McConica, James. "The Fate of Erasmian Humanism." Pp. 37–61 in Nicholas Phillipson, ed., *Universities, Society, and the Future.* Edinburgh: Edinburgh University Press, 1983.

Medvedev, Zhores A., and Roy A. Medvedev. *A Question of Madness,* trans. Ellen de Kadt. New York: Knopf, 1971.

Mendus, Susan. "Harm, Offence and Censorship." Pp. 99–112 in John Horton and Susan Mendus, eds., *Aspects of Toleration.* London: Methuen, 1985.

————. *Toleration and the Limits of Liberalism.* London: Macmillan 1989.

Menkel-Meadow, Carrie. Review of Catharine MacKinnon, *Toward a Feminist Theory of the State. Signs* 16 (1991): 603–7.

Merck, Mandy. "From Minneapolis to Westminster." Pp. 50–61 in Lynne Segal and Mary McIntosh, eds., *Sex Exposed: Sexuality and the Pornography Debate.* London: Virago, 1992.

Mill, John Stuart. *On Liberty,* ed. Gertrude Himmelfarb. Harmondsworth: Penguin, 1974.

————. *The Subjection of Women.* Cambridge, Mass.: MIT Press, 1970.

Miller, Henry. *The World of D. H. Lawrence.* Santa Barbara: Capra Press, 1980.

Miller, Richard B. "Violent Pornography: Mimetic Nihilism and the Eclipse of Differences." *Soundings* 69 (1986): 326–46.

Milosz, Czeslaw, ed. *Postwar Polish Poetry.* 3d ed. Berkeley and Los Angeles: University of California Press, 1983.

Milton, John. *Areopagitica,* ed. J. C. Suffolk. London: University Tutorial Press, 1968.

Moi, Toril. "Patriarchal Thought and the Drive for Knowledge." Pp. 189–205 in Teresa Brennan, ed., *Between Feminism and Psychoanalysis.* London: Routledge, 1989.

Monas, Sidney, "Censorship as a Way of Life." Pp. 7–22 in Geoffrey A. Hosking and George F. Cushing, eds., *Perspectives on Literature and Society in Eastern and Western Europe.* New York: St. Martin's, 1989.

———. *The Third Section.* Cambridge, Mass.: Harvard University Press, 1961.

Moodie, T. Dunbar. *The Rise of Afrikanerdom.* Berkeley and Los Angeles: University of California Press, 1975.

Mulvey, Laura. "Visual Pleasure and Narrative Cinema." Pp. 303–15 in Bill Nichols, ed., *Movies and Methods,* vol. 2. Berkeley and Los Angeles: University of California Press, 1985.

Nairn, Tom. *The Break-Up of Britain.* 2d ed. London: Verso, 1981.

Nicholson, Michael. "Solzhenitsyn and *Samizdat.*" Pp. 63–93 in John Dunlop et al., eds., *Aleksandr Solzhenitsyn.* 2d ed. New York: Macmillan, 1975.

Nikitenko, Aleksandr. *The Diary of a Russian Censor,* ed. and trans. Helen S. Jacobson. Amherst: University of Massachusetts Press, 1975.

O'Meara, Dan. *Volkskapitalisme.* Johannesburg: Ravan, 1983.

Oramus, Marek, and Maria Szmidt. "A Poet of Exact Meaning." *PN Review* 8/6, no. 26 (1982): 8–12.

Ortega y Gasset, José. *Meditations on Quixote,* trans. Evelyn Rugg and Diego Marin. New York: Norton, 1961.

Orwell, George. *1984,* ed. Bernard Crick. Oxford: Clarendon Press, 1984.

Pally, Marcia. "Out of Sight and Out of Harm's Way." *Index on Censorship* 22/1, no. 146 (January 1993): 4–7.

Pateman, Carole. "Sex and Power" [Review of Catharine MacKinnon, *Feminism Unmodified*]. *Ethics* 100 (1990): 398–407.

Patterson, Annabel. *Censorship and Interpretation.* Madison: University of Wisconsin Press, 1984.

———. *Fables of Power: Aesopian Writing and Political History.* Durham: Duke University Press, 1991.

Pelzer, A. N. *Die Afrikaner-Broederbond: eerste 50 jaar.* Cape Town: Tafelberg, 1979.

Pirie, Donald P. A. "Engineering the People's Dreams: An Assessment of Socialist Realist Poetry in Poland, 1949–1955." Pp. 135–59 in Adam

Czerniawski, ed., *The Mature Laurel: Essays on Modern Polish Poetry.* Chester Springs, Pa.: Dufour, 1991.

Pitt-Rivers, Julian. "Honour and Shame." Pp. 19–78 in J. G. Peristiany, ed., *Honour and Shame: The Values of Mediterranean Society.* Chicago: University of Chicago Press, 1966.

Plato. *Republic,* ed. James Adam. 2d ed., 2 vols. Cambridge: Cambridge University Press, 1963.

——. *The Republic,* trans. H. D. P. Lee. Harmondsworth: Penguin, 1955.

Pomeranzev, Igor. "The Right to Read." *Partisan Review* 49 (1982): 54–67.

Poole, Howard. "Obscenity and Censorship." *Ethics* 93 (1982): 39–44.

Popper, Karl. "Toleration and Intellectual Responsibility." Pp. 17–34 in Susan Mendus and David Edwards, eds., *On Toleration.* Oxford: Clarendon Press, 1987.

Pszenicki, Chris. "Freedom of Expression in Jaruzelski's Poland." *Index on Censorship* 12/6 (December 1983): 19–24.

——. "Polish Publishing, 1980–81." *Index on Censorship* 11/1 (February 1982): 8–11.

Publications Control Board. "Die tweede beslissing oor *Magersfontein, o Magersfontein!" Standpunte* 33/4, no. 148 (1980): 3–15.

Rancour-Laferriere, Daniel. "The Deranged Birthday Boy: Solzhenitsyn's Portrait of Stalin in *The First Circle." Mosaic* 18 (1985): 61–72.

Randall, Richard S. *Freedom and Taboo: Pornography and the Politics of a Self Divided.* Berkeley and Los Angeles: University of California Press, 1989.

Rees, John C. *John Stuart Mill's "On Liberty."* Oxford: Clarendon Press, 1985.

Rhoodie, N. J. "G. Cronje se beskouing van die Suid-Afrikaanse Blank-Bantoe-problematiek, soos weerspieël in sy onmiddellik na-oorlogse geskrifte." Pp. 41–81 in J. E. Pieterse et al., eds., *Mens en gemeenskap.* Pretoria: Academica, 1969.

Ripoll, Carlos. *The Heresy of Words in Cuba.* New York: Freedom House, 1985.

Roberts, Sheila. "Breyten Breytenbach's Prison Literature." *Centennial Review* 30 (1986): 304–13.

Rolph, C. H., ed. *The Trial of Lady Chatterley.* London: privately printed, 1961.

Rothberg, Abraham. *The Heirs of Stalin: Dissidence and the Soviet Regime, 1953–1970.* Ithaca, N.Y.: Cornell University Press, 1972.

Rowe, Eleanor. *Hamlet: A Window on Russia.* New York: New York University Press, 1976.

Ruud, Charles A. *Fighting Words: Imperial Censorship and the Russian Press, 1804–1906.* Toronto: University of Toronto Press, 1982.

Sanday, Peggy Reeves. "The Social Context of Rape." *New Society* 61, no. 1037 (20 September 1982): 540–42.

Sartre, Jean-Paul. *Being and Nothingness*, trans. Hazel Barnes. New York: Washington Square Press, 1966.

Saunders, David. "Copyright, Obscenity and Literary History." *ELH* 57 (1990): 431–44.

———. "The Trial of *Lady Chatterley's Lover:* Limiting Cases and Literary Canons." *Southern Review* (Adelaide) 15 (1982): 161–77.

Scammell, Michael. *Solzhenitsyn: A Biography*. New York: Norton, 1984.

Schauer, Frederick. *Free Speech: A Philosophical Enquiry*. New York: Cambridge University Press, 1982.

Scheler, Max. *Person and Self-Value: Three Essays*, ed. and trans. M. S. Frings. Dordrecht: Martinus Nijhoff, 1987.

Schlereth, Thomas J. *The Cosmopolitan Idea in Enlightenment Thought*. South Bend: Notre Dame University Press, 1978.

Schmemann, Aleksandr. "On Solzhenitsyn." Pp. 28–44 in John Dunlop et al., eds., *Aleksandr Solzhenitsyn*. 2d ed. New York: Macmillan, 1975.

Schöpflin, George. "The Black Book of Polish Censorship." Pp. 33–101 in George Schöpflin, ed., *Censorship and Political Communication in Eastern Europe: A Collection of Documents*. New York: St Martin's, 1983.

Schweppenhauser, Gerhard. "Narrenschelte und Pathos der Vernunft: Zum Narrenmotiv bei Sebastian Brant und Erasmus von Rotterdam." *Neophilologus* 71 (1987): 559–74.

Screech, M. A. "Good Madness in Christendom." Pp. 25–39 in W. F. Bynum, et al., eds., *The Anatomy of Madness*, vol. 1. London: Tavistock, 1985.

Segal, Lynne. Introduction. Pp. 1–13 in Lynne Segal and Mary McIntosh, eds., *Sex Exposed*. London: Virago, 1992.

Sharp, John. "The Roots and Development of *Volkekunde* in South Africa." *Journal of Southern African Studies* 8/1 (1981): 16–36.

Shatz, Marshall S. *Soviet Dissent in Historical Perspective*. Cambridge: Cambridge University Press, 1980.

Siegel, Paul N. "The Political Implications of Solzhenitsyn's Novels." *Clio* 12 (1983): 211–32.

Simmons, Ernest J. "The Organization Writer (1934–46)." Pp. 74–98 in Max Hayward and Leo Labedz, eds., *Literature and Revolution in Soviet Russia 1917–62*. London: Oxford University Press, 1963.

Smart, Carol. *Feminism and the Power of Law*. London: Routledge, 1989.

———. "Unquestionably a Moral Issue: Rhetorical Devices and Regulatory Imperatives." Pp. 184–98 in Lynne Segal and Mary McIntosh, eds., *Sex Exposed*. London: Virago, 1992.

Smith, Anthony D. *The Ethnic Revival*. Cambridge: Cambridge University Press, 1981.

Smolla, Rodney A. "Academic Freedom, Hate Speech, and the Idea of a University." *Law and Contemporary Problems* 53 (1990): 195–225.

Solzhenitsyn, Aleksandr. *The First Circle*. Augmented edition, trans. Thomas P. Whitney. New York: Harper and Row, 1978.

———. Nobel Lecture, trans. Alexis Klimoff. Pp. 570–75 in John Dunlop et al., eds., *Aleksandr Solzhenitsyn* 2d ed. New York: Macmillan, 1975.

———. *The Oak and the Calf*, trans. Harry Willetts. London: Collins, 1980.

Sontag, Susan. *Styles of Radical Will*. London: Secker and Warburg, 1969.

Sparrow, John. "Regina vs. Penguin Books, Limited." *Encounter* 18/2 (February 1962): 35–43.

Spechler, Dina R. *Permitted Dissent in the USSR*. New York: Praeger, 1982.

Squire, P. S. *The Third Section*. Cambridge: Cambridge University Press, 1968.

Stout, Jeffrey. *Ethics after Babel: The Languages of Morals and their Discontents*. Boston: Beacon Press, 1988.

Strauss, Leo. *Persecution and the Art of Writing*. Glencoe: Free Press, 1952.

Swanson, Maynard. "The Sanitation Syndrome: Bubonic Plague and Urban Native Policy in the Cape Colony, 1900–09." *Journal of African History* 18 (1977): 387–410.

Swayze, Harold. *Political Control of Literature in the USSR, 1946–1959*. Cambridge, Mass.: Harvard University Press, 1962.

Swift, Jonathan. *Complete Poems*, ed. Pat Rogers. New Haven: Yale University Press, 1983.

Tanner, Tony. "Licence and Licencing." *Journal of the History of Ideas* 38 (1977): 3–18.

Taylor, Gabriele. *Pride, Shame, and Guilt. Emotions of Self-Assessment*. Oxford: Clarendon Press, 1985.

Tempest, Richard. "Madman or Criminal: Government Attitudes to Petr Chaadaev in 1836." *Slavic Review* 43 (1984): 281–87.

Thompson, Leonard. *The Political Mythology of Apartheid*. New Haven: Yale University Press, 1985.

Trilling, Lionel. "The Poet as Hero: Keats in His Letters." Pp. 3–49 in *The Opposing Self*. London: Secker and Warburg, 1955.

Trznadel, Jacek. "An Interview with Zbigniew Herbert." *Partisan Review* 54 (1987): 557–75.

Turchin, Valentin. *The Inertia of Fear*, trans. Guy Daniels. Oxford: Martin Robertson, 1981.

Twarog, Leon I. "Literary Censorship in Russia and the Soviet Union." Pp. 100–108 in Leon B. Blair, ed., *Essays on Russian Intellectual History*. Austin: University of Texas Press, 1971.

Van Heerden, Etienne. "Seur en kleur: Oor neo-sensuur, kwetswoorde en lesers." *Tydskrif vir Letterkunde* 24/4 (1986): 58–65.

Van Rooyen, J. C. W. *Censorship in South Africa*. Cape Town: Juta, 1987.

———. *Publikasiebeheer in Suid-Afrika*. Cape Town: Juta, 1978.

Vargas Llosa, Mario. "The Writer in Latin America." Pp. 161–71 in George Theiner, ed., *They Shoot Writers, Don't They?* London: Faber, 1984.

Viala, Alain. *Naissance de l'écrivain.* Paris: Editions de minuit, 1985.

Viviers, Jack. *Breytenbach.* Cape Town: Tafelberg, 1978.

Waldron, Jeremy. "Mill and the Value of Moral Distress." *Political Studies* 35 (1987): 410–23.

Weale, Albert. "Toleration, Individual Differences and Respect for Persons." Pp. 16–35 in John Horton and Susan Mendus, eds., *Aspects of Toleration.* London: Methuen, 1985.

Webster, Richard. *A Brief History of Blasphemy: Liberalism, Censorship and "The Satanic Verses."* London: Orwell Press, 1990.

Weil, Simone. *Gravity and Grace,* ed. G. Thibon. London: Routledge, 1952.

Welz, Martin. *Breyten en die bewaarder.* Johannesburg: McGraw-Hill, 1977.

Westermarck, Edward. *The Origin and Development of the Moral Ideas.* 2 vols. London: Macmillan, 1924.

Williams, Bernard, ed. *Obscenity and Film Censorship: An Abridgement of the Williams Report.* Cambridge: Cambridge University Press, 1981.

Williams, Linda. "Fetishism and Hard Core." Pp. 198–217 in Susan Gubar and Joan Hoff, eds., *For Adult Users Only: The Dilemma of Violent Pornography.* Bloomington: Indiana University Press, 1989.

Zeeman, Peter. *The Later Poetry of Osip Mandelstam: Text and Context.* Amsterdam: Rodopi, 1988.

Zweig, Stefan. "Erasmus." In *Erasmus [and] The Right to Heresy,* trans. Eden and Cedar Paul. London: Souvenir Press, 1979.

Index